Wakefield Press

THE FIERCE COUNTRY

Stephen Orr is the author of seven novels,
a short story collection and a book of non-fiction.
He writes features and occasional columns, and
teaches part-time. He lives in Adelaide.

By the same author

Fiction
Attempts to Draw Jesus
Hill of Grace
Time's Long Ruin
Dissonance
One Boy Missing
The Hands
Datsunland
Incredible Floridas

Non-fiction
The Cruel City

The *FIERCE* COUNTRY

True stories from Australia's unsettled heart, 1830 to today

Stephen Orr

Wakefield Press

Wakefield Press
16 Rose Street
Mile End
South Australia 5031
www.wakefieldpress.com.au

First published 2018
Reprinted 2019

Copyright © Stephen Orr, 2018

All rights reserved. This book is copyright. Apart from any fair dealing for the purposes of private study, research, criticism or review, as permitted under the Copyright Act, no part may be reproduced without written permission. Enquiries should be addressed to the publisher.

Cover designed by Liz Nicholson, designBITE
Edited by Julia Beaven, Wakefield Press
Typeset by Michael Deves, Wakefield Press

ISBN 978 1 74305 574 8

A catalogue record for this book is available from the National Library of Australia

Wakefield Press thanks Coriole Vineyards for continued support

CONTENTS

Preface	ix
CHAPTER 1	
The Fierce Country	1
Coal and Cracked Masonry: Dr Hill's Eye Hospital	1
The 'iron solitude of the hills'	6
The 'black line'	7
Myall Creek	8
Frank Hawson	12
Eliza Fraser	14
Daisy Bates	16
CHAPTER 2	
Point Puer Boys' Prison	21
CHAPTER 3	
Jandamarra	30
CHAPTER 4	
The Calvert Expedition	38
CHAPTER 5	
'… the police seem unable to get any clue': The Gatton Murders	51
CHAPTER 6	
The Tea and Sugar	59
CHAPTER 7	
Ingkaia: Carl and Theodor Strehlow's journey to Horseshoe Bend	65
CHAPTER 8	
The Murchison Murders: 'Snowy' Rowles and Arthur Upfield	74
CHAPTER 9	
Lasseter's Reef	89

CHAPTER 10
1 2 3: The Search for Nicholas Bannon 100

CHAPTER 11
'Ran out of Petrel': The Page Family 109

CHAPTER 12
The Faraday School Kidnapping 124

CHAPTER 13
'I Found Peece': Simon Amos and James Annetts 133

CHAPTER 14
Clinton Liebelt 145

CHAPTER 15
Caroline Grossmueller 160

CHAPTER 16
Robert Bogucki 168

CHAPTER 17
The Disappearance of Peter Falconio 175

CHAPTER 18
'We believe he is sinless': The Murder of Imran Zilic 189

CHAPTER 19
Wake in Fright: The Fierce Country Made Real 199

Sources 205
Acknowledgements 211

Three hundred miles to Birdsville from Marree
Man makes his mark across a fierce country
That has no flower but the whitening bone and skull
Of long-dead cattle, no word but 'I will kill'.
Here the world ends in a shield of purple stone
Naked in its long war against the sun;
The white stones flash, the red stones leap with fire:
It wants no interlopers to come here.

from *The Birdsville Track and other poems*
Douglas Stewart

Preface

The Fierce Country starts on the fringes of our big cities and extends through market gardens and wheatbelt, moving into the outback. It begins in 1830s Van Diemen's Land, where primary-school-aged children were sent to be 'reformed', continuing into the Western Australian desert, full of cut-snake explorers, to a murder mystery in a Gatton paddock and a journey along the No. 1 Rabbit Proof Fence. On to stories of lost children, stranded backpackers, Christ-like figures searching for God on the gibbers, Peter Falconio pulling over beside the highway, Imran Zilic hurtling across the Nullarbor beside his father.

This volume describes the friction between man, woman, child and landscape. It's a rough edge, continually wearing. In this zone farmers fix fences, foreign students drive for days to see waterless lakes, drug runners ferry their wares between cities and pink roadhouses serve Chiko rolls, lined up like trucks waiting for a bowser. A folklore begins to smoke and catch among the shavings of our history.

These stories are all worth the telling, but for every lost child and wandering explorer there were, and are, dozens, hundreds more.

PREFACE

CHAPTER 1

The Fierce Country

Opening remarks – In the national consciousness – Nathaniel Hailes – Terowie, and Dr Alfred Hill – 'I came out of Bataan' – Native Americans and 'sacred land' – The 'black line' – Myall Creek – Frank Hawson – Eliza Fraser – Daisy Bates

Coal and Cracked Masonry:
Dr Hill's Eye Hospital

If the maxim is true that you never know what you've got till it's gone, then the Australian outback, in all of its red-sand, snowy mountain manifestations, is a treasure that continues to seep into the darkest recesses of our national consciousness. For example, the stockman – high saddle and felt hat, mustering shorthorns in the last gasp of late winter light – now more cinematic cliché than reality in a world of Robinson helicopters and trail bikes. He is someone we want to believe in, a Chips Rafferty who stands for and protects values we praise in Lawson and Paterson verses recited at school assemblies. A character whose hand-split shingles we see on display in farming museums in small towns on the verge of extinction.

He is not just a farmer. He's a kid riding to school along the Birdsville Track, falling, grazing his arm, getting up and continuing; he's a boundary rider, fixing fence posts at the 183 mile peg on the rabbit-proof fence; he's a paddle-steamer captain, watching for snags along the sun-dried Murray; he's a Croatian opal miner, driving towards a new shaft, a box of dynamite on the seat beside him; he's a 13-year-old kid in the wheatbelt, working up a few paddocks for Dad after tea, stopping to wrestle an International into low range; *she's* the small town matriarch, displaying her sultana slab in a glass case, smiling, proud of her latest blue ribbon; she's a Katherine School of the Air student, reciting her six-times-tables in a hot, dusty room that smells of Glanvac and scones.

They're all part of the legacy, the stories that city folk admire but dismiss, find (in an old-fashioned sort of way) charming, but can't understand, failing to grasp why country people choose to live the way they do. No shops, no hospitals, no cafes, no air-conditioned cinemas.

For most coastal dwellers the outback is more notion than reality. The colour, smell and memories of these regions ossify, become sepia, and drift into a landscape of old kerosene tins and country shows. We realise we're losing something, but we can live with that. We cling to the stories (Ned Kelly, Burke and Wills, Amos and Annetts) but we'd never go to these places. We are spectators of our own past; it lies dormant, rusting, forgotten.

But in the great contradiction of modern Australian life we can't imagine ever letting our past disappear. We feel these places in our bones, see them in the Drysdale prints on our dentist's wall, and taste them in the lamb we slow cook. We are jealous of the freedoms these dry creek beds, paddocks and small towns offer, their opportunities, their child-friendly streets and cheap houses. We are drawn to documentaries about them, and even films showing crinoline-clad schoolgirls sucked into giant rocks cast off from Dreamtimes we've never grasped.

At the beginning it was an awfully big adventure.

Nathaniel Hailes arrived in Adelaide in 1839, three years after the city's settlement at the hands of pious Dissenters and a few stray Catholics. As a journalist he saw the city grow and prosper. He travelled widely across the state, writing about the experiences of free settlers – outback murders, attacks by Aboriginal people, but mostly, what it was like to be there at the beginning. In 1878, looking back on these early days, he wrote in the *South Australian Register*:

'With your back towards men of your own colour, and your horse's head in the direction of a vast, untraversed country ... a pleasurable excitement is experienced which was previously unknown. The very vagueness heightens the enjoyment ... in the interior of this irregular country every mile of progress is the penetration of a mystery.'

Pioneers were a special type: self-sufficient, ambitious, driven, often escaping an unremarkable or difficult past. And for the most ambitious, the empty acres, studded with bush that would be made to yield to the plough, called to them. As Hailes explained: 'The breezes that meet you as they sigh amid the apparently interminable forest seem whispering secrets of the enigmatical regions beyond. The path which probably your horse chooses, his rider only deciding the direction, is perpetually presenting something interesting, because [it is] new to you. There are so many unfamiliar flowers beneath your horse's hoofs; so many strange yet simple and melodious notes hailing you from branches and shrubs which border your course ...'

Most of the people who inhabit the pages of *The Fierce Country* shared some of this spirit: Ernie Page, driving his family north along the Birdsville Track; Robert Bogucki, searching for God in the desert; young jackaroos Simon Amos and James Annetts following their dreams in the Kimberley. Each shared a restlessness, a feeling that there must be something better just around the corner. Hailes put it like this: 'What splendid castles in the air the mind of a traveller in the bush constructs, whether of the fervid sunbeams overhead, of the silver rays of the shadowless moon ... Most of my colonial castles have been built at night. My sweetest waking dreams have been enjoyed when those of slumber would have been more seasonable ...'

The frontier soon recedes, the spirit diminishes with time. In describing the 'advances which settlement and cultivation have made', Hailes (less than 40 years after his arrival) said, 'Much of the transformation [which one beholds] was effected by muscular arms which are no longer counted in our census – by able and industrious men, some of whom are in their graves.'

The Fierce Country

Legacies, lives, cities and towns were made, myths forged, fortunes gathered.

One example was the small, Mid North South Australian town of Terowie. In the 19th century it was a key element in the colony's rail network, a supply town for far-flung pastoral properties as well as communities in the booming mining regions of Broken Hill and Silverton. By the 1880s, just over ten years after its settlement, Terowie boasted several pubs, an agricultural implements factory, a timber store, tailor, baker, monthly cattle sales, brass band, solicitor, saddle and harness maker, jeweller, a piano teacher (Mrs G. Dawson, reasonable rates), and even an eye hospital, operated by a Dr Alfred Hill who, strangely, conducted experiments on rabbits to further his ophthalmological knowledge.

Soon Terowie's population passed 2000, most of whom were employed by the Railways. As late as World War II it was an important 'break-of-gauge' town, once visited by General Douglas MacArthur, who stood on the railway station and famously declared, 'I came out of Bataan and I shall return.'

This was the sort of frontier town to which many young men and women fresh off the boat from the slums of London, or the recently cleared Highlands of Scotland, would have been drawn. In an Australian version of the famous 'Go West, Young Man!' thousands quickly headed to the outback, a vast, khaki Xanadu where they imagined they'd make their fortune, or at least, forge a new life. For many, farming or mining was all they knew, for others, it was a break with the past.

But, as Hailes explained, the figures tell their own story.

In the 2006 Census Terowie had a total of 145 residents: 18 people had a job (6 in agriculture, 4 in 'fuel retailing' – the local servo – 4 in accommodation and 4 in manufacturing), 9 were unemployed and 77 were 'not in the labour force'; the median household income was $339 per week, compared to a national average of $1027 per week.

Times had changed. The railway bypassed Terowie in the 1970s. In 1985 the government declared it an 'historic town', a label no one wants. The once-thriving railway station was a peeling, crumbling ghost of its former self, Bleechmore Brothers, General Storekeepers had long since gone and the Rechabites and Odd Fellows had given up on finding new members, odd or otherwise.

On 16 December 2009 the Clare-based *Northern Argus* reported: 'Terowie farewells school after 132 years.' A photo showed the remaining 11 students at Terowie Rural School (TRS) standing outside their old classroom. Parents had been gradually sending their children to larger schools in nearby towns and TRS, once one of two schools in the town educating 200 kids, had given in to the inevitable. The principal, Des Deuter, explained that some winter days when there was illness about there were as few as two kids at school. 'What it came down to in the end was parents realising their children weren't getting the socialisation that they needed,' he explained.

The article finished by saying the school's equipment would be shared between neighbouring schools and, in a story that had become familiar to the citizens of Terowie, 'All the school's windows will be boarded up and the building secured against vandals while its future use is assessed.'

The great promises of the 1880s – of Dr Hill and his eye hospital, of flour mills and dramatic societies, of dozens of bullock teams camped around town waiting to be loaded with goods for the mines – came to nothing. Full of eternal optimism, the Terowie Citizens' Association bought and preserved six old buildings, but time has, and will, continue marching on.

For most passing through Terowie today there is little reason to stop. Again, people slow down, look, admire and feel sentimental, but that's no longer enough. L.P. Hartley was right in saying the past is a foreign country, but it's one we still long to rediscover.

The 'iron solitude of the hills'

Culture shapes attitude; attitude shapes action. Nowhere is this more clearly seen than in the way humans interact with landscape. In her article 'Mountains made alive: Native American relationships with sacred land', American writer Emily Cousins compared the 'mystique of private property', in the Western sense, with the ancient idea, still held by many aboriginal peoples, that, 'When people recognise a spiritual essence shared by the world around them, their interactions with the land take on a quality of reverence and respect. Instead of being one-sided, with the humans taking what they need and not giving back, these relationships become mutual ...'

Cousins described a time, reaching its peak in the late 19th century, when these two world views locked horns. She quoted the American senator Henry L. Dawes, who in 1885 said that Native Americans 'have gone as far as they can go, because they own their land in common. There is no enterprise to make your home any better than that of your neighbour's. There is no selfishness, which is at the bottom of civilization. Till this people will consent to give up their lands, and divide them among their citizens, so that each can own the land he cultivates, they will not make much progress.'

To the modern reader, these words seem dated and dangerous. They need to be seen in the context of their time – big men trawling a big land for opportunities. We need to look to Europe, and the history of feudalism, of wars fought and blood spilt over small patches of productive land; of industrialisation, of Mr Gradgrind's Facts, and boys sent down mines to maximise profits for the few at the expense of hundreds of thousands dead from black lung disease. In the 19th century wealth was taken, not earned; the future belonged to those who could wrestle it from the past. None more so than those who set out across the American prairies, or the Australian outback, in search of land.

The *'black line'*

In 1826 the governor of Van Diemen's Land, George Arthur, had tired of trying to make peace with the local Aboriginal population. Settlers had been attacked and killed and livestock was regularly taken by 'hostile tribes' (Arthur's words) who had lost their traditional hunting grounds. Although Arthur had pleaded with locals to show compassion and understanding, in April 1830 he wrote, 'The aboriginal natives of this colony are and ever have been a most treacherous race.'

In October 1830 he decided to drive all Aboriginal people from the 'settled country' onto the Tasman Peninsula, an isolated area 75 kilometres south-east of Hobart connected to the mainland by a narrow, easily regulated isthmus. Arthur spent £30,000 and used thousands of men to make his 'black line' but only managed to capture two Aboriginal people. The next year he sent George Robinson to capture and remove 'natives' to a mission on Gun Carriage Island, and later, in 1831, to Flinders Island. This helped but certainly didn't end Arthur's problems, mostly caused by the white settlers' treatment of Aboriginal people in the first place.

Arthur's actions were a response to intense criticism from settlers and the press. On 1 May 1828 Andrew Bent of the *Hobart Town Colonial Advocate* warned his readers: 'By a fatality, over which we have no control, accounts of the outrages of these surely most savage of all savages in human shape are destined to pollute our pages of record, every succeeding month.'

Bent pulled no punches. 'Unless the blacks are exterminated or removed, it is plainly proved, by fatal and sanguinary experience, that all hope of their ceasing in their aggressions, is the height of absurdity. All the conciliations – all the mercy – all the kindness ... that have been bestowed to render these unhappy tribes sensible of the benefits of civilisation, have been thrown away, and the only return they have made is to murder and plunder, and express their determination to exterminate every white man that comes in their way.'

At which point Bent made his weekly inventory of 'outrages' perpetrated upon Englishmen by 'a handful of black barbarians', starting with:
1. Mr Giles's hut attacked; the inmates saving their lives by flight.
2. A servant of Mr Cotterel's killed at his hut ...

And finishing with a flurry of exclamation marks:
10. A man of Mr Robertson's speared, and is missing!
11. Another man, in the same neighbourhood, dangerously speared in five places!

We might laugh, and pass judgement, but Arthur was in a fix. Civil strife, and chaos, were real possibilities. Although Bent said, 'The *lex talionis* [an eye for an eye] is by no means what we are about,' he went on to say, 'We predict, that unless the blacks are removed ... the whole of the Settlers ... will set about the dreadful work of Aboriginal extermination.'

Myall Creek

On 7 June 1838, Charles Reid and Andrew Burrows arrived at Bengari Station, 60 kilometres south of Myall Creek Station, west of Inverell, New South Wales. Both men were employed as farmhands at Myall Creek. Reid and Burrows were in charge of a herd of a hundred cattle that William Hobbs, Myall Creek's manager, wanted moved to fresh pasture. That night they met a group of six men, mostly convict settlers, armed with swords and muskets. The leader of this group, John Russell, and his offsider, George Palliser, asked Reid and Burrows if there were any Aboriginal people at Myall Creek. They replied that yes, there was a small group of men, women and children. When asked how long they had been there they told Russell and the others about five weeks, although the group had only just arrived.

Reid and Burrows were concerned about what these men were planning. A few weeks before a group of about 40 Kwiambal Aboriginal people had moved and settled on land at Myall

Creek Station, a run owned by Henry Dangar. They had kept to themselves, hunting traditional foods, fishing in the river, and the station hands had shared tea, sugar and flour with them. Often the two groups would get together to dance and sing. George Anderson, an assigned convict at Myall Creek, was sleeping with a Kwiambal girl named Impeta.

Over the next 24 hours the group of six men rode along the Gwydir River towards Myall Creek. As they went they picked up more convict settlers, and a free man, John Fleming, who would play a major role in the forthcoming events, although he was the only member of the group to escape punishment. Late on 9 June the group arrived at Dangar's property. They split into two groups and approached the Kwiambal camp. The frightened group of Aboriginal people fled, seeking protection near Anderson's hut. The group of 12 men approached Anderson and told him they were 'rounding up' Aboriginal people in retaliation for cattle stealing, although they couldn't say if any of the assembled group were responsible.

Anderson could do little. He was sent to fetch milk, and when he returned the Kwiambal had been roped together. He watched as the group was led towards nearby hills. Twenty minutes later he and several other hands heard rifle shots.

Yintayintin, an Aboriginal servant who had been left behind at Myall Creek, followed the party and later that night discovered 28 bodies in the bush. In his book *Blood on the Wattle*, Bruce Elder described what Yintayintin saw: 'It seemed that the murderers, not wanting to waste ammunition, had drawn the swords and cut the Kwiambal to pieces. They had decapitated most of the babies and children. Heads had been hurled far from the bodies ... Sickened by what he saw ... he fled. Arriving back at the hut, he blurted out the news to Anderson.'

Reid's group had spared an Aboriginal girl. After she'd been made to watch her family and tribe massacred, she was raped by members of the group.

The following morning the group set out to search for ten Kwiambal men who had been out cutting bark the pervious day.

They found Thomas Foster, who had been with the men, but he lied to protect them. The next day these men, perhaps becoming aware of the enormity of their act, returned to Myall Creek. They gathered branches and foliage and attempted to burn the bodies.

Meanwhile, William Hobbs, who had been helping Reid and Burrows move cattle, heard a rumour about the massacre and started back for Myall Creek. Upon arrival the next day he investigated the Kwiambal camp, strewn with clothes and cooking implements, and knew that something was wrong. He questioned Anderson and Yintayintin. They were reluctant to describe what had happened. He then questioned Charles Kilmeister, a Myall Creek stockman who had been among the group of 12, but he too denied any knowledge.

Later that day Yintayintin took Hobbs to the scene of the massacre. According to Elder, 'It was, as Hobbs was later to describe it, horrible beyond description. The fires had been only partially successful. Spread around the stock-yard were piles of half-burned bodies. The stench of death and decay was overwhelming.'

Hobbs spent several days deciding what to do. He searched Myall Creek for any sign of the missing cattle but found none. He wrote a letter to his boss, Henry Dangar, but didn't send it. He was partly indignant, partly cautious, wrestling with his conscience, trying to find a path forward. Eventually he rode 400 kilometres to Muswellbrook and reported the massacre to the local magistrate, Captain Edward Day. Day then contacted Edward Thomson, the Colonial Secretary, who in turn reported the events to Governor George Gipps.

A month after the massacre, Gipps ordered Day to investigate. Day arrived at the scene and found charred and crushed bones and skulls, despite the area having been 'cleared up'. Eventually he identified at least 27 remains. Over the next seven weeks he completed an investigation, arrested most of the group (excluding John Fleming) and returned to Sydney.

The trial of the men began in November 1838. Lawyers were provided and paid for by a coalition of local landowners called The

Black Association. One of this group, a magistrate, gained access to the accused and helped them construct a single version of events. Therefore, in court, the men managed to display a unified front. After all, as Elder explained, the group felt that 'according to the non-laws of the frontier, their actions were justified. They saw themselves as heroes – not as murderers'. It's clear that large numbers of the population, especially on the 'frontier', shared these sentiments. As one of the jurors later told a newspaper, 'I look on the blacks as a set of monkeys and the sooner they are exterminated from the face of the earth, the better.' Justice was vague, open to interpretation, to the actions of interest groups, to long-held opinions, and grudges. The juror stated: 'I knew the men were guilty of murder but I would never see a white man hanged for killing a black.'

The men were found not guilty. Then, according to Elder, 'to the amazement of everyone in the court, it was announced that the eleven men would be held in custody and retried using the same evidence'.

Seven of the men were eventually retried and sentenced to death. Anderson, who had been a key witness in the first trial, spoke out against the group. Despite an appeal to the Executive Council of New South Wales the men were hanged at Darlinghurst Prison on 18 December 1838.

The government was sending a message: murder is murder, black or white. In the following years the killing went underground, carried out on a smaller scale, more discreetly, using poison and other means in an unwritten practice named 'death by stealth'. Myall Creek was only one in hundreds of instances of a slow, creeping genocide that continued well into the 20th century. From the 1857 massacre of the Yeeman people in Queensland to the 1928 Coniston massacre, where 32 Aboriginal people were killed after attacking a dingo trapper and station owner. From the murder of up to 170 Aboriginal people in Queensland's central highlands in the 1860s to the 1924 Bedford Downs massacre, where a group of Kija men were poisoned by strychnine-laced food, and shot and burned by station hands.

The Fierce Country

Frank Hawson

Life on Australia's frontiers was marked by loneliness, struggle and cruelty. Even children weren't immune. On 5 October 1840, 12-year-old Frank Hawson was tending a flock of sheep just outside Port Lincoln, 640 kilometres from Adelaide. He was working near a log hut filled with food supplies and other provisions. Early that morning he was approached by a dozen or so Aboriginal men and boys who asked him to come with them on a kangaroo hunt. He declined, and as Nathaniel Hailes recalled in 1878, 'Had he done otherwise there can be little doubt that his life would have been saved, although the provisions or a substantial proportion of them would have been stolen.'

The Aboriginal people asked for food and Hawson gave them flour, rice, and a lighted stick to make a fire. Some of the Aboriginal people noticed a sword and gun in the hut, and asked for the firearm. Hawson refused and the men demanded to be let in. By now the boy must have been terrified – alone, miles from any help, unsure whether to stand up to the group or let them take what they want. Maybe he thought he could scare them off, for next, he took the gun, closed the door, and stood outside the hut. Two of the Aboriginal men threw spears which hit him in the chest. He fired and hit one of the men, at which point the whole group ran away.

That evening Hawson's brother arrived to find Frank adding wood to his fire, resting the shafts of the spears in the flames and trying to burn them away. As Hailes explained, 'The jagged heads of the spears could not be withdrawn, but his brother in some way relieved him by cutting away the external parts as near to the flesh as possible.'

In what must have been an agonising journey, Hawson's brother took Frank to Port Lincoln on horseback. Without any surgical help he survived for six days before dying.

Eighteen months later it all happened again. On 29 March 1842 two men named Biddle and Fastins, as well as an old couple named Tubbs, were gathered in a hut near Port Lincoln. A group of Aboriginal people had been camped nearby for several days. Just as Biddle, Fastins and the Tubbs were eating their evening meal a large group of Aboriginal people approached the hut. Fastins went out to talk to them, but was met with a 'shower of spears'. He went back inside, found some bread and potatoes, went out and threw the food to the assembled group, who soon dispersed.

An hour later 40 Aboriginal men returned. This time all three men went out, but again they were greeted by a shower of spears, one of which hit Fastins in the leg. Biddle fired a pistol at the group, which only got them angrier, and they started to come closer.

The three men barricaded themselves in the hut. The attackers made a hole in the wall and continued throwing spears. Soon the group broke into the hut and continued spearing the four. Mrs Tubbs hid under a bed. Mr Biddle was speared through the chest and died with 'one exclamatory sentence'. One of the group started attacking Fastins with a pitchfork that had been kept in the hut. In a scene from a *Boys' Own* adventure Fastins turned to Tubbs, pointed to a pistol on the ground, and asked him to shoot him. Tubbs didn't need to. Fastins died from the spear wounds moments later.

The group pulled Mrs Tubbs from under the bed and attacked her with the pitchfork and a pair of sheep shears. Hailes said, 'When the natives had finally retired, Mrs Tubbs observing that her husband, who had withdrawn no fewer than six spears from different parts of his body, appeared to have escaped a mortal wound, but feeling that her own recovery was hopeless ... made him promise that he would return to England as soon as possible.'

Hours later Tubbs awoke, severely wounded, blinded in one eye by a spear. His wife and the others were dead. Later that night he was found by shepherds, who raised the alarm. Eventually he recovered and did return to England, happy to tell his story to anyone who'd listen. Two Aboriginal men named Narrabie and Nultia were captured, tried and executed at the site of the massacre.

The Fierce Country

Eliza Fraser

Not every frontier encounter took place on land claimed by Europeans for agriculture. The sounds of spears slicing the air, of muskets discharging, was not always heard in stockyards or along dry creek beds, witnessed by a few indifferent crows along wheatbelt tracks. Sometimes these tragedies played out in what we today call paradise.

The town of Stromness is a small, windblown village on the Orkney Islands, off the coast of Scotland. In the 17th and 18th century its harbour, Hamnavoe, was crammed with ships plying the Atlantic, especially vessels from the Hudson's Bay Company. Stromness itself is built around the harbour, and its main flagstone-paved street follows the bay. The old stone homes and shops, with their small windows and large chimneys, are old world, picture-postcard, vastly different from the red desert and white beaches of what in the early 19th century was the unknown world of Australia.

But it was here that 37-year-old mother of three Eliza Fraser lived with her husband, James, a ship's captain. In 1835 Mrs Fraser decided, or perhaps was persuaded by her husband, to accompany him on a voyage to the Antipodes – a journey that would end in shipwreck, murder, and the creation of one of Australia's strangest frontier myths.

Eliza and James left their daughter and two sons in Scotland and boarded the brig *Stirling Castle* bound for Hobart. Over the next eight months they sailed from London to Hobart Town, to Sydney, and north towards Singapore. Then, on a dark night in May 1836, off Australia's north-east coast, their ship struck a coral reef and sank. The 18 crew and passengers boarded a longboat and a pinnace and headed south for Moreton Bay.

Eventually the boats drifted apart. One came ashore at the Tweed River, near present-day Coolangatta. The other, carrying Eliza, James and several seamen, drifted for 32 days before landing on the northern tip of what was then the Great Sandy Island (Fraser Island, later named in honour of Captain Fraser).

During their time at sea, Fraser gave birth to a child who died.

The Frasers and the others met a group of Kabi Aboriginal people who, at first, were happy to trade with them. For 11 days the Europeans swapped their few goods for food. Then, believing they were on the mainland, four of them tried to walk south to Moreton Bay. That night the Kabi, tired of their visitors, surrounded the others and stripped them of clothes and possessions. Later, they decided to put them to work, taking the men into family groups to help with hunting and fishing. Kabi women 'adopted' Fraser. They cleaned her body with charcoal and grease then decorated her with ochres and feathers. She was expected to help look after the children and gather food.

The fiery Scotswoman wasn't happy about this. She wasn't about to become anyone's slave. We can imagine her lecturing these 'savages', refusing to help, and we can hear the women laughing, but eventually tiring of her rantings. Fraser, though, was determined to survive. Her husband had been speared for not helping, and buried by Kabi men in a shallow grave. The brig's first mate had died and several seamen had drowned attempting to escape the island.

Eventually the Kabi Aboriginal people took her by canoe to the mainland. She remained with them and other tribes until she was found, and helped, by John Graham, an escaped convict who had lived in the confidence of the Kabi for six years. Graham found Fraser near Lake Cootharaba and, assisted by Aboriginal men, returned her to civilisation. She was eventually taken to Sydney where she became a minor celebrity, staying in the home of the colonial secretary, receiving £400 raised for her by a public appeal, and having her (highly embellished) story told in newspapers. The following year she married Captain John Greene and returned to her family in Scotland.

This starchy Presbyterian has come to symbolise the yawning chasm that existed between black and white in the first few decades of colonisation. Mrs Fraser – with her bonnet and shawl, reciting Bible verses in her thick Orcadian accent, refusing, but being forced to submit to a new culture – embodies everything stubborn, indignant and doomed to irrelevance, in our early history. Fraser wasn't about to compromise. Ultimately, she had to learn the hard way. In the end, she preferred to return to Scotland than face the challenges of the New World.

Fraser was one of the first to enter, and re-emerge, alive, from the Fierce Country. She was only aware of one type of man, one landscape, one way of organising families, and communities, one god, one explanation for Heaven and Earth, one morality, and one set of laws. We can't judge her but we can listen to the old stories again and try to make sense of them, to find a new way forward, a set of common values that ignores fence lines and mining rights.

Daisy Bates

Daisy Bates, or Kabbarli (grandmother) as her 'natives' called her, is best remembered as an eccentric Edwardian, done up in a white blouse, stiff collar and ribbon tie; a dark skirt, sailor hat and flyveil. Bates always maintained a 'fastidious toilet … to the simple but exact dictates of fashion as I left it when Victoria was Queen'. Most people would visualise her waiting for the train at Ooldea Siding, or back at Yooldilya gabbi (Ooldea Soak), bringing her charity and strong, healing hands to the local Wirangu people. In an inhospitable chunk of desert, 190 kilometres north of Fowlers Bay, Bates lived alone in a tent with her collection of Dickens novels from 1919 to 1935.

Bates was a mass of contradictions: conservative Edwardian and bigamist; ethnographer and shonky journalist (in 1908 she met a group of Aboriginal women in the Murchison district, every one of whom, she claimed 'killed and ate her newborn baby, sharing it with every other woman in her group'); an inspiring, outback proto-feminist, but in the end sad; loving, but impossible to love.

In her day, she was almost as well known as Don Bradman. She was the original Geraldine Cox, running a one-woman mission for a people who were, in her opinion, destined for extinction.

Whereas Cox's Sunrise Children's Villages are all about creating futures, Bates' work was more about soothing the fatal wound of history.

In 1935 Bates was brought to Adelaide by the writer Ernestine Hill. She had persuaded the *Advertiser*'s managing editor, Lloyd Dumas, to offer Bates money to write a series of features about her desert experiences. Hill would be employed to help her. Bates was more than happy to oblige. She had come to believe that she'd gathered as much material about the desert Aboriginal people as she could. Also, the United Aborigines Mission (UAM) had set up in Ooldea Soak in 1933 and stolen at least some of her thunder. With typical temerity she explained that 'the mission's coming has brought my work of investigation to a dead end. Of course, I encourage my natives to go to the mission and stay there ... one must play the game, you know'.

Bates was soon set up in the *Advertiser*'s offices in King William Street. A local journalist described the scene: 'She had a glass-lined cubby about ten by eight ... Mrs Hill had the air of a nurse maid, utterly unable to control her charge ... she did not seem to have the right feeling for Mrs Bates.'

Hill was being paid to 'assist' Bates but it is now generally accepted she had much more than a secretarial role in helping prepare the features that were published as 'My Natives and I'. Bates was 76 years old, with failing eyes, a 'sallow and thin' face and hoarse whisper. Still, Hill later claimed, 'I was careful, and she would have wished it, that all the material ... was exclusively hers.'

Bates was soon making up for a lifetime in the desert. Of an evening she would walk to her room at the South Australian Hotel on North Terrace, where she was the in-house celebrity. Hill later wrote of this period: 'The house phones at the South Australian were carolling all day, flowers, letters, notes to be delivered ... she was the friend of the world, inviting it to dinner, luncheon and tea. Greeting a dozen at a time she mustered them all to the dining room at the bang of a gong.'

Bates was invited across the road to Government House (but

turned down the invitation) and went for a shopping spree on the proceeds of her writing. After years of tent life the temptations of the city were too much. Just before Christmas 1935 she worked her way along Rundle Street's department stores. Her young companion on that day, Josephine Wylde (daughter of an *Advertiser* editor), said 'she flitted from counter to counter ... collecting things she thought we would like as she went. My mother worried that she may not realise how much she was spending ... but she sailed on majestically: "It might be my last Christmas and I am enjoying it with children."'

It seems she loved children. Her own son, Arnold Bates, was born in 1886. At the time she was bigamously married to Jack Bates. Arnold fought in World War I and later moved to New Zealand. When Daisy attempted to contact him in 1949 he wanted nothing to do with her. Arnold realised he had always come a distant second to his mother's 'natives'.

Such was Daisy's mindset, and determination. She had been a self-declared ethnographer since 1904 when she began collecting Aboriginal vocabularies for the Western Australian registrar-general. It's likely this is where she first learnt of the plight of indigenous Australians: exploited by station owners, living in poor conditions, far from decent health and education services. Perhaps not all that different from today. Bates often expressed her opinion of well-meaning government agencies and missionary societies. 'The most that can be said of these efforts is that the native exists, or, perhaps the better would be, *suffers*, a little longer; his ultimate disappearance is only a matter of time.' This statement must be taken in the context of the time. It's not that Bates *wanted* them gone (after all, she devoted her life to their welfare), but she always believed there was 'no way of protecting the Stone Age from the twentieth century'.

By January 1937, with her bank account overdrawn, and intending to research a new book, Bates moved to Pyap, in the Riverland. She'd recently sent her collected articles to a London publisher, but on the way the plane had crashed into the sea. The bags were salvaged and the articles forwarded to John Murray Publishers who released them as *The Passing of the Aborigines*. Although out of print today (for obvious reasons), in 1938 this book was read and admired throughout the world, affirming Bates's reputation as an authority on Australian Aboriginal people.

After years in the Riverland, and a mental and physical breakdown, Bates was hospitalised in Adelaide in 1945. The old wanderlust soon kicked in and she went to live at Streaky Bay, hoping she might run into some of her old wards.

A friend, Beatrice Raine, invited her back to Adelaide in 1948 to share a house. Bates was almost 90, but showed no signs of slowing. Upon her return to the city she tried to contact her son in New Zealand. She always carried a picture of him as a seven-year-old. When he refused to talk to her, Bates told a friend that 'he must have lost his memory'. This, she convinced herself, was the only way to explain his rejection. But according to a journalist who met Arnold Bates, he had no feeling for her or her 'legend' at all.

Bates could be seen parading Adelaide's city streets. Cars would slow to look and kids would ask mums, 'Is that Mrs Bates?' She would often get lost, confused, and ask for directions. She'd wander onto roads and have to be helped, but no man or woman alive was about to tell Daisy Bates she should be home beside the wireless.

One day she stood outside Government House demanding to see the governor. To save everyone embarrassment, a local police woman, Alvis Brooks, convinced her that her car was the governor's own limousine, and Bates allowed her to drive her home.

Bates died on 19 April 1951. She was almost blind from sand blight, small, weak, but still proudly defiant and mentally sharp. She was buried at North Road Cemetery with a sprig of desert pea on her coffin.

This book, with its stories of lost children, murder and wrong turnings, is an attempt to relate individuals to their landscape. Are we made by the desert, the beach, the heat waves, the droughts? Are we still trying to forge a national character, to put forward a version of history we think might stick? Or are we just a race of illywhackers, clutching at headlines, at gossip, that might define us; and is this attempt at fiction, passing from Adam Lindsay Gordon to Lawson, from Boldrewood to Bail, really just a way of us saying, Well, take a look around, this is Australia, for better or worse?

The single most poignant image of our colonial past is that of the lost child, wandering the outback in search of his or her parents. Peter Pierce, author of *The Country of Lost Children: An Australian Anxiety*, has tried to explain the plethora of stories, poems and paintings about children expiring in the bush as whisky-warmed voices – part Dickens, part Lawson – retell their tragic final moments around campfires. In a 2001 speech, Pierce explained 'in the first instance the child was a surrogate figure for the adult generation which had not yet begun to feel that it belonged in this country ... What this seemed to speak of in part was a fear of the future into which they might be born in Australia'.

Pierce told the story of three boys who disappeared in the bush near Daylesford, Victoria, in 1867. Ten weeks later their decomposed bodies were found near a hollow tree. Pierce described the triple funeral attended by a thousand people filing past the boys' single, open grave. The local community, and beyond, searched for an outlet for their grief. Soon there were poems ('In Memoriam. The Lost Children of Daylesford'), newspaper articles and engravings (one by Samuel Calvert showing the hollow tree and suggestions of the small bodies), and even a short story by Marcus Clarke ('Pretty Dick'). In this sentimental tale, a child wanders 'across a creek into the beckoning land of promise beyond ...'

As did so many of the victims of the Fierce Country.

CHAPTER 2

Point Puer Boys' Prison
1834–1849

The journey to Australia – Arrival, and the 'efficiency of this system' – Walter Paisley – Discipline and Rations – Description of geography – Little Boy Lost – '68 Urchins' – Lashes to the buttocks

Imagine: ten years old, brought up in the East End of Victorian London, abandoned by your parents, left to find an Artful Dodger and make your way in the world. Your first picked pocket and you're up in front of the 'beak'. He looks at you and tells you you're no good and suggests a few years in Van Diemen's Land. Five months later you and a hundred other boys are lined up in Hobart Town and inspected by farmers and factory owners in search of free labour. It's called the Assignment Scheme, but you've got another name for it. After a hellish journey, packed into a dark hold, fed on gruel and biscuits (just in case you were in any sort of condition), the government has decided you are, after all, no good for coal mining, quarrying or building roads. So it's back to the barracks, and the thieves and murderers destined for the Port Arthur penal colony.

By now you're learning how to protect yourself from abuse, to obtain your share of food and water, to stay sane at an age when other children are playing with tin soldiers and paper windmills.

Soon, you learn you'll be sent to Point Puer Boys' Prison. The name is muttered as some sort of omen, a warning or damnation. You realise it doesn't sound good.

In 1843 Benjamin Horne visited Point Puer to observe and write a report on conditions for the governor, Sir John Franklin.

His notes make it clear that this wasn't a place for the faint-hearted:

> In the sleeping apartments lights are kept burning during the night, and they [the boys] are constantly watched by Overseers, but the efficiency of this system must depend wholly upon the moral character and vigilance of these Officers. Sometimes the Overseer relaxes his vigilance and falls asleep, and, if he is not a favourite with the boys, they put out the lights and invert and empty a night-tub over his head and shoulders. This trick which is called 'Crowning the Overseer' has occurred once during my visit.

Point Puer was established to cater for boys who had been sentenced to transportation. It's difficult for us to fathom a government and judiciary who could treat children as the worst sorts of criminals. To some extent, English society thought itself better off without these 'types', but there was also an idea that these boys needed to be saved from themselves. They could be reformed, taught to fix shoes, bind books, mill wood and contribute to the future of their new colonial home. Horne believed the juvenile prisoner is 'deplorably ignorant of religious and moral duties ... or of reading and understanding good books ...' In other words, these 'rascals' just needed a firm hand.

Thirteen-year-old Walter Paisley was sentenced to seven years' transportation for housebreaking. He was one of Point Puer's first arrivals. He was no angel. During his time at the prison 44 charges were brought against him for insubordination, stealing and assaulting overseers and superintendents. Mostly, the punishment was solitary confinement, but this didn't bother him. A few weeks after his arrival he was sentenced to the cells for a week for insubordination. A few months later he was back for smuggling tobacco. He sat singing, shouting obscenities, determined to make life difficult for his captors. After his release he struck the schoolmaster, stole a chicken from the superintendent's garden and assaulted boys who had given evidence against him.

The first few years at Point Puer were tough. Discipline was strict. The boys were mostly a product of the slums within growing cities such as London, Birmingham and Manchester. Either this, or used as free farm labour from an early age. Despite not having chosen their path through childhood they were seen by authorities as 'very depraved and difficult to manage, perhaps more so than grown men'.

Boys were up at five am, rolling their mattresses and washing in tanks of Point Puer's scarce water. Six o'clock meant prayers. 'Singing is not taught, and the consequence is that this part of the Divine Service is very badly conducted. In fact the screaming is almost intolerable to any person whose ears have not by rendered callous by hearing it continually.' Then:

½ past 6	Breakfast
½ past 7	Musters
8 to 12	Workshops and General Labor
12 to 1	Play and washing for dinner
1	Dinner
¼ to 2	Muster for School and Work
2 o'clock	One half goes to School and the other half to work on alternate days from 2 to ½ past 5
½ past 6	Supper
7 to 8	In summer play. During the winter Months they are mustered earlier and some time is spent in reading aloud to them in their barracks etc.
8 o'clock	General muster in the different buildings. After this reading the scriptures and prayer
By 9 o'clock	All are in bed

If it was warm enough, and tide permitting, the boys could take a 'sea bath' between five and six in the morning. A near freezing dip would be enough to get anyone's day started. As with Port Arthur, the location of Point Puer, on a fat finger of land stretching into the bay, was meant to deter thoughts of escape. The south-eastern tip of Tasmania is rugged, ocean-beaten, windswept. On the journey from Hobart boys would have passed Two Island, Curio, Tunnel and Raoul bays, the latter with its 180-metre-high dolerite columns soaring into the sub-Arctic sky as a warning of what's to come. At one point Cape Raoul had its own signal station. Years after it was closed, due to inaccessibility, the skeleton of an escaped convict who'd starved to death was found in the signalman's hut.

The boys would have sailed north past heavily wooded country, eventually arriving at their new home, a rocky peninsula pointing to the Isle of the Dead, Port Arthur's burial island. They would have looked across Carnarvon Bay and seen Port Arthur itself, its grim face warning them there would be no escape.

Their prison was surrounded on three sides by water, and strong currents that carried small, underfed bodies out to sea. This 'Junior Port Arthur' was an early version of San Francisco's Alcatraz prison. To the west, sheer cliffs and a rock pavement ensured no one was going anywhere.

Point Puer features in Marcus Clarke's novel *For the Term of His Natural Life*. The story was published in the *Australian Journal* between 1870 and 1872. It concerns Rufus Dawes, a young man transported for a murder he didn't commit. The loosely connected stories outline his struggles as a convict in Van Diemen's Land. In the novel, Clarke introduces 12-year-old Peter Brown, a 'refractory little thief' who jumps off the Point Puer rocks and drowns himself. Clarke's sense of drama is laced with social conscience. 'Just so! The magnificent system starved and tortured a child of twelve until he killed himself. That was the way of it.' His indignant superintendent, Burgess, is enraged at this 'jumping off'. 'If he could by any possibility have brought the corpse of poor little Peter Brown to life again, he would have soundly whipped it for impertinence ...'

Childhood suicide was probably the extreme. Many boys tried to escape but the road to Port Arthur was patrolled by soldiers stationed in a barracks on a 'demarcation' line between the two prisons. There were three recorded successes, but there were probably more, and probably more small bodies lost in the bush.

One commandant, William Champ, described the location as a 'bleak, barren spot without water, wood for fuel, or an inch of soil ...'

Benjamin Horne agreed. His report said that water was brought from the mainland in a ditch but 'from the porous nature of the soil this could scarcely have succeeded ... At present water is brought from Port Arthur by sea ...' He described how an attempt had been made to improve the soil using 'seaweed, night soil etc'. Also, 'the wood on the Point is exhausted and firewood is also brought from the Penal settlement'.

None of this was good news for the boys.

Rations (daily)
¾ lb flour
¾ lb fresh or salt meat

Dinner (lunch)
1 Pint Soup
12 oz meat, reduced by boiling and extraction of bone to 6 oz
9 oz bread
9 oz dumpling

Supper (dinner)
1 Pint gruel
9 oz bread

Mostly, the Point Puer inmates were not misunderstood angels. Several months after Horne forwarded his report an overseer was murdered by two boys. Discipline included confinement on bread and water for up to 14 days, corporal punishment (up to 36 lashes) and, 'in very bad cases', transfer to Port Arthur itself. It's hard to imagine how bad a boy would have to be to warrant removal to one of the toughest prisons in the world. The weekly magistrate's visit attracted between ten and 60 hearings. Horne explained, 'A removal to the Jail is very little feared by a bad boy ... A boy who has perhaps a little moral principle remaining is sent to the Jail for two or three Months, associates daily with other boys still worse than himself, and returns to the General Class thoroughly corrupted.'

He goes on to explain the pointlessness of corporal punishment. 'It tends to degrade and harden, and after having been twice or thrice inflicted is evidently useless.'

There was a growing view in England, America and Australia that locking up increasing numbers of 'criminals' would achieve nothing. Dickens had already visited American prisons to study new ways forward for the British system, full to overflowing, sucking in hundreds of thousands of poor and spitting them out in the Antipodes. Here was Oliver Twist in Van Diemen's Land. Meanwhile, William Blake and the Romantics were de-industrialising childhood in poems such as *Little Boy Lost*.

> The weeping child could not be heard,
> The weeping parents wept in vain:
> They stripped him to his little shirt,
> And bound him in an iron chain.

Years later, Marcus Clarke would leave no doubt what sent little Peter Brown to his death: '20th November, disorderly conduct, 12 lashes. 24th November, insolence to hospital attendant, diet reduced. 4th December, stealing cap from another prisoner, 12 lashes. 15th December, absenting himself from roll call, two days' cells. 23rd December, insolence and insubordination, two days' cells. 8th January, insolence and insubordination, 12 lashes.'

And so it continues. Later in the book, Brown's friends, Tommy and Billy, succumb to the same horror: 'And so the two babies knelt on the brink of the cliff, and raising their bound hands together, looked up at the sky, and ungrammatically said, "Lord, have pity on we two fatherless children!" and then they kidded each other, and "did it".'

Horne explained that instruction 'in trades and various industrial employment is valuable both as a means of reforming the juvenile delinquent and of preparing him after his liberation to preserve his subsistence by honest labour'. Colonial authorities believed the problem was the boys' 'love of wandering'. If they could be trained and kept working they would become 'habituated' to a life without crime and vagrancy. Soon after its establishment Point Puer was producing junior shoemakers, tailors, sawyers, coopers, blacksmiths, boat builders, book binders and carpenters. All trades that would be in demand by the developing economy.

In 1837 the barque *Frances Charlotte* brought boys to Van Diemen's Land. They were all from poor backgrounds, uneducated, part of the *residuum*, or lowest strata of Victorian society. On the journey an attempt was made to train them in manual arts. Instead of learning bad habits from older inmates these young convicts would be taught skills to aid both them and the Colonial authorities during and after their term of incarceration.

Up to 20 per cent of convicts arriving in Australia in the 1830s were boys aged between ten and 14. In Van Diemen's Land, lieutenant-governors Arthur and Franklin and prison commandant Captain O'Hara Booth knew what would come from putting these boys with adult prisoners: apprentice criminals would become master crooks, gangs would form, power cliques take over and the dreaded *vice l'anglais* spread (older and younger boys were separated at night in their Point Puer barracks).

In January 1834 the brig *Tamar* arrived from Hobart Town. Aboard were 21 adults and 68, mostly drunk, boys. Booth explained in his diary:

> January 10: Tamar signalized – found on board an increase of 21 Adults and 68 Urchins – on the way down the latter evinced their dexterity by foraging out in the Hold of the Vessel a six dozen Case of Wine for me, had abstracted all but one Bottle – some of which they had handed in to the Adults – the consequences a scene of general intoxication – some of the Boys and Men brutal – landed all Men that were drunk ...

It was obvious that men and boys had to be kept separate. Horne explained that 'boys and men are frequently out as absconders at the same time and may meet ... Very lately, no fewer than 6 men and 10 boys were missing from the two places on the same evening'.

Point Puer's first inmates arrived in December 1833 and started building their own accommodation. By the time of Horne's visit, ten years later, there was a 'Barrack' for the now 716 boys, workshops, bake-house, a building used as a school and chapel, and a gaol with one building for 'boys under sentence for faults' and another for those sentenced for more serious offences. The prison was run by officers, a 'Catechist' (who also ran the school), a superintendent of the gaol, and various tradesmen, most of whom had been or were still prisoners or 'Ticket of Leave' men. This carried its own risk, although perhaps these men were determined to give the boys the sorts of opportunities they'd lacked.

Then again …

The 1840s saw the demise of transportation to Australia. New South Wales (then most of eastern Australia) stopped the practice in 1840 and convicts were diverted to Van Diemen's Land. Public opinion there led to the formation of the Anti-Transportation League in the late 1840s and the last convict transport was sent from England in 1853. Four years earlier, in March 1849, the last 162 Point Puer boys were loaded onto a ship and sent to the Cascades in Hobart Town.

Walter Paisley had been released in 1838. Less than a year later he was arrested for housebreaking in Launceston. He was sentenced to transportation for life and sent to Port Arthur, across the bay from his old home. Here he was up on charges six times before being sent to the Colonial Hospital in Hobart in 1844.

Paisley's life was typical of thousands. A society that had failed so many children had dealt with them in the harshest possible way. These early encounters between child and landscape, menacing convicts and ruthless authority, were some of the starkest in the history of our fierce continent. Nightly, the Point Puer boys heard waves crashing on the cliffs beside their barracks. They thought of lost parents and siblings, friends, lives that seemed so distant they might have never happened. Benjamin Horne's report to Sir John

Franklin is full of statistics and opinions ('the criminal should not find that he has improved his condition by breaking the laws of God and man ...'). But nowhere are the boys talked about as children. In a way, they had forfeited their childhoods.

Marcus Clarke knew he had the perfect setting for a novel about man versus nature. He describes the Tasman Peninsula as a 'wild and terrible coastline, into whose bowels the ravenous sea had bored strange caverns, resonant with perpetual roar of tortured billows ... Forrestier's Peninsula was an almost impenetrable thicket, growing to the brink of a perpendicular cliff of basalt'.

The boys knew there wasn't much point attempting to escape. Some tried. Eleven-year-old William Bickle had his sentence extended by two years for insubordination and being 'illegally at large'. During his time at Point Puer he faced 65 charges, served 172 days in solitary confinement and suffered 300 lashes to his buttocks.

Today, Point Puer is gum trees and native grasses, the ruins of bread ovens and a few crumbling walls from workshops where boys carved stone for Port Arthur's buildings. If you try you can hear Paisley singing inside his cell, the sound of 12-year-olds reciting from their primers, perhaps even the sounds of happy voices playing in their hour off.

CHAPTER 3

Jandamarra
1894

Comments regarding Bunuba land – Lennard River station – Meat and money – 'Wrong skin' and the consequences – Work as a tracker – The first crime – 'An outrage by the natives' – The uprising, and what it led to – An aside: Jimmy Governor – The years of conflict – What happened to Tho. Jasper – Tracked by Mingo Mick – Final indignities

Two worlds. Banuba Land. Southern Kimberley. The Lennard River cutting through 350-million-year-old limestone. Tunnel Creek, enlarging subterranean caverns and passages the Banuba people have known, and followed, for hundreds of generations. Windjana Gorge. Sheer cliffs and a hundred places to hide, if you need to. A few miles away, cattle, fences, barbed wire that encloses and defines an entirely different mindset. Shorthorn dreams feeding on unimproved pasture, fattening *Bos taurus*, white men making racehorse-chandelier fortunes. And somewhere in between, an indigenous population whose culture is being stripped, layer by layer, song by song, dance by dance, until only the photographs and wax-cylinder recordings remain. The slow, gentle suffocation of traditions that have persisted and sustained since the beginning of time.

Something has to give.

In 1873 or 1874 a boy is born into this rapidly changing world. He learns the way of his people, listens to the elders describe Creation – and the way a man should behave, take care of his skeletal world, and pay tribute to his ever-present ancestors. Soon he and his mother come to live on Lennard River Station. The boy Jandamarra learns to ride, shoot, and speak English. Here he sees another way of explaining the world. Meat. Money. Things that belong to one man, not many. The self, and its preservation, versus the importance of skin.

There are no photographs of Jandamarra, a man who embodied the struggle against Colonial power. During his short life his own people came to believe he had the powers of a Jalgangurru, a man-as-spirit residing in a water soak around Tunnel Creek. Turning into a bird, flying away from danger. Protected from bullets. Police pursuing him couldn't work out how he kept escaping, although they had no idea what lay beneath the Napier Range. How he could cross hot, rocky land with bare feet, gather food, disappear without a trace. To them, he was 'Pigeon'.

Jandamarra was six years old when his mother, Jinny, took him to live on a cattle property that covered most of the Lennard River Flats. According to Queen Victoria's laws, these spinifex acres belonged to Mr William Lukin. But they were really part of Jinny's world: Djumbud country. Lukin watched Jandamarra at work and knew he was on to a good thing. He was a hard worker. Lukin taught him to become an expert marksman, stockman. But soon the boy's time was up. Jandamarra's other world was calling. Now he had to return to his people, to be initiated.

Jandamarra reconnected. His uncle, Ellamarra, taught him the 'law'. This ancient connection awakened new feelings in the teenager. Voices started calling. The frontier struggle for land and power, the 'killing time', raged around him, but he came to sense he was part of something bigger, and more ancient. Like the mineralised waters that flowed beneath the Napier Range. As the Western Australian government continued arresting hundreds of Aboriginal men and boys, sending them to Rottnest Island prison to keep them from slowing the march of progress, Jandamarra and his uncle returned to their lives as stockmen. Ellamarra was the single most important influence in the young man's life. As Jandamarra continued growing – physically, emotionally, spiritually – he began to understand the nature of the black–white divide.

Then things started going wrong. Jandamarra and his uncle were arrested for spearing a sheep. To them it was food, but to the white man, property. Jandamarra served a prison term but was allowed some freedom helping look after police horses. During this time, Jandamarra had 'relations' with women of 'wrong skin' under Banuba law. When word got out he was banished from his own people. He was a sort of plastic spirit, bending, twisting, attempting to live in two worlds, but failing to graft to either. He was confused, tormented, angry.

Jandamarra returned to what he knew best: cattle and sheep. He obtained work on Lillmaloora Station, at the base of the Napier Range. Here he met Bill Richardson, who took the place of his uncle as sage and friend. Jandamarra became his right-hand man. When Richardson joined the police as a freshly minted constable, Jandamarra became his tracker. Now he helped find and arrest his own people, mostly for taking stock. According to one estimate, 4000 sheep had already been stolen. Much easier to catch than kangaroos. Local Aboriginal people knew when they were on to a good thing. Including Ellamarra, who, along with other Banuba people, was tracked down and apprehended by Richardson and his offsider. But one night, Ellamarra escaped. Richardson put it down to super-human strength, but he must have suspected Jandamarra had released him.

Jandamarra was still drifting between two worlds. Caught up. Unable to reconcile differences he could feel on his skin, taste, sense, deep down, in a way that defied words and explanation.

In October 1894 Jandamarra finally decided. He and Richardson had rounded up most of the Banuba leaders and elders. They'd taken them to the Lillmaloora Police Post; watched them for seven days. It's likely that during this time these men spoke to Jandamarra, reminded him of his obligations, where he'd come from, who he really was. On 31 October Jandamarra shot Richardson and released the group, all of whom returned to their families and Banuba land.

Police and pastoralists were worried. Not only had the rule of law been broken, but the Banuba men were armed.

Jandamarra, his uncle and a group of men decided enough was enough. This was the beginning of three years of conflict; a ragged, improvised guerilla war that the *West Australian* (and newspapers the country over) characterised as 'an outrage by the natives in the north'. Lightning raids, not so much to kill, as to frighten pastoralists and townfolk. Footprints. A few stolen sheep. Speared cattle.

The first major conflict took place on 10 November 1894. Jandamarra and his followers attacked a group of five stockmen driving cattle across Banuba land. Two of these men were killed. According to the *West Australian*, 'a body of wild natives arrived at Leonard [sic] Station, and depredations as well as personal injury to the station people were feared. A party of native police were [sic] sent out to preserve order with Police Constable Richardson at their head. When they arrived at Lillmaloora they were met by a body of the blacks, who immediately attacked the police ...' A group of native police and trackers deserted, changing sides. 'Constable Richardson was killed in the affray which followed, whilst the rest of the party endeavoured to get back for reinforcements ...'

The Banuba War had begun. For the first time, indigenous men had decided to stand their ground, defend themselves with firearms, protect their land, families and way of life against an invader who, they must have assumed, had no intention of comprising. The report explained that 'police have been sent out from Derby and other stations, but as yet no information has been received as to whether they have been successful in arresting any of the murderers'.

It had been decided. Murderers. Written in Indian ink. Published in gazettes. Discussed in the front bars of small hotels. So now, frontier justice would have its way.

More bloodshed. Police and local stockmen organised a raiding party. Thirty men set out after Jandamarra. On 16 November 1894 they arrived in Windjana Gorge. Gun shots rang out. A battle followed. Jandamarra was badly wounded but escaped with up to a hundred of his people through tunnels and caves. His uncle, Ellamarra, was killed.

The raiding party continued attacking Aboriginal camps. Guilt by association. Retaliation. Scores were settled.

Jandamarra knew he had nothing to lose. He was a marked man. His closest connections to the black and white world, Ellamarra and Richardson, were dead. His people were looking to him. He'd brought the police down upon them. Indiscriminate killings. City and civilisation were far away, but newspaper reports suggested these folk weren't too concerned, anyway. They only believed what they read about these 'murderers'.

Another indigenous 'outlaw' who enjoyed an even shorter career, and life, than Jandamarra, was Jimmy Governor. The subject of Thomas Keneally's 1972 novel, *The Chant of Jimmie Blacksmith*, Governor was also torn between two worlds. Forced into a position where he had to choose sides.

Governor was born in New South Wales on the Talbragar River in 1875. As with Jandamarra, minimal education, then 'two years at Cassilis police station, employed as a tracker ... After a time I went to Gulgong, wood-cutting for a man named Starr; then I went wool-rolling at Digilbar, then back to Gulgong'.

Then: 'I got married.' A white girl, Ethel Page. A proper service at the Gulgong Church of England.

It's likely this was something at least resembling love. Although Jimmy was part-white, his hair tinged with red, taboos had been broken. Gossips whispered. Eyebrows were raised. Governor was aware of what black and white were saying. The worm was wriggling, uncomfortably. But it wasn't until a day, years later, when he heard the words 'Pooh, you black rubbish, you want shooting for marrying a white woman' that things turned sour.

By April 1900 Governor was working for John Mawbey of Breelong, Gilgandra. Splitting posts, digging post holes and raising fences. He was soon joined by one of his four brothers,

Joe, his nephew Peter, a man named Jacky Underwood, and other Aboriginal people. They were Mawbey's men, claiming rations, becoming part of the settler's family. But they were never really accepted. Kept at a distance. Governor repeatedly asked Mawbey for extra rations but he wouldn't hand anything over until the fencing contract was completed.

All went well until Jimmy learnt that Mrs Mawbey, and Helen Kerz, a teacher residing with the family, had been giving Ethel grief over marrying him. On 20 July 1900 Helen, Mrs Mawbey, and her 18-year-old sister, Elsie Clarke, were home alone with the seven Mawbey children. Governor and Underwood confronted them. Governor later claimed they mocked and laughed at him, told him he wanted shooting. He wasn't about to take this. He had a Jandamarra–Richardson moment. He later said, 'My wife and me had a word or two ... Everything I said to her she said, "Pooh, that's nothing." With that me and Underwood cleared out. I thought I might as well die, so the Mawbey murders were committed.'

Ethel, it seems, had had a change of heart.

Governor and Underwood killed the two women with a tomahawk and nulla-nullas. They then killed three of the children and seriously injured Elsie Clarke.

The men fled, aware of the repercussions. Like Jandamarra, Governor had decided. Underwood was soon caught but Jimmy and Joe spent several months roaming north-central New South Wales. During this time they travelled thousands of kilometres, set upon nothing but revenge. Jimmy had a list of people with whom he needed to settle scores: Alexander McKay, Elizabeth O'Brien and her son, Kieran Fitzpatrick. All murdered. They committed robberies and hid in rugged country around the Hastings and Manning rivers. They were pursued by trackers, police and armed civilians, most aware of the generous reward for their capture.

On 13 October Jimmy was shot in the mouth by a hunter, Herbert Byers. He fled but, in a weakened condition, was captured two weeks later. Joe kept going, but was tracked down and shot dead near Singleton four days after his brother.

In a statement published in the *Maitland Daily* on 29 October 1900, Governor explained: 'I was shot in the mouth and the hip. The shot in the mouth tore four teeth away and passed out through the cheek ... [later] they fired till they disabled me ... I did not fire because I was tired of the whole thing, and was thinking of giving myself up ...'

Governor went to trial and was convicted of the murder of Helen Kerz. As he awaited his fate he read the Bible, sang traditional songs and cursed his wife. He was hanged on 19 January 1901 (after a two-month delay because of 'Federation celebrations'). He was buried in Rookwood Cemetery.

Meanwhile Ethel carried on, undeterred. She re-married and had nine more children.

The following three years were uncertain times for Jandamarra and his followers. They waited, developed strategies, chose their fights. Stalked homesteads, stole, intimidated. Retreated to the caves around Windjana Gorge and Tunnel Creek. There was no political will to solve the problem, find common ground, accommodate the Banuba people.

For a while, Jandamarra was winning. Some pastoralists left their stations, retreated to Derby and other towns.

In March 1897, the final act began. Jandamarra and his followers attacked Oscar Station on the Fitzroy River. On the 22nd of that month the Adelaide *Advertiser* told its readers: '[Thomas Jasper] was sleeping near Collin's Oscar station homestead when he was shot through the head with a bullet and speared in three places. The station hands next morning found the dead man's belongings in possession of a notorious native named Pidgeon [*sic*] and a hand of warlike followers ...' Two constables arrived and, with help from local trackers, surrounded the group. 'Pidgeon opened fire with a Winchester repeater, but did not hit anyone! The police replied and Pidgeon decamped, it is alleged, through a subterranean passage ...'

The chase was on. Police used a tracker from the Pilbara region,

Mingo Mick, to locate Jandamarra. They soon found a camp. The *Kalgoorlie Western Argus* explained that: 'there were nine separate native camps with "Pigeon's" camp cleverly located. Double-barreled guns, a large quantity of Webley revolver ammunition, and an immense quantity of native weapons were secured by the police.'

Finally, police trapped Jandamarra at Tunnel Creek. He was wounded and, perhaps, realising the endgame, emerged from a cave and stood on an outcrop of limestone. He fired at his pursuers but perhaps his spirit faltered. Was he tired? Had he come to believe there was no point continuing? On 9 April the *Sydney Morning Herald* reported: 'News received from the Lennard River states that the head of the police, Constable Chisholm … after following the native "Pigeon" for some days, came on him on the morning of the 1st. After a severe contest they shot him. This ends the career of the most desperate native the colony has known.'

Jandamarra's body was recovered, his head removed, preserved and sent to London where it was put on display by a firearms company. For politicians, police and pastoralists, order had been restored. But no questions had been answered, no bridges built, no justice dispensed for the victims of the Banuba War.

Jandamarra was eventually buried in the Napier Range. His was a short life, but filled with passion: for his people, his land, and justice that was still a long time coming. Jandamarra has become myth. Spirit. The subject of novels, documentaries, a play. A man who tried to live in two worlds. Who came to see that the compromises this required were just too great.

CHAPTER 4

The Calvert Expedition
1896–1897

A short history of Albert Calvert – Westralia's Golden Prophet – Lawrence Allen Wells – Dervish Bejah, cameleer – 'Filling the blanks' – The expedition splits – Separation Well – 'I can hardly remember how I got back' – Sandy Blight – Arrival at Fitzroy River – The five rescue attempts – Last words of Jones – Wells returns to the desert

The Calvert Scientific Exploring Expedition ('equipped at the request and expense of Albert Calvert Esq., F.R.G.S., London, for the purpose of exploring the remaining blanks of Australia') was made up of a group of determined men who, by design or accident, or both, wrote their names in one of the lesser volumes of Australian history. This book is filled with facts, figures, tragedies and triumphs, all described on a thousand yellowing pages. A mould-stained, ink-rendered frontispiece shows a big-bearded explorer looking out to posterity. All of the requisite elements are there: a Voss-like leader, camels, 'sandy-blight', mercury thermometers that try but can't get beyond 120 degrees, a few bad decisions, lots of persistence and, finally, the discovery of a pair of mummified bodies.

The challenge of filling unexplored blanks on the map of Australia loomed large in the 19th-century psyche. There was a type of man who, to paraphrase Patrick White, was already lost before he set off on his voyage of discovery. Perhaps a case of will, or ego, locking horns with nature; men aware that they were somehow fated (as the Romantic poets echoed in their ears) to search for their own destiny as much as cattle country, gold or copper. Perhaps the blanks were their own voids. Or perhaps, in the spirit of Victorian scientific, technological and cultural endeavour, guided by their ever-present sense of duty, they took it for granted they would be successful.

The English 'author, traveller and mining engineer' Albert Calvert was more interested in gold than filling blanks on maps. He first visited Australia in 1890 to undertake two expeditions from South Australia's Lake Gairdner to the upper Murchison River. He then circumnavigated the continent before returning to London and publishing his ambitiously titled *The Discovery of Australia* in 1893. He was back in 1895 with his brother and two servants and, along with a mining engineer, artist and private secretary, made an extensive tour of Western Australia's eastern goldfields. When he returned to London he published *My Fourth Tour in Western Australia*.

Meanwhile, in January 1896, taken with the idea of opening a stock route from the Northern Territory to the Western Australian goldfields, as well as finding the missing explorer Ludwig Leichhardt, 'Westralia's golden prophet' (as he'd become known in London) offered the South Australian branch of the Royal Geographical Society funds to mount an expedition into Australia's heart of darkness, the pink bits that weren't quite pink.

Calvert's offer was accepted and the Royal Geographical Society set about organising the Calvert Exploring Expedition (the 'Scientific' came later). The Society appointed Lawrence Allen Wells as the expedition's leader. Wells was principally a surveyor. He was born in 1860 in Penola, South Australia, and worked for the colony's Survey Department. At age 23 he helped Augustus Poeppel map and peg the South Australian–Queensland border between the Simpson Desert and the Gulf of Carpentaria. In 1891 he worked as surveyor and eventually leader of the Elder Scientific Exploring Expedition. This expedition, from Warrina, South Australia, to the Western Australian coast, discovered the East

Murchison goldfields, making Wells, in Calvert's eyes at least, the perfect man for the job.

Calvert was ambitious, but flawed. He saw (or made his own) opportunities, took risks and showed a type of vision peculiar to his time. Australia was ripe for the picking. There were fortunes to be made, but also legacies to be forged.

The Calvert expedition soon grew to include Charles Wells (Lawrence Wells's cousin, and second-in-command), George Jones (mineralogist and photographer), James Trainor, and naturalist George Keartland. Hoping to avoid any prejudice, Larry Wells tried to find a white camel driver but, luckily, failed. He then appointed a man who would later become known as the greatest of all Afghan cameleers: Dervish Bejah. Bejah was helped by another cameleer, Said Ameer.

Bejah was born in present-day Pakistan and served in the Indian army under Lord Roberts, rising to the rank of sergeant. After his arrival in Australia in 1890 he worked as a cameleer in Western Australia and South Australia before joining Wells.

From 1838 until the 1960s Afghans were crucial in helping 'open up' the interior of Australia. They played an important role in exploration, the development of railways and the Overland Telegraph, as well as providing access to large tracts of grazing land. They were not always welcomed, having to live in separate camps in towns such as Marree and Farina, and there were occasional conflicts with whites.

In 1933 the journalist and novelist Ernestine Hill wrote: 'Within the high tin walls of the Afghan camps ... white women are living, the only ones in Australia who have blended to any extent with the alien in our midst. Renouncing the association of the women of their own race, they have forsaken their own religion for the teachings of the Prophet and the life of the cities for the desert trail.'

Still, the Afghans were vital in areas where horse and cart was impractical. If anything was needed in Birdsville or Stuart (Alice Springs), Broken Hill or the Western Australian goldfields,

The Calvert Expedition

Oodnadatta or along the Strzelecki Track, there was only one option. The largest group of Afghans arrived in Australia in 1893. The 94 cameleers came without wives or family, expecting to return to their native land as rich men, although very few did. Some married Aboriginal women, and some, as we have seen, Anglo-Saxon women who, most guessed, had completely lost their moral compass.

In May 1896 the seven men and 20 camels of the Calvert expedition left Adelaide by sea. They landed at Geraldton, 424 kilometres north of Perth, and made their way inland another 100 kilometres to Mullewa. From here, on 13 June 1896, they headed north towards the Fitzroy River. Wells followed the practice of establishing a base from which he would scout ahead for water. Food and water for both men and animals were plentiful in these sparsely settled regions but once they headed further inland things changed. On 21 July they filled kegs of water and started moving into unexplored territory. Now they were about to start filling in the blanks.

As Keartland busied himself collecting specimens, Wells started a journal in which he recorded their daily movements, compass bearings, and general observations. The expedition passed to the north of Lake Way (near present-day Wiluna) and on 23 July Wells named a lagoon after the poet Adam Lindsay Gordon. The lagoon, north of the present-day Gunbarrel Highway and east of Lake Carnegie, was full of native birds. Wells found signs of Aboriginal people, although he didn't see any. The expedition pushed on through late July, over hills Wells named the Princess Range.

On 29, July Wells, his cousin Charles and George Jones left Bejah and the others to look after sick camels that had eaten 'poisonous' bushes, while they scouted ahead for a suitable depot. They found a waterhole north-east of Lake Way and returned for the others. The expedition and sick camels recuperated here for a week while Wells, Jones, Bejah and seven healthy camels scouted ahead for another source of water. During this time Wells discovered and named Bejah Hill.

Bejah was busy caring for his animals. He tried to gather suitable feed so they wouldn't eat toxic grass and shrubs. He, in a sense, ate, drunk, thought and slept like his charges. If there was no feed for the animals he too would refuse to eat ('Camel no eat, me no eat'). He was also seen 'talking to and playing with them in a most excited manner'.

On 25 August the scouting party found water by digging in sand where they'd seen birds circling. Wells named this location, halfway between their existing depot and Joanna Spring, Midway Well. The next day they headed back to camp, stopping to let the camels feed on fresh grass. They also found a grove of quandong trees and filled a large sack with fruit. The weary travellers were forced to cross high sand ridges, which caused the water-laden camels problems. All the time, Wells kept meticulous notes about geography, minerals, flora and fauna. He noted, 'The same disheartening outlook everywhere! Although there is no doubt that something fairer to look upon existed here before this terrible sand hid it from view.'

On 8 September, 30 days and 800 kilometres after they'd left the depot, they arrived back to find the other men and camels rested. A week later the whole expedition set off for Midway Well. After arriving on 29 September, Wells and Bejah set off on yet another scouting mission. On 3 October they located more water at what would become known as Separation Well. They returned to Midway Well, gathered their party and travelled to Separation Well, arriving on 8 October.

By now they had entered the Great Sandy Desert. They travelled mostly by night. Wells wrote that 'the sand becomes so hot after 11 am that the poor [camels] can barely endure walking over it'. The expedition came across a small group of Aboriginal people but they fled when they saw the camels.

Wells started relying heavily on Bejah's bush skills as well as his expertise with the animals. During the course of the mission they would often scout together. As they travelled during the night Wells trusted Bejah to navigate by the stars as he slept in his saddle. After the completion of the expedition the two men remained good friends. The Australian poet, Douglas Stewart, immortalised their relationship in his poem 'Afghan'.

> Mopping his coppery forehead under his turban,
> Old Bejah in baggy trousers, bearded, immense ...
> Old camel-driver, explorer, the giant Afghan
> Who steered his life by compass and by Koran ...
> And fondled his box of brass and kissed his book
> So passionately, with such a lover's look,
> He whirled in deserts still, too wild for human.

Eight days after the party arrived at Separation Well, Lawrence Wells made a fateful decision. He wrote, 'My cousin [Charles] and Mr Jones will leave us, here, for a trip to the north-west, and we hope to meet eventually, somewhere in the vicinity of Joanna Spring.' In line with accepted practice, Wells decided to split his party to cover more ground, to see if he could find suitable land for stock, alternative water sources, even mineral deposits. He had often followed this format on the Elder Expedition. He figured he'd take 12 days to reach Joanna Spring, and that it would take his cousin and George Jones a few days more to cover the slightly longer route. He explained that, 'They propose proceeding along the flats or troughs between the sand-ridges, generally bearing north ...'

Wells reasoned that if either party failed to locate Joanna Spring they would continue on to the Fitzroy River, which led north to Derby and the coast, thereby fulfilling Calvert's brief of securing a stock route from the goldfields to a northern port.

On the morning of 11 October Wells wrote: 'We experienced thunderstorms all around us last night but only a few drops of rain fell here ... At 7.15 am we wished my cousin and George goodbye and god speed and each party left the well at the same time, my cousin starting on a bearing of 280 degrees (true) whilst I bore 356 mag. or 358 true.'

Wells and Jones took three healthy camels, 230 litres of water and enough food for a month, and set off into the Great Sandy Desert. Before the main party left they buried supplies at Separation Well. The morning was already hot. The first 12 kilometres were sandy flats, but eventually they encountered more sand ridges, which again slowed the camels. They travelled in the early morning and camped during the day to avoid the heat. Wells wrote, 'The days are now so frightfully hot that during the early morning they [the camels] refuse to pass a shade of any kind, and when the caravan halts they all huddle together, trying to stand in one another's shade.'

By 26 October: 'I found we were in a more critical position than ever.' The party had managed to locate a well they named Adverse Well, but it yielded only a small amount of water. One camel died and another six were in extremely poor condition. Wells decided to abandon most of his equipment before they moved on to Joanna Spring. They were only able to travel 15 kilometres each night. At that rate it would take them another four days to arrive. 'We left all the tents, most of the tools, provision boxes … small firearms and other articles which we can do without for the present, also all personal property, taking only bare necessities … I felt this step to be absolutely necessary, as otherwise we should get nothing through this fiery furnace.'

Both parties continued on through late October. The main party approached the location of Joanna Spring as it had been incorrectly given in Peter Warburton's account of his 1873 expedition from the Overland Telegraph to Perth (his chronometer was faulty). As they approached these coordinates Wells wrote, 'We are now within two miles of the computed latitude of Joanna Spring but there is nothing about to indicate its position no birds such as gala's pigeons or finches we saw …'

On 30 October Wells saw smoke to their east and, hoping it might be his cousin and Jones, set off to investigate. 'Starting off towards it at once taking no firearms and only a pint of cold tea in a bottle I walked for four hours, quite 12 miles, without reaching it and feeling quite done up with the heat I felt I could go no further so retraced my steps as best I could. I can hardly remember how I got back ...'

Unable to locate the spring, and dangerously low on water, Wells and his party decided to keep heading north to the Fitzroy River. On 31 October they set off, abandoning several more camels. Wells was nearly blind with a form of ophthalmia known as 'sandy blight' (probably actinic conjunctivitis, the result of prolonged exposure to light). Bejah was keeping them alive with his ability to find water and food, and to keep the majority of the camels moving.

The main party arrived and crossed the Fitzroy River on 6 November.

Lawrence Wells and his men now had fresh water, fish, birds and shelter. He was disappointed they had been forced to abandon so much equipment, especially Keartland's specimens. 'It seems to me a cruel blow to have to abandon the whole of our outfit and collection. Mr Keartland who has displayed such energy in attending to his part must also feel it hard to lose all his treasures ...'

Nonetheless, he knew they were lucky to be alive: 'Now that I know the nature of the country and climate, I feel we did well to get through at all ...' His only anxiety, he wrote, 'was for my cousin Charles and Mr Jones'.

The main party followed the Fitzroy River until, on 9 November, they reached the track from Derby to Fitzroy Crossing. Here they watered and fed the camels then met a mail contractor who agreed to send two telegrams for Wells – one to the Royal Geographic Society in Adelaide and the other to the Fitzroy telegraph station asking if they'd heard news of Charles and George Jones.

Wells moved on to Quanbun Station, north of the Cunningham River, a tributary of the Fitzroy River. While resting here he wrote a full report of the expedition for the Royal Geographical Society. A few days later he received word from the telegraph station that nothing had been heard of or from Charles Wells and George Jones. A further telegram from Adelaide instructed him to take water back along the route he'd followed and leave it in the desert for the others. His party attempted to do this but had to turn back because of extreme heat and the still poor condition of the camels. They did manage to leave some water under a tree, perhaps even then realising the futility of the gesture.

A few days later they tried again, accompanied by a police trooper, but had to turn back again. They were just too tired, their bodies unable to cope with the 'furnace' they'd just escaped.

A third attempt began on 4 December with Wells, Bejah, a searcher named Nat Buchanan, an Aboriginal tracker and eight camels. This time they managed to travel 140 kilometres south from the Fitzroy River before being forced back by the heat. In the process they lost another two camels to toxic bushes.

Wells was nothing if not determined. By now he was aware that his searches were more about recovery than rescue, but he wanted to find his cousin and George Jones, perhaps out of a sense of guilt, or perhaps duty and obligation towards both families. He decided to wait for cooler weather before trying again.

His fourth attempt began on 14 March 1897. His party, and ten camels, headed back into the Great Sandy Desert and arrived at Joanna Spring on 9 April. They found no evidence that Charles and George had been there although they did find an Aboriginal man who was wearing some of Charles's clothes. He explained he'd got them from two men 'killed by the sun'.

Wells turned back again. His fifth and final expedition set off from Fitzroy Crossing on 14 May 1897 with several white and Aboriginal police troopers led by Sub Inspector Ord. Twelve days into their journey, a short distance from the path followed on the fourth expedition, they found the bodies of Charles Wells and George Jones. 'I could then see my cousin's iron-grey beard,' Wells wrote, 'and we were at last at the scene of their terrible death, with its horrible surroundings.'

Wells found Jones's belongings, including a compass and sextant, a watch and a small box of medicine containing an unused vial of arsenic. He also discovered a notebook in which the 22-year-old Jones had written to his parents:

My dearest Mother and Father,

I am writing this short note the last one I shall ever write I expect. We left the main party at the well and after 5 days travelling had to return being away 9 days as we were both far from well I had hardly any strength. After 5 days spell we started to follow the main party after severe trials some of the camels died so we had to walk we are both very weak and ill the other two camels are gone and neither of us have the strength to go after them I managed to struggle half a mile yesterday but returned utterly exhausted. There is no sign of water near here, and we have nearly finished our small supply have about two quarts left so we cannot last long. Somehow or other I do not fear death itself I trust in the Almighty God. We have been hoping for relief from the main party but I am afraid they will be too late. Any money of mine I think I should like divided between Eve Laurie and Beatrice. Now my darling parents I wish you goodbye, but I trust we will meet again in heaven. You both have always been so good to me I should like to see you again. Mr Charles has been very good indeed to me during this trip he is not to blame that we are in this fix. It is Gods will so we should not object. Goodbye to Evie Joe and Beat and all our friends. And now darlings God give me strength till our next meeting. God's will be done.

I remain,
Your loving son,
George Lindsay Jones

In his poem 'Afghan' Douglas Stewart imagined the moment Dervish Bejah discovered the two lost explorers.

> 'Oh ya, oh ya, the young man dead in the sands,
> I dig with my hands, I find him, and fifty yards further
> The other, both dead, so young; no water, no water.'
> The gestures, the voice, all larger and wilder than human,
> Some whirlwind out of the desert. 'Two days in the sun,

Done when I sight the camp. I shoot off my gun
And Larry Wells he carry me over his shoulder;
Looking for water out there; oh ya, no water.'

The bodies of George Jones and Charles Wells had been mummified by the desert heat. Both men were wrapped in sheets and eventually returned to Adelaide, where they were given a state funeral on 18 July 1897.

After his return to Adelaide, Wells was roundly criticised in newspapers and by segments of the community for the failure of at least part of his expedition. In 1899 a parliamentary select committee reviewed his actions and cleared him of any blame, praising him for completing a long and difficult mission. Meanwhile, Calvert informed the Royal Geographical Society that he was unable to meet his financial commitments to the venture he had first suggested. These costs were eventually covered by the South Australian and Western Australian governments. By the time Larry Wells paid his men's wages he was also out of pocket. The South Australian government agreed to pay him a small amount as 'a recognition of the intrepid and courageous conduct of a public servant, as well as on humanitarian grounds'.

Lawrence Allen Wells, with his bushy moustache, square head and no-nonsense demeanour, was a big man with a big vision, a character full of frontier spirit, charged by a restlessness that drove him beyond the confines of towns and cities. Although he lived until 1938, when he was hit and killed by a rail car in the Adelaide suburb of Mitcham, he was the archetypal Victorian explorer, stumbling through the desert with his gummy eyes, keeping meticulous notes, encouraging his men to keep going, convinced that great discoveries lay just beyond the horizon. He, like Leichhardt, or Burke, was a man whose mantra was *Facts, Progress and Industry*. He was aware that fortune favoured the brave. He knew that within a decade or two the blanks would all be filled in, and his shot at glory gone. There was no time to waste.

Back in Adelaide, Wells worked for the South Australian Pastoral Board until 1903, at which time the South Australian government convinced him to lead the North-West Prospecting Expedition to explore the Musgrave, Mann and Tomkinson ranges for any sign of gold or mineral resources. He, along with his second-in-command, Frank George, accompanied four prospectors, 20 camels (with two drivers) and three Aboriginal guides from Oodnadatta to just beyond the Western Australian border. Five-and-a-half months later they returned without having found any significant mineral deposits.

In 1908 he was off again, this time conducting a trigonometrical survey of the Victoria River district in the Northern Territory. In the 1910s and 1920s he worked with both state and federal governments in the area of land tax (he was the chair of South Australia's Land Board from 1918). He eventually retired at age 70 in 1930, but soon got the itch again. At 72 he led the Endeavour Expedition through the Great Victoria Desert, where he and his party almost died of thirst near McDouall Peak.

Wells was awarded an OBE in 1937, and it took a rail car to eventually stop him in 1938. Today he is buried in Mitcham Cemetery.

At the completion of their journey, Wells gave Dervish Bejah the expedition compass as a sign of gratitude for his help and dedication. Bejah settled at Hergott Springs, near Marree, and married a widow, Amelia Shaw, in 1909, and they had one son, Abdul 'Jack' Bejah. Bejah ran camels through the outback, carrying wool and general provisions, until the 1930s. After his retirement he became well known for his interest in growing date palms on his property.

Bejah was a devout Moslem and spent hours each day reading and studying the Koran. This, he believed, had brought him long life and good health. He can be seen praying in the film *Back of Beyond*, a 1954 documentary about outback postman Tom Kruse and the Birdsville Track 'mail run'. He was tall, with a sun-bleached face and white beard, standing still, a man of few words. But it was he, Wells admitted, who had saved the Calvert expedition from even greater tragedy – his devotion to his camels, his knowledge of the desert, his uncanny ability to find water, to drive the others on, to navigate by the stars.

When Bejah died in the Port Augusta Hospital on 6 May 1957 an obituary was published in, among many other newspapers, *The Times* of London.

Albert Calvert was publicly disgraced when he revealed he couldn't cover his expedition's costs. It's tempting to remember him as nothing more than a misguided capitalist, but this must be balanced with his interest, research, explorations and writings about geography, minerals, flora, fauna and Aboriginal people. In the early 1890s he published his *West Australian Review* but eventually lost interest in Australia after his bankruptcy, brought on by management difficulties with several Western Australian mining interests, as well as some large losses on the ponies in 1898.

By any reckoning, the Calvert Expedition was successful. It did help fill 'the remaining blanks', building on the work of Warburton and David Carnegie, who, a year before, had led an expedition from Coolgardie through the Gibson and Great Sandy deserts to Halls Creek in search of gold and pastoral land. Ironically, after the successful completion of his mission, Carnegie learnt of the two missing members of the Calvert expedition and offered to help search for them, going as far as formulating a detailed plan. He was put on stand-by in Halls Creek but, 15 weeks later, after hearing nothing, withdrew his offer.

CHAPTER 5

'... the police seem unable to get any clue': The Gatton Murders
1898

Boxing Day 1898 – Michael, Norah and Ellen – 'Some ants were on her face' – The crime scene is disturbed – An unsuccessful search – Reports of several farmers – Richard Burgess, suspect – A second autopsy – *In memoriam*

The outback is littered with unsolved murders. In the remotest corners of the continent, in and around small settlements, beneath endless stretches of lancewood and saltbush, lie the bodies of people who, a hundred years later, are still missing, or in some cases, were never missed at all.

Perhaps Australia's most famous unsolved outback murder occurred late on Boxing Day, or early on Tuesday 27 December, 1898, near Gatton, a small town 70 kilometres west of Brisbane. Although remembered as unsolved, the Gatton Murders (also known as the Gatton Tragedy or the Gatton Mystery) probably would have had a resolution if not for some second-rate police work in the hours and days after the discovery of the victims' bodies. Twenty-nine-year-old Michael Murphy and his sisters, Norah, 27, and Ellen, 18, were found in a field two kilometres from Gatton. According to a *Cairns Post* journalist, writing in 1928, this triple murder 'created an interest and a horror unparalleled in the history of crime in Australia'. This 'Old Journalist', as he described himself, stated that 'little more is known about the crime today (though much is strongly suspected) than was known on the day the bodies of the three ... were found'. Thirty years after the murder he was still blaming 'the consistent blundering on the part of the police'.

At eight o'clock on the evening of Monday 26 December 1898, Michael, Norah and Ellen Murphy set out from their family farm at Blackfellow Creek in a dogcart belonging to their brother-in-law, William McNeill, who was staying at the Murphy farm. The trio was heading for a dance at the Gatton Divisional Hall. When they arrived an hour later they discovered the dance had been cancelled due to a lack of female partners. They then headed back to the farm.

Next morning, the siblings' mother, Mary Murphy, became anxious about her children's whereabouts. According to a contemporary article in the *Queensland Times*, McNeill then 'caught a horse to go and look for Michael, Norah and Ellen. He started along the Tent Hill Road towards Gatton. He called at the creamery two miles from Murphy's place, and asked if a trap had passed along the road to Murphy's. The people said they had not seen it. He then proceeded towards Gatton, another two mile[s], until reaching Moran's slip rails'.

Close to the slip rails (a rough, wooden fence with easily removable rails) McNeill noticed the distinctive wobble of wheel tracks from his cart. He dismounted, took down some rails, followed the tracks into a paddock, then remounted and searched the area for a house he believed to be close by. Unable to find it he returned to the tracks and started following them on foot, leading his horse. Further along he saw 'what looked like heaps of clothes on the ground, and the cart and horse. The horse was lying down … He went right up to the heap of clothes … and then he saw that Norah Murphy was there, and that she was dead. Some ants were on her face'.

Norah was lying face down on a rug, with her feet pointing west, a feature that would later intrigue police and public alike, although the distinctive positioning of the body was never explained. McNeill also noticed the bodies of Michael and Ellen 'eight or ten yards further off', but, strangely, 'did not go up to them'.

McNeill rode off for Gatton, reaching Gilbert's Hotel around 10 am. In the bar he asked the publican, Charles Gilbert, if he knew where the police sergeant was, and Gilbert told him. When later asked why he hadn't gone straight to the police barracks, McNeill said, 'I did not know where they were.' He found the local sergeant, William Arrell, and told him about his discovery. Arrell accompanied him to the paddock and, according to the *Cairns Post*, 'when they arrived they found four of the town's residents, including a justice of the peace, already there'.

The local grapevine was incredibly efficient. This 'ghoulish rush to the scene' was responsible for the disturbance and destruction of much crucial information. 'The importance of leaving the bodies undisturbed until they could be seen by skilled detectives and a doctor, and the necessity of preventing any obliteration of the tracks ... would hardly be overlooked by one policeman in a thousand. The sergeant happened to be the thousandth.'

As Sergeant Arrell examined the scene he allowed a growing crowd to enter the paddock and view the bodies before he rode back to Gatton (leaving the area unsecured) to telegraph the commissioner of police in Brisbane. The officer who took the message failed to pass it on. It wasn't seen or acted upon until the following day. Arrell, receiving no reply, didn't think to send a second telegram. In the meantime, back in the paddock, the sightseers just kept coming.

Arrell then made his way to the Murphy farm, informed the family of the tragedy, harnessed two horses and drove Mary Murphy to the scene. The sergeant examined the bodies and found that all three had been bound with sections of the harness and beaten around the head with a large piece of wood. Michael Murphy had also been shot and at least one of the girls had been raped. Tom, the horse, had been shot and killed. Michael's 'purse' was found in his hand and 15 shillings were missing.

The *Cairns Post* reported, 'There were signs of a terrific struggle near the spot where Norah Murphy lay. The murderer had taken a rug from the dogcart, spread it out carefully on the grass, and placed Norah's body upon it – all this, apparently, after he had killed all three ... The paddock was overgrown with young scrub, with the exception of the clearing' in which the bodies were found.

Mary Murphy asked the sergeant if her children's bodies could be taken to Gatton. Arrell agreed after the local chemist convinced him the bodies should be moved because of 'the ants and the sun'. By now there were at least 40 people in the paddock and any possible tracks or footprints had been disturbed.

At 1.30 pm Norah and Ellen's bodies were placed in the Murphy's buggy, Michael's in another cart, and the corpses driven to Gilbert's Hotel. A post-mortem was carried out by a Dr von Lossberg, who failed to find the bullet in Michael Murphy's head. He also assumed that both girls had been 'outraged'. He certified that all three had died from a fractured skull, and the bodies were given to local women to clean and re-dress in preparation for a burial.

The following day, Wednesday 28 December, the news of the murders made front page news. The *Queenslander* reported: 'Today the whole town is in mourning, flags on different buildings flying half-mast. The bodies, which were lying in Gilbert's Hotel all yesterday, were removed to the Roman Catholic Church this morning. The funeral takes place at half past 11 o'clock.'

By now the police commissioner, a chief inspector, inspector and several detectives had arrived from Brisbane. They were 'heavily handicapped by grave faults of commission and omission'. The locals were in a state of 'intense excitement' as police and black-trackers were brought in to search for any remaining clues. Paddy Perkins and 'another black fellow named Colquhan' searched the bush surrounding the murder scene without success.

Initial inquiries on Wednesday and Thursday discovered several possible leads. One report suggested, 'It had transpired that the victims were seen by a constable about half a mile the Gatton side of the track where the vehicle left the main road. At that time they were at a standstill, speaking to their brother, who was riding into Gatton on horseback.' A farmer, living near the crime scene, reported hearing a 'sharp, decisive report' at approximately 9.30 pm on the Monday and a second farmer said he heard several screams around the same time. Also, 'a farmer residing some three miles out of Gatton states that when riding home between 9 and 10 o'clock he heard someone splashing in the waterhole [making a noise] similar to that which would be made by a person washing clothes'. Two girls who lived near the scene also heard rifle shots and a voice screaming, 'Father, father.'

A 'special reporter' for the *Queenslander* described the scene of the murders as 'a very quiet spot – as quiet a one, in fact, as could be found in the district. The paddock is a very dry one, and the track through it is rarely used … the leaves and sticks in the vicinity of where the bodies were found have been very little disturbed, and Sergeant King, who is an experienced bushman, gives it as his opinion that there was very little struggling'.

By Wednesday afternoon police had 'already examined one man as to his doings on Tuesday [*sic*] night, but up to the present no arrests have been made'. The reporter informed his readers that Tom was already being 'boiled down' to try and secure the bullet. He speculated on why and how a strong man such as Michael Murphy might have allowed himself and his sisters to be taken, bound, and murdered. It would have been dark, and the Murphys would have had to wait as the murderer took down the slip rails to let them in the paddock. They must have followed him for some distance, believing, perhaps, a story about an accident, or a lost child. Maybe the person was someone they knew. Or perhaps they were being threatened with a revolver? Either way, by the time they caught on it was too late.

On Friday 30 December the *Sydney Morning Herald* reported that Aboriginal trackers had found 'the tracks of … two horses … leading around the paddock inside the fence … emerg[ing] into the main road by the slip rails through which the cart had been taken into the paddock'. Although the tracks were 'lost among the traffic' this raised the very real possibility that two murderers had been involved. This theory might explain how one man had overcome three people. Later that morning, police obtained a small bullet from Tom's carcass.

During the day a more in-depth search of the area was undertaken, including waterholes. A heavy hammer and riding whip were found near the slip rails, as well as footprints, so someone had been waiting near this junction with the road. A local woman named Florence Lowe came forward to tell police she was approached by a man near the rails just after 9 pm on Monday. She was walking slowly at the time but as soon as she saw the man she 'spurred her horse and galloped on'. Later, other locals would claim to have seen him lingering near the slip rails between 7.45 pm and 9.15 pm.

This man became the prime suspect for the murder. Witnesses described him as approximately 5'9" with a large moustache and a low voice, wearing blue clothes, a coat and a felt hat drawn down over his face. No one recognised him as a local. Some said he carried a parcel in his hand. The *Cairns Post* explained, 'The man at the slip rails spoke to Miss Lowe, and made as if to grasp her bridle, but she urged the horse forward.'

Lucky for her. If not for her sense that something wasn't quite right, Miss Lowe well may have been the evening's first casualty.

'Apparently when the Murphys reached this spot the man had lowered the slip rails ready for their entrance ... A few yards from the slip rails there was a slight dip in the roadway ... Either Michael Murphy was shot here, or else the murderer fired in the air to show that he was armed, and then ordered Murphy to drive through the slip rails, and pointed the revolver at him for the whole of the distance to the clearing.'

Soon the police had their first suspect. They were told that Richard Burgess, a man well known to them (he had 14 assault convictions) had been seen drinking in a hotel in Gatton on the evening of the murders. Burgess roughly matched the description given by Lowe and the other witnesses. When police tracked and attempted to arrest Burgess in the Bunya Mountains there was a violent standoff. After his arrest Burgess claimed that on the evening of the murders he was nowhere near Gatton. Police checked and confirmed his story.

By now newspapers across the country had picked up the story. Theories abounded as to what had happened to the Murphys. Most believed the murderer had forced all three to drive into the paddock at gunpoint before forcing Michael to bind his sisters' hands using part of the bridle. He was then shot dead.

By week's end a correspondent for the *Mercury* stated, 'The police have two or three young men under surveillance, and it is possible some arrests will shortly be made.' In an attempt to fill the gaps between the facts, traces of a morbid bloodlust started appearing in the reporting. 'Murphy's frontal bone was crushed in by a blow from a large stick ... at one end of the stick there was a quantity of clotted blood and hair sticking to it.' Euphemisms abounded. 'Both the girls had been struck from behind and they had also been brutally treated in other respects ... The elder had a deep cut over one eye, penetrating to the bone, evidently inflicted with a sharp instrument ...'

Police had not ruled out McNeill as a suspect. He was the first person to leave the Murphy's farm in search of his brother- and sisters-in-law; he had found the paddock; recognised the cart marks and tracked them; discovered the bodies. But, McNeill was happy living with the Murphys. He'd never argued with any member of his extended family. Why would he want to kill Michael and his sisters?

Nine days after the murder, in response to statements that there had been at least two shots, police obtained an order to exhume the bodies. A second autopsy was held, carried out by the government medical officer, Dr Wray, assisted by Dr von Lossberg. This time the bullet in Michael Murphy's head was found.

By now the Gatton Murders had become a curiosity. One reporter stated, 'Many people from all parts of Australia visited the scene of the murder and took away mementoes of the crime, such as bloodstained leaves, twigs, and pieces of bark ... Mr "Jack" Hoolan, a member of the Queensland Parliament, acquired and kept as a souvenir, another sapling, blood-stained, which he declared was the weapon used.'

The drama surrounding the Gatton Murders eventually died down. The newspapers moved on, and an inquest was held. Witnesses – relatives, locals, police officers and medical professionals – were called, all to no avail. The *Mercury*'s correspondent summed up by saying, 'The impression is growing that the outrage is the work of persons well acquainted with all parts of the district, but the police seem unable to get any clue.' Most believed the crime would never be solved because of the 'consistent blundering on the part of the police'.

In late 1899, nearly a year after the murders, a Royal Commission was called. New suspects, theories, witnesses and evidence were produced. Over the next century, the case took on myth status, leading to books, articles and dozens of theories about who murdered whom, why, and how they got away with it.

The Australian outback has a way of keeping secrets – there are a million quiet spots, overgrown with scrub, forgotten, waiting. In the end, all that's left is regrets, and memories: a brother and two sisters on their way to a dance.

CHAPTER 6

The Tea and Sugar
1917–1996

The Trans-Australian Railway – For the fettlers – Places like Mungala – The Pay Van – The Butcher Van – The Provision Store – Breaking the isolation – 'without even taking my shoes off' – Alf Harris as Santa – Cook, and mothballed

The Nullarbor is a place of extremes. No trees, of course. Hot. Forty-nine in summer. A distance of 1675 kilometres from Port Augusta to Norseman (including Australia's straightest stretch of road). A few kangaroos, wombats, camels. Not much else. But it had to be crossed. Firstly, on horseback, then railway. It was a big job. Nation building. States were too poor, so the Commonwealth Railways stepped in. The Trans-Australian Railway, between Port Augusta and Kalgoorlie, started stretching east-west in September 1912. Slowly. Expensively. By 1915 the two converging ends were still a thousand kilometres apart and, on the South Australian side, the workers were hungry, thirsty, in need of the consolations of civilisation.

And from the beginning, the 'Tea and Sugar' was there. A train, steaming from Port Augusta, to supply the fettlers. At first, a simple service to provide the basics, but by 1917, when the line opened, a more organised service providing meat, provisions, fruit and vegetables, health services and, most importantly, wages.

Andrew Fisher had got his way. The country was united, at last. But for years to come, hundreds of men and women would be needed to replace the wooden sleepers, fix the sun-warped rails, man the repeater stations, work in the hospitals and shops, and keep the trains running. At first, small settlements sprung up along the line: Hesso, Kultanaby, Malbooma and Mungala. Stops as rough and ready as they sounded. Men (and wives and kids) in tents, and later, asbestos and cream brick buildings, working to unite the country. Life was a constant improvisation. News came from up the track, the bigger town, cities, the world, via the Tea and Sugar.

Once a week. Departing Port Augusta at 10.47 every Thursday morning. Loaded with everything from lettuces to light globes. Trawling the seemingly endless standard gauge track. Stopping at work camps for twenty or thirty minutes to deliver orders, have a quick yarn, make sure everyone was still functioning. The whole camp would arrive, and gangers, working up and down the line. Faces washed and belts tightened, as the shop girls explained what Hitler, or Mao, or Pol Pot was up to. Who was running the country, had won a million quid, or stood on the town hall balcony waving to the girls (John, Paul, Ringo, and some other fella?).

Like Daisy Bates, who lived at Ooldea siding, looking after the local Aboriginal people, the 'Trans' became an Australian institution. Now, an icon, but back then, a necessity. For most of its life the Tea and Sugar was made up of a locomotive and four specialised cars. First, the Pay Car. The men would arrive here first, receive their money, and count it (probably). Later, this van doubled as an agency for the Commonwealth Bank. Railway mums and kids could save their pennies and pounds, and each week, come to check their compounded fortunes. Then, to the Butcher Van. Orders were ready and waiting. Steak tonight, snags tomorrow, a lump of corned beef for Sunday. At first, the Tea and Sugar included a stock wagon (meat-on-legs – the refrigeration wasn't that good). A few unlucky beasts would be unloaded, or the butcher would step out with his knife ready. Stock killed and dressed on the run (as the Nullarbor's billion stars slid by).

Next, a visit to the Provision Store. Flour, sugar and vanilla essence. Oats and writing paper. A few books, ordered especially, to ward off the boredom. And in the refrigerated compartment, ice-cream and frozen peas (after they'd started freezing them).

The Tea and Sugar ran for over eighty years. Well past the time when it was needed by the Railways (wooden sleepers replaced by concrete). When it left on its final run on 30 August 1996 many were sad to see it go. Not that there weren't other (and easier) ways to keep supplied in the modern age, but more because this train had come to symbolise hope, an umbilical connection to civilisation, something to look forward to every week, as the vibrations travelled the tracks, the diesel's big engines grew louder, the purple slug appeared over the horizon and crawled, inch by inch, over the thousands of empty acres.

In 1954 the Australian Commonwealth Film Unit jumped aboard. Recorded a small memento, for the future. Mostly, simple black-and-white images that needed no narration: a Greek ganger explaining how he loved 'the sight of the paymaster. My name is Papadopoulos. My brother and I make about £26 a fortnight and send back about £15 to Greece so that our mamma and poppa can come out to Australia too.' Kids, waiting for the train to stop, so they could smell the liquorice in the store, see the cow's eyes looking down at them. One woman explained why they needed the train. 'We have news from everyone along the line and I remember, just recently, I was so very ill I had to be taken by section car down to Tarcoola. There was no sister there so they sent across to Ceduna and the Flying Doctor came along. We stayed there overnight and she took me back to Ceduna with the train sister and they had the ambulance waiting. Took me straight into the hospital and onto the operating table without even taking my shoes off.'

That's how it was done along the Nullarbor. You made the best of things. As another railway wife explained, 'What you lose on the roundabout you gain on the swings ... life's not so bad.'

Here's the rub. Those that had nothing were happiest, in a way. You valued what you had, and those around you. Avis French, who grew up along the line, explained, 'In the bush you don't shun people. Whoever they are, whatever colour their skin.'

The idea being, perhaps, that eventually everyone would need to rely on someone else. There were no Aboriginal people, Afghans, wogs – just people. The desert had dissolved walls, suburbs, class, education, employment, everything. You were just a fettler, or his wife, or kid, or the fella that brought the meat, or furniture.

Later, after the butcher knocks off, he cleans his face, changes his shirt, and goes to lie down. In the Relay Van. Simple, with a railway rug, and a small fan to blow hot air over his tired body. Wakes, visits the rumbling toilet (nothing between him and the sleepers), cleans up and heads into the kitchenette. Plenty of meat, as he helps a tired driver cook a few eggs, chops and rashers of bacon. After the dishes (and a stop at Bates) they retire to the lounge to play cards, read about Lasseter, before retiring to bed. Another big day tomorrow, and more people relying on them. It's important they're well-stocked, and on time. Mums will be waiting with their wheelbarrows, seeking self-raising for a week of scones.

On 24 February 1943 Broken Hill's *Barrier Miner* explained why they couldn't be late. 'Workers on the Trans-Australian Railway have been complaining that they have been left for days without essential supplies, including bread and meat. On Wednesday they threatened to stop work if provisions were not sent …' Turned out the bread was taking longer to cook, the provisions, to be packed. The system was fixed, and the Tea and Sugar was soon back on time.

The train provided more than basics. Every six weeks a medical van was hooked up and a nurse sent to check on the locals' wellbeing. Babies were weighed, examined and vaccinated, wounds treated, men and women's plumbing discussed and antibiotics provided for blighted eyes. One mum explained, 'The young mothers never miss a chance to take their children to the health centre coach for a check-up. There's never much to worry about. Where there are no people you just don't get epidemics.'

Some consolation. And the soothing hand of civilisation didn't rest there. Jimmy Stewart and Shirley Temple visited the outback, too. In the form of a film car that ran once a month. Here, everyone could gather for a few hours as a grainy, black-and-white

George Wallace walloped across the Western Australian goldfields in *Wherever She Goes*, or a young Julie Andrews described her favourite things. Strange to imagine, now, but children brought up along the line had no television, cinema, Doris Day, or the cascading strings of Mantovani. These were other worlds, piped into their diesel-smelling desert, their corrugated iron bedrooms and bread-and-dripping kitchens. It must have seemed wonderful: to escape, just for a while, from a dun-coloured world of dingoes and flies.

Then, at Christmas, the train's engineer, Alf Harris, would put on his Santa suit and greet the kids as they ran towards the train. They'd gather inside, and presents would be distributed. It didn't matter whether your mum had remembered to order a gift – station kids, local Aboriginal people, everyone was a winner. Alf played the part for thirty-six years, a generation of railway offspring, just as excited, involved, as any city kid. The plain-wrapped gift, a soft drink, lollies. One Tea and Sugar veteran explained, 'You get a list of what children you are to give presents to but … a lot more would roll up so you had to have surplus.'

But, it couldn't last forever. In 1981 the Tea and Sugar service was restricted to railway camps. The following year the butcher's van was removed and meat delivered in prepacked portions. The twentieth century had finally caught up with the 'Sugar'. Soon, there'd be no more water delivered, no fuel, no small, ecstatic (but necessary) moments in the lives of thousands of people who'd chosen to work and live along the Nullarbor railway.

Today, the Trans-Australian Railway is the Indian Pacific. A three-night, 4300-kilometre journey from Sydney to Perth. Apart from the big cities, the train stops at Cook, 130 kilometres shy of the Western Australian border (the Tea and Sugar's last stop in the terminal years prior to 1996). Cook is typical of most of the train's old haunts: a handful of inhabitants, a muddle of disused railway buildings (at its peak two hundred people lived here), a few dogs and a kangaroo. There are medical supplies (in case of a railway disaster), accommodation for drivers, fuel tanks and a shop that opens (not surprisingly) only when the train pulls in. It's ten hours' drive to the nearest town, so the Indian Pacific does what its predecessor did, and provides food and other supplies to the locals.

Cook was mothballed in 1997 when the railway's new owners realised it was surplus to need. Like so many of the old places that kept our transport infrastructure going: surplus to need. Indian Pacific passengers have ninety minutes to stretch their legs and marvel at a living relic that once had a swimming pool, school and hospital (with its famous sign: 'If you're crook, come to Cook'). Then, the train sounds its horn and it's all aboard. As fascinating as it is, no one wants to get left behind. A little bit of history, clinging to the edge of the desert, its abandoned vans and government houses narrating the story of when this place (and the other Tea and Sugar stops) were alive and kicking.

Thankfully, the Tea and Sugar vans have been saved from the desert, restored and housed at the National Railway Museum, Port Adelaide. Now, kids still climb aboard, although they have no idea about pounds, shillings and pence, or why a plastic leg of mutton sits gathering dust in the Butcher Van. Excellent interactive displays keep the stories alive, although only as long as we're interested. A bed remains made up in the Provision Store. The same table with the same crossword books, the same fan and radio. The Tea and Sugar is still running, carrying us away from city, to land, and its own little Gravox dreamings.

CHAPTER 7

Ingkaia:
Carl and Theodor Strehlow's journey to Horseshoe Bend

1922

Pastor Strehlow falls ill – Frieda and Ted – A brief history of Hermannsburg – Ted's brothers and sisters – Hesekiel runs for help – The party sets off – Offer of help – Ted Strehlow's later life – Towards Idracowra – Mrs Elliot on horseback – Horseshoe Bend – *Wachet Auf, ruft uns die Stimme!*

October 1922. Finke River, Central Australia. At this stage, God and his Son are being animated in the outback. In this instance, by Carl Strehlow, a Lutheran pastor who has, for the past twenty-eight years, broadcast the Word to the 'natives' living on Hermannsburg Mission in this driest, most forbidding part of the continent. But now, aged fifty, Strehlow is ill. Prayer won't help, even calls to the Lutheran Mission Board in Adelaide. As it becomes apparent to the local Arrernte (or Aranda) people, Carl's wife, Frieda, and fourteen year old son, Theodor George Henry Strehlow, that drastic action will be required to save the pastor.

This is a story that mightn't have been remembered. If not for the super-human, if not saint-like qualities of Carl Strehlow, strapped to an upholstered chair, carried through the desert as his son – Theodor, Ted, TGH, this boy with multiple names, and dimensions – travelling on a dray in his father's wake, faced the real possibility that fire and brimstone wouldn't be enough to save his father from a combination of pleurisy and dropsy (oedema). Most of a life spent evangelising, singing hymns and sweating in a desert surrounded by its own Dead Sea. As Barry Hill outlined in a 2016 review of the reissue of Theodor Strehlow's biblical trek,

Journey to Horseshoe Bend, the boy suffered 'as the lonely soul he always felt himself to be.'

This is a story about faith. Trust. Love. But more than anything, the bond between a father and son. A boy who was to see death for the first time, and seek its meaning in the gaps between Christianity and traditional Arrernte beliefs (both of which he'd spend his life attempting to reconcile).

Carl Strehlow began his stint as pastor and superintendent at the Hermannsburg Mission, 130 kilometres south-west of Alice Springs, in 1896. Theodor was born in 1908, the youngest of six children. His was a complex childhood, brought up speaking German with his missionary parents, Arrernte with the Aboriginal kids and women who helped raise him, and English. An unhealthy baby, he was born a month premature and quickly baptised, just in case. He was raised between and within cultures, soon forming a kinship with his 'Aboriginal mothers', a sort of cross-cultural and -spiritual pollination. As Michael Kirby explained in 2003: 'Whilst the language of his home was German, the young Theodor was cradled into the Aranda language. Only a person with this insight could connect so seamlessly with the very essence of Aboriginal existence. His mastery of language allowed him to feel the poetry of the people, not as translation but his own native tongue.'

At the time of his father's illness in October 1922, Ted had only recently been confirmed in the rites of the Lutheran church. His two childhoods would soon graft to form a unique world view that would make the man, the teacher, the anthropologist, and a father for whom words were keys to other cultures. As Barry Hill observed, in *Journey*, Theodor refers to himself in the third-person, 'and the journey left him plagued by romantic agonies and a childish sense of entitlement.'

Why? Growing up without his brothers and sister. After a family trip to Germany in 1911 when Ted was three years old, the boy returned to Hermannsburg with his parents while his brothers and sister (Frederick, Karl, Rudolf, Hermann and Martha) stayed in Germany for a Lutheran education. Making Ted the most,

Ingkaia: Carl and Theodor Strehlow's journey to Horseshoe Bend

or least, important of the six Strehlow children. Forever in the shadow of his father, adopting the local Hermannsburg kids as de facto brothers and sisters. Isolated, full of his own thoughts, ideas and connections to Dreamtime stories. Homer, Ulysses and the songs of the Aranda, floating around Hermannsburg (*Ntaria*). A Latin primer, and *ingkaia:* Ted Strehlow's last word, as he died in the arms of Michael Kirby in 1978. Australia's Justice of the High Court later wrote: 'I had never seen a dead person before ... His last utterance was 'ingkaia'. This was the Aranda word for bandicoot, driven from the land by the invading rabbit introduced by the Europeans. It was a kind of metaphor. He was describing to me a bridal headpiece made of bandicoot tails. But he was actually talking of the way the Europeans had disrupted the lives of the Aranda people, their society and their laws.'

At Hermannsburg in 1922, Carl's health worsened. Theodor observed, and fretted over his father. One of the senior Aboriginal men, Hesekiel, was sent to Alice Springs on foot to telegraph the Lutheran Mission Board (LMB) in Adelaide to ask for a car to take Carl south for medical treatment. Hesekiel eventually arrived, waited, before the LMB replied that they had no transport available.

Faced with this news, a decision was made to transport Carl to the railhead at Oodnadatta where he could be placed on a train to Adelaide. A cart was hastily organised for *ingkata* (ceremonial 'father') and on Tuesday 10 October 1922 fifty-year-old Carl, racked with pain, was loaded onto an improvised seat strapped to a cart for the journey. He was accompanied by Frieda, Theodor, a Hermannsburg teacher named Hermann Heinrich, Hesekiel, and two other Aboriginal men: Jacobus and Titus. The party set off in two carts in what Shane Heresy described as a parallel 'to Christ's journey to the cross ... there is an unmistakable relationship between Christ's agonising death nailed to a cross and the pastor's equally agonising journey "strapped" in his chair.'

On the first day the party only managed to cover twenty kilometres. They following day they stopped at Irbmangkara

(Running Waters) where they met Jack Fountain, the mail carrier, travelling in the opposite direction. The party read their letters, hoping for any offers of help from Adelaide. TGH later explained: 'The message that had brought them [his parents] most joy was a telegram giving fairly full details about the proposed journey by Mr Gotthold Wurst, the wheat farmer who had accepted the challenge to come to Strehlow's rescue after all other appeals for help had failed.' Wurst planned to truck his car to Oodnadatta, fetch Strehlow and drive him south. 'This heartening telegram brought tears of joy into the sick man's eyes: his clerical colleagues had failed him in his hour of need but here was a man of goodwill and humanity who was prepared to risk his car and come to the rescue.' At two pm the party packed up and continued, travelling across stone country towards Iltjanmalitnjaka (Parke's Pass). Just before sundown they approached the Krichauff Ranges, raised their tents, fed and watered the horses and prepared a hot meal. Theo tells how, 'Theo in particular was fascinated by it [the country]; for he could not remember having seen table mountains before.'

Theodor Strehlow, years after *Journey*, was educated at Adelaide's Immanuel College, where he topped the state in Latin, Greek and German, before winning a bursary to The University of Adelaide in 1926. Followed by an Honours degree in English Language and Literature, then a return to Central Australia in 1932, where he used a grant from the Australian National Research Council to collect and document Arrernte language, songs and stories. Continuing his work through the early 1930s (including the Tindale and Stocker Expedition) before the Commonwealth Government appointed him Patrol Officer for the southern Northern Territory in 1936. After marrying in December 1935 he travelled with his new wife, Bertha, across Central Australia, before joining the army in 1942. After the war, he and Bertha settled in Adelaide with their three children (Theo, John and Shirley), although the marriage ended in 1968.

Ted's life was not without controversy. In 1946 he was appointed lecturer in English and Linguistics at his old university, and the 1947 publication of *Aranda Traditions* (assembled in 1934 but not published until his informants were dead) earned him serious academic kudos. This book was the result of thousands of miles of travelling, and witnessing 166 sacred ceremonies. But, according to Kirby, 'Perhaps it led him into the mistakes that were later to affront the Aranda people. A film he displayed on his return to Hermannsburg portrayed a number of sacred objects. The film clip caused chaos, the women rushing into the night with the children; the men angry and resentful.' Years later, according to Kirby, the Strehlows (by now Ted had remarried) 'became very suspicious about what they saw as a threat that the Government would seize their precious collection of Aboriginal treasures. Indeed, Aboriginal groups demanded the return of hundreds of sacred objects kept at the Strehlows' Adelaide home. Things came to a head when, in 1978, the German magazine *Stern* published colour photographs of naked Aboriginal men in glorious headgear and body paint. To many Aboriginal people the photographs of people and objects in secret ceremonies and the fact that Strehlow had received $6,000 as an "honorarium" for the photographs caused deep affront.'

Day three. The horses plodded as the party followed the northern bank of the Finke River. Strehlow's memories of the crossing were full of drama and description. 'The pull across the channel was a heavy one; and long before the southern bank had been reached, the lashes of the whips started falling sharply on the backs of the sweating, panting horses.' But later, 'the drivers pulled up their foamy mouthed teams under some shady box gums for the sake of the passengers.' That afternoon the party continued beside the Finke, setting camp before sunset at Tunga, a sheltered waterhole upriver from Henbury Station. Both horses and travellers were exhausted. Men from the Henbury Aboriginal camp soon notified the station staff and 'it was not long before a large group of men, women and children came down to the travellers' camp, both to greet Strehlow and exchange gossip with the Hermannsburg drivers.'

Two white men, Bob Buck and Alf Butler, shared a meal with the Strehlows. Butler, a frequent visitor to Hermannsburg, said he thought Strehlow's horses looked too tired to cross the Britannia Sandhills. 'And those last bloody miles along the Finke from Hell's Gate to Idracowra [Station] are not a bit better.' He offered eight donkeys, better suited to the loose sand, and eight 'loose donks' in reserve.

The following morning the party set out on the next leg of the journey. Young Theo sat, watched, and helped, but must have had deep concerns for his father. 'On leaving Henbury [Carl] had still been hopeful of reaching at least the Overland Telegraph line at Horseshoe Bend. But the fifty-five mile journey from Henbury to Idracowra had shattered even his iron will. Travelling through the Britannia Sandhills had been for him one long nightmare.' Again, the travellers rested. The chances of Carl surviving must have seemed increasingly remote to all. According to Walter Veit, Carl had always been 'strong-willed, with a high opinion of his own ability; his rigid self-discipline made him a stern pedagogue and a strict parent.' So maybe little passed between father and son; maybe young Theodor's questions were answered by his mother, or the Aboriginal men. According to Veit, Carl was a missionary 'who placed his obligations to God above all else.' Decades of 'pastoral, teaching, accounting and administrative duties, tending of the sick and management of the missionary farm' had produced a formidable character. Ted lived in his shadow, always.

The party continued, stopping to rest at waterholes, tending to Carl. On 17 October, they were met by Mrs Elliot, from Horsehoe Bend, who had ridden seven hours on horseback to meet them. She explained that the car coming from Oodnadatta to meet them had broken down. According to Hersey, Mrs Elliot organised a night trip 'through the scrub guided only by kerosene lanterns so as to avoid the scorching heat of the day. The plan is to get Carl to Horseshoe Bend, which has a phone, so that he can get medical advice from a doctor at Oodnadatta.' According to Ted, Carl 'had led till now far too active a life to have given much thought to the problems of pain, of suffering, and of calamities in a world governed by an omnipotent God of Love.' The pastor sought solace in the Book of Job, searching for signs of the 'strong faith of the afflicted'. *Why hast Thou set me as a mark against Thee, so that I am a burden to myself?* Theo thought his father 'felt obliged to defend the Almighty and the justice of His ways.'

The party continued, arriving at Horseshoe Bend. Carl lingered for another day, hoping help might arrive. A doctor from Marree, staying in Oodnadatta, was contacted but his medical advice wasn't helpful. There were no medicines available, and no one with any medical training. It was a hundred and ten in the shade, and according to Theo, 'Strehlow was much lower in point of physical strength and mental alertness than he had been only the day before. Mercifully perhaps, his overwrought mind began to wander everywhere now and then; and in his moments of delirium he did not seem to be conscious of those excruciating pains that had begun to wrack his body most of the time.' Carl asked his wife to fetch Mrs Elliot (Gus Elliot had ridden off in search of help). Frieda was surprised, but went out to find her.

Frieda: Mrs Elliot, my husband wants to speak to you. And he wants to speak to you alone. I will wait here. Please go – he is almost too weak to talk this afternoon.

Elliot: *(entering)*
Mr Strehlow, I believe you asked for me to come. Is there anything I can do to help you?

Carl: Please, do sit down. Yes, Mrs Elliot, I want to ask you to help me please. There are several things I want to talk to you about.
Elliot pulls up a chair and sits.
I must be brief. My strength has almost gone. Mrs Elliot, I am dying. I have not many more hours to live.

Elliot: Don't say that. You are much stronger than you think. Gus'll bring the doctor back by Saturday afternoon, and after that everything will be alright with you.

Carl: No, Mrs Elliot. I know that I am dying. And I think you know too. And so does your husband. But my wife does not. And she must not be told. I want her to have peace while I am still alive. I'm afraid that she will break down completely when I'm gone. It will be hard on her. She has always relied on me in everything. She will not know what to do once she is a widow.

The drama continues, full of the best and worst Victorian melodrama, values of duty and loyalty, almost as though the older Theodor is channelling his fourteen-year-old self. *Journey to Horseshoe Bend* is narrated by a man trying to say what he feels can't, or perhaps shouldn't, be said. The book has what Barry Hill calls a 'melancholic burden'. The words that Ted might've wanted to say to his father, if that was at all possible. Instead, while Carl implored Mrs Elliot to 'let the men in your hotel have a few rounds of drinks in your bar on my account', young TGH was outside, as always, playing with the Aboriginal kids.

At four o'clock in the afternoon Frieda started singing a hymn to her suffering husband.

> *Help He today has suspended*
> *He has not forever ended*
> *Though at times in vain we plead*
> *Help He gives in deepest need.*

Carl asked her to stop. 'Don't sing that hymn any more, Frieda. God doesn't help.' As if God had said no to all his prayers. Strehlow slept for half an hour then took a deep breath, and another, before his body slumped back onto his bed. Again, Ted later filled in the gaps. 'Then all movements stopped in the body, and a bluish tinge began to spread over the face.' Frieda cried, 'Oh, my God, he's dead!' before collapsing in tears.

If Carl Strehlow was a sort of tintype missionary, then his son was something less focused, stranger, more divided. He spent the rest of his life studying Aboriginal culture, completing his father's work. His books – *Aranda Traditions, Songs of Central Australia* (finished in 1956 but not published until 1971) and others – reflect a love and deep connection to a culture and mythosphere the young boy accepted as self-evident truth, alongside the Book of Job, and Bach's *Wachet Auf, ruft uns die Stimme!* All of this, thrown into a difficult socio-religious framework that seems deeply problematic to many today. But people are always a product of their time, culture, friends and family. Young Ted, growing up with only a few lines from his siblings in Germany, bright, curious, always alone. In 1969 he wrote, 'The Aranda folk of Central Australia had always lived and died secure in the belief that their immortal totemic ancestors, too, were living and sleeping in their very midst of this Eternal Land.' Maybe that describes Ted Strehlow's journey: an attempt at reconciliation, long before that word took on other meanings.

Finally, Ted has himself standing in the rain beside his father's grave. Just the two of them, at last, talking. 'To the boy the rain that was falling ... had come to represent the symbol of life, the promise of life, the assurance of life, and the certainty of life. Life could not be finally conquered by death; for the power of life was greater than the destructiveness of death.' Michael Kirby pointed out that Ted Strehlow 'could never be a full member of any of the communities that claimed him – the German Lutherans, the English educators or the Aranda of his childhood. His soul was divided.' An interesting insight, in these days of division, as Australians continue the search for who *they* really are.

CHAPTER 8

The Murchison Murders: 'Snowy' Rowles and Arthur Upfield

1929–1930

The No. 1 Rabbit Proof Fence – Arthur Upfield on patrol – 'Snowy' Rowles – The Murchison district – Ritchie describes the perfect murder – Upfield gets an idea – Rowles at Narndee Station – Ryan's motor-truck – Rowles gets busy – Act II: Louis Carron – Another murder – Detective Sergeant Manning – Chain of evidence – The endgame – Upfield gets his man

The No. 1 Rabbit Proof Fence, or as it's less poetically known today, the State Barrier Fence of Western Australia, is one of three 'pest exclusion fences' built between 1901 and 1907 to keep rabbits and other agricultural pests out of the state's pastoral zones. The No. 1 fence, the longest, runs north–south from Wallal Downs, south of Broome, to Jerdacuttup, west of Esperance. Its rough posts were first made from salmon gum and gimlet wood, but these were soon eaten out by white ants, and the hardier mulga and ti-tree were used where they could be harvested from adjacent scrub.

After its completion the fence was patrolled by boundary riders on bicycles, and later, camels, although these proved impractical for inspection purposes. A car was tried, but kept getting punctures or bogged. Eventually a solution was found. Two camels were used to pull a buggy up and down the length of the fence. Twenty-five boundary riders each patrolled a 160-kilometre stretch of fence, often in pairs if there was a threat of violence from local Aboriginal people. It was hot, challenging work but, for a time at least, it suited Arthur Upfield.

Arthur William Upfield was a writer of mystery and suspense

novels, 29 of which featured the half-caste Aboriginal man, Detective Inspector Napoleon 'Bony' Bonaparte of the Queensland police. Upfield wrote from the late 1920s until his death in 1964. Although his Bony stories were hugely popular in their day, most are now forgotten and out of print. At the time of the Murchison murders Upfield, who wrote on a fold-down desk attached to the dray on which he patrolled the rabbit fence, had enjoyed a modest success with three mysteries: *The House of Cain* (1928), *The Barrakee Mystery* (1929) and *The Beach of Atonement* (1930). Now, he was casting about for a new idea, something captivating, a story that would make his name in Australia and beyond. At the time Upfield had no way of knowing that the search for this idea (which would become *The Sands of Windee*) would lead to the murders of three men.

Upfield, like many writers past and present, needed to find an income to supplement his writing. He worked as a boundary rider for the Western Australian 'Rabbit Department' between October 1928 and September 1931. Between May and June 1929 he was based near the '163 mile' post on the No. 1 rabbit fence at Camel Station (so called because camels were bred here for use on the fences) with a man named George Ritchie. Another man, an itinerant stock worker known as 'Snowy' Rowles, often passed through Camel Station on the way to outlying stations, and knew both Upfield and Ritchie.

Rowles was a free spirit, a frontier character who spent his days roaming and his nights camped alone, who'd often stop at Camel Station for a drink and a yarn. Upfield and Ritchie knew little about him. For instance, that his real name was John Thomas Smith; that he was a wanted man, having escaped from the cells of the Dalwallinu courthouse in 1928 while awaiting trial for housebreaking. They knew little about his cunning or propensity for violence.

The setting for these murders was the desolate, isolated Murchison district of Western Australia. Writing in 1932, journalist Desmond Robinson invoked the scene for readers of Melbourne's *Argus*: 'It is a country of vast distances, isolated station homesteads, and lonely camps. In this wild area men may wander for weeks without encountering another human being.' Robinson warned his readers that the 'story of [this] case surpasses in dramatic interest many sensational novels of the "thriller" type'.

Upfield wanted his next book to start with the 'perfect murder'. He cast about for ideas and eventually Ritchie came up with a scheme. Over a period of weeks they discussed and refined it. Rowles was present at least once during these conversations. What if, Ritchie proposed, the victim was shot and his body burned in a fire? What if the murderer then gathered the bones and crushed them in a 'dolly', a container used for grinding minerals? What if he scattered the powdered bones to the wind? What if he then gathered any remaining clues such as bone fragments, buttons, dental plates or tooth fillings, and dissolved them in sulphuric acid? What if he burnt kangaroo carcasses on the same fire to divert any suspicion?

Upfield was pleased, but had a problem. Ritchie's method was just too efficient. Detective Bony wouldn't be left with anything to go on. Determined to keep Ritchie thinking, Upfield offered him a pound if he could find a flaw in his own scheme. Unluckily for Upfield, he couldn't.

Some time after Upfield's and Ritchie's initial conversation, Ritchie discussed his ideas at least once with Rowles. Then, on 5 October 1929, in the men's hut at Camel Station, the 'murder' was discussed among a larger group of men; 'Snowy' Rowles was one of them.

During this discussion Rowles said nothing. He sat quietly, listening, taking it all in, remembering the details. Later, Upfield would make it clear that Rowles knew of Ritchie's 'idea' before this evening.

Jessica Hawke, Upfield's de facto partner (for whom he left his wife in 1946), wrote Upfield's biography, *Follow My Dust*, in 1957. In this book she reconstructed the conversation that took place in the hut at Camel Station on the evening of 5 October. She has Ritchie saying, 'Supposing I wanted to do you in, I'd kid you into the bush a bit and when you were nice and handy to plenty of dry wood, I'd shoot you dead and burn your body.' She then has Ritchie explaining his scheme, finishing with, 'Easy, Arthur, me lad, easy. On the fire site you burn a couple of kangaroo carcasses. We always burn carcasses around a camp or homestead to keep the flies down. Burning a carcass would also shunt suspicion of why the fire was lit in the first place. Getting away with murder is as easy as falling off a log if only you use your brain. Try it some time and see.'

If the conversation did run anything like this (and it well may have, given Hawke was living with Upfield when these words were written, or, as has been suggested by some, Upfield himself may have written parts of the 'biography'), we can imagine Rowles sitting listening, the cogs in his brain turning, as he tried to convince himself that murder was as easy as 'falling off a log'.

A few weeks after the conversation Rowles took a job on Narndee Station, approximately 100 kilometres south-east of Mount Magnet, 300 kilometres inland from Geraldton. He was employed by Charles Bogle, Narndee's manager and part-owner, and sent out to sink a well at Challi bore with two other men – 50-year-old James Ryan from Kalgoorlie, and 32-year-old George Lloyd from South Australia and later Burracoppin in Western Australia.

The three men set off in Ryan's motor-truck on 8 December. After a few days Bogle decided to visit the bore. When he arrived Rowles was alone. Bogle found this strange as Rowles had been 'paid off' on the understanding he'd leave Narndee when the job was finished. Bogle asked what had happened to Ryan and Lloyd and Rowles told him Ryan had offered him a job, and that he was now working for him, but that he'd since gone off with Lloyd to 'do some work'. Bogle stayed for lunch, but Ryan and Lloyd did not return.

Several days later, George Ritchie told Upfield he'd met a miner, James Yates, who'd told him he'd seen Rowles driving Ryan's vehicle, and that Rowles had told him he was with Ryan and

Lloyd, but that they were off gathering timber. When asked about the vehicle, Rowles told locals Ryan had sold it to him because it was always breaking down. This surprised no one. These were all itinerant men, selling up and moving on to new jobs.

On Christmas Eve 1929, three weeks after Rowles had set off from Narndee Station with Ryan and Lloyd, Upfield came across him in the town of Youanmi. Rowles told the writer that Ryan was still in Mount Magnet and had lent him the car. Later he would tell another local he'd bought the truck from Ryan for £80.

It was only after Rowles had been arrested for his next murder that police found cooking utensils, bones, buttons, tools, eyelets from tents and boots, belt buckles and parts of an accordion (which Lloyd had played) in eight separate camp fires close to where the three men had been working. The identity of the bones was never established but, assuming they did belong to Ryan and Lloyd, it's interesting to note that Rowles hadn't quite perfected Ritchie's technique.

Although it seemed likely Rowles had murdered the other men, and attempted to dispose of their bodies, it hadn't occurred to him to hide the vehicle, keep a low profile, or move to an area where Ryan and Lloyd were less well known. Indeed, the promise of a new 'motor-truck' had probably motivated him to kill both men. Although he'd borrowed Ritchie's and Upfield's ideas, he hadn't been so clever on the follow-up.

Journalist Desmond Robinson later commented on Rowles's lack of any sense of self-preservation. 'If Rowles, having apparently committed two callous murders to obtain possession of a motor-truck, had remained content, he might never have been detected. He made the inevitable mistake of all criminals – he believed that he was proof against detection.'

Leslie George Brown was a 27-year-old French Canadian who migrated to New Zealand in 1925. In the same year he married in Auckland and over the next four years had two children, Desmond and Fay. Later, he and his wife, Minnie, agreed to separate. In

February 1930 Brown, now calling himself Louis Carron, arrived in the Murchison district of Western Australia broke and in search of a new life. He soon obtained work at Wydgee Station, 90 kilometres south of Mount Magnet, where he met Rowles.

In May 1930 the newly renamed Carron left Wydgee Station, intent upon finding a new job. He was carrying a cheque for £25 in his pocket. He went to visit a friend, boundary rider John Lemon, who was working at Fountain outcamp on Narndee Station. A day later Rowles arrived at the same camp in Ryan's motor-truck. He convinced Carron to go kangaroo shooting (or prospecting, depending on which source is believed) with him. It's likely he'd followed Carron to the outcamp with one idea in mind: murdering the New Zealander and stealing his cheque.

The two men set off in the motor-truck, telling Lemon they were heading east to Paynesville, and then Wiluna. As they left, Carron told Lemon he would write to him soon. At that stage Carron was still wearing his gold wedding ring, a clue that would later become vitally important. A week later Rowles was seen alone in Youanmi.

It took two months before Lemon, not having received the promised letter from Carron, became concerned enough to telegraph Rowles at Youanmi asking about his friend. Weeks later Rowles replied explaining that Carron had moved on to Geraldton. More time passed and Lemon became increasingly worried. Eventually, in January 1931, he visited the Mount Magnet police station and reported his friend missing. The police, meanwhile, had received a letter from one of Carron's New Zealand friends who was similarly concerned about not having heard from him. Even at this stage, over a year after the disappearance of Ryan and Lloyd, no connection was made to the other missing men.

Meanwhile, Upfield, unaware of the fate of Ryan, Lloyd or Carron, or the fact that Rowles had been turning his ideas into actions, was completing his fourth novel, *The Sands of Windee*, which was published a few months later by Hutchinson, London (the normal path for authors in a country lacking its own publishing industry).

Back in Mount Magnet, Constable William Hearn, who was about to leave for holidays, was taking John Lemon's concerns very seriously. He decided to spend his holidays searching for the missing man. After obtaining permission to use a police car he took a constable named McArthur and headed south, slowly searching the country he assumed Rowles and Carron would have covered. He made enquiries, visited outcamps and stations, looked in dry creeks and gullies, and used his considerable bush skills to find any clues. One evening the two constables visited a small shack the local Aboriginal people called the 'haunted hut' (the '183 mile' hut along the rabbit-proof fence).

Desmond Robinson told his readers: 'Outside the hut they found the ashes of a fire many months old. About 40 feet away was another pile of ashes. In both ... the constables found what appeared to be the remains of a human body. There were several blackened teeth – natural and artificial – the charred remains of a dental plate, some small curved pieces of bone, several buttons and press studs, a Hong Kong coin, and a gold wedding ring of an unusual shape. There was also a bullet and a discharged cartridge shell. Leading to and from the hut were motor tracks.'

The two officers packed these items in a box and quickly returned to Mount Magnet where they telegraphed their news to Perth detectives. Then, like the beginning of the second act of a detective novel, 'A few days later Detective Sergeant Manning arrived'.

Manning was an old-school policeman. After he was apprehended, Rowles claimed that when he was first interviewed by Manning, the detective said to him, 'You will wish you were dead after I have finished with you.'

Henry Manning, a Victorian by birth, joined the Western Australian police in 1897. He was strictly 'by the rules'. Locals at one of his early postings, Burtville Station community, tried to have him removed for breaking up gambling rings. He spent years working in Kalgoorlie tracking down gold thieves, as well as investigating the disappearance of Inspector Walsh and Sergeant Pitman, who had been murdered, beheaded and thrown down an abandoned mine shaft. Manning soon apprehended the local gold thieves turned murderers. It was this experience that made him the obvious choice to investigate the Murchison murders.

On 5 March 1931 Manning tracked Rowles to Hill View Station. He immediately recognised him as John Thomas Smith, wanted for escaping the lockup in the wheatbelt town of Dalwallinu in 1928. In his report Manning said, 'When he got into the car I said "How long have you been known as Rowles?" He said, "You know fucking well who I am and if I had known who you were you would not have got me so easy."'

Rowles told Manning he didn't know where Carron was. He explained they had gone their separate ways because Carron couldn't stand Rowles's drinking. Manning then searched Rowles's hut and found a watch, shirt and other articles he believed might belong to Carron. He arrested Rowles for escaping custody and sent him to the Meekatharra lock-up. That night Rowles attempted to commit suicide by strangling himself with a blanket.

Yet again, he failed.

Manning had bought himself some time, but realised he had a difficult job. He had no body, no eyewitnesses. Apart from a detailed investigation of the crime scene he would need to interview witnesses from all over Australia and New Zealand. He would spend the next 11 months establishing a 'chain-of-evidence' before he was confident enough to charge Rowles with Carron's murder. In his article on the murder, 'The Extraordinary Case of "Snowy" Rowles: A Classic of Patient Detective Work', Desmond Bailey summarised Manning's five main leads. They are reproduced here as Bailey presented them.

1. The cheque for £25, which Carron had in his possession when he left Lennon's camp with Rowles, was cashed by Rowles at a hotel at Paynesville.

2. The remains of the false teeth found in the ashes at the 'haunted hut' were similar to teeth made for Carron by Arthur William Sims, a dentist from Hamilton, New Zealand. From his records Sims was able to swear that he had drilled a hole in one of Carron's teeth in exactly the same position as a hole in one of the teeth in the ashes.
3. Several articles found in Rowles's hut were the property of Carron.
4. The wedding ring of unusual shape found in the ashes was similar to a ring given by Carron to his wife before their marriage in New Zealand. She had returned it to him when they separated [a jeweller in New Zealand identified the ring as one he had cut and re-sized, accidentally using the wrong type of solder when he rejoined it; he had been too busy to fix his mistake, and the ring now had different coloured solders].
5. Two watches were sent for repairs to a jeweller in Perth by Carron before his disappearance. Subsequently the same two watches were sent to the same jeweller by Rowles.

Meanwhile, Rowles had been tried for housebreaking and escaping custody, and sentenced to three years' gaol. On 7 January 1932 Detective Sergeant Manning visited Fremantle Gaol and charged him with Carron's murder near the '183 mile gate' of the rabbit-proof fence.

The Sands of Windee was now being read across Australia. Over the next few months, as Rowles's trial began, it was serialised in the *Western Mail*. Fact and fiction lived side-by-side in the streets, front bars, law courts and living rooms of Perth, and beyond.

For Upfield, it was a godsend. Born in Hampshire, England, in 1890, he was sent to Australia on a one-way ticket by his father in 1910. He fought at Gallipoli and in France with the Australian Imperial Force (AIF). After his discharge, and the birth of his son in 1920, he spent years wandering the outback, working at jobs including boundary riding, and learning about Aboriginal culture.

For an Englishman, Upfield was the quintessential Australian: Gallipoli veteran, bushy, practical, no-nonsense fence-mender, good husband and father, quick with a yarn or to offer help, but at the same time able to withdraw into his own private world, to wipe the day's dirt from his hands and start writing by gaslight. He knew the outback and its characters intimately. This was the coalface of stories he would mine for over 30 years. Upfield was no aloof artist; he inherited the legacies of Lawson and Paterson and harnessed them to his own distinct vision. He was a prolific storyteller, crafting his characters and plot-lines in the same way he would build a fire, patch a roof or fix a fence post.

A coroner's inquest into the death of Leslie George Brown began in January 1932. The first witness to take the stand was Arthur Upfield. He told the inquiry Rowles had been present when he talked about the 'perfect murder' with George Ritchie, and that he'd had a further conversation with Rowles on 6 October 1929 when the method was discussed in the context of a book he planned to write. An article in the *Canberra Times* on 19 January 1932 stated: 'Evidence by the police showed that human bones, thought to be those of Brown, were found in the ashes of a fire. A pathologist giving evidence said that he had examined some of the bones found in the fire, but they were so broken they could not be recognised as human. However, several teeth found were human.'

A few weeks later, Arthur Sims, Carron's New Zealand dentist, appeared as a witness. He identified several of the teeth found in the ashes as belonging to Carron. On the same day, Andrew Long, the New Zealand jeweller who had fixed Carron's wife's wedding ring, said the ring found by police was similar to one he'd sold to the Browns. The *Canberra Times* correspondent explained, 'Minnie Alice Brown said when she and her husband parted he took his mother's name of Carron. With tears in her eyes she examined the wedding ring and said it was similar to one her husband gave her. When she placed it on her finger, it fitted exactly.'

Another witness identified a shirt found in Rowles's hut as one manufactured in New Zealand, and John Worth, the bookkeeper at Wydgee Station, told the inquiry that he had given Carron a cheque for £25 when he'd finished working there. Police alleged this was the same cheque Rowles later cashed at a hotel at Paynesville, buying beer he claimed was for Carron (although he later claimed Carron was a teetotaller).

The coroner's inquest finished and Rowles's trial began. In March 1932, Rowles, now referred to as John Smith, took the stand in his own defence. He'd had plenty of time to get his story straight. He explained that he and Carron had gone kangaroo hunting, and one morning he [Rowles] had gone to Paynesville for stores. Carron agreed to pay half, and had given him his £25 cheque to cash. The Melbourne *Argus* reported that Rowles claimed he 'got the goods and received a cheque for £16 as part of the change. He then returned to Windimurra homestead and gave Brown the change. They went to Mount Magnet on the following night and had supper together at Slavin's shop. Brown, who was a teetotaller, objected to Smith having a few drinks that night and said that he could do better alone, and took his gear off Smith's motor-truck ... Smith had not seen Brown since that night ... a man named O'Dea would say that he saw Smith and Brown having supper in Slavin's shop ... after the date of the alleged murder'.

Rowles accounted for Carron's possessions found in his hut by saying Carron must have left them there when he departed in a rush. Rowles's lawyer, Fred Curran, had done his homework, managing to track down Rowles's brother, George Smith, who claimed that a camera found on Rowles, alleged by the prosecution to have belonged to Carron, was the same as one he'd sent to his brother as a birthday present. This, together with O'Dea's questionable evidence, cast some (slight) doubt on the prosecution case. Another witness, Robert Broadbent, claimed John Lemon had told him he'd offered to testify in favour of Rowles if Rowles gave him £200.

Australia's Wild West was still a place of mixed allegiances.

The trial judge, Mr Justice Draper, eventually summed up, saying: 'Upfield, who is a budding author ... says he remembers a discussion one night in a small room when the accused, among others, was present ... It was proposed by Mr George Ritchie that the best way [to dispose of a body] would be to burn the body, and crush the bones remaining ... The bones found in the ashes I have referred to were certainly crushed up.'

In the days before DNA testing there was no way to be certain whose they were. Draper explained that police had advertised for Carron in New Zealand, but not Canada. But, he countered, a letter Carron had posted to his sister in New Zealand showed that he had no intentions of returning to Canada. Therefore, he told the jury, their decision would rely to a great extent on the presence of bones in the ashes, as well as Carron's belongings in the hut. He went on to say, 'If the ring is not enough to satisfy you that the remains in the ashes were Carron's, what if other belongings of Carron's were found in the ashes? It would indeed be a strange coincidence. We have the teeth, and it is for you to decide if they were Carron's.'

The jury in the Criminal Court was out for two hours. When they returned, Ronald Monson, a reporter for the *West Australian*, described the scene: 'All eyes turned on their faces, and most read from their grim expressions what the verdict would be. Rowles, who had borne himself with great fortitude throughout the trial, stood on the steps leading from the dock to the cells below ... When Mr Justice Draper took his seat in court Rowles mounted to the dock and stared at the jury. He was seen to shake his head, as if he knew that he was doomed.'

Rowles had guessed right. The foreman read out the verdict: Guilty. Monson continued: 'For a few seconds there was a deathly silence in court, and then the judge's associate asked Rowles if he had anything to say before sentence of death was pronounced.'

Rowles: I have never been guilty of a crime that has never been committed.

Draper: Is that all? Is that all you have to say?

Rowles refused to answer. Draper then donned his black cap, and sentenced 'Snowy' Rowles to death.

Rowles refused to go to the gallows without a fight. Within days Curran had lodged an appeal against the sentence. These proceedings were heard by the Full Court of Western Australia, which upheld the conviction. The appeal was then taken to the High Court which, on Thursday 26 May 1932, spent a full day hearing submissions. Curran asked for a new trial, claiming there had been 'an undue emphasis of the case for the Crown and an inadequate presentation of the case for the defence'.

Curran argued there had been three problems with the trial. Firstly, the judge heard 'irrelevant' evidence about Ryan and Lloyd; secondly, Upfield was wrong about him [Rowles] being present when the 'perfect murder' was discussed; and, thirdly, there was no evidence proving that the bones in the fire belonged to Carron or, indeed, that Carron was actually dead.

Rowles's appeal was dismissed.

Then, a few days later, Rowles made a statement claiming that Carron had been 'accidentally poisoned'. He described how he had eaten poisoned butter intended for foxes. He said he had found Carron's body when he had returned from Paynesville and, not expecting to be believed because of his criminal record, had disposed of it in the fire. Rowles's statement was presented to the Western Australian attorney general, who dismissed it out of hand.

Rowles was getting desperate, running out of time, thinking on his feet. He'd told Curran about the poisoned butter when he'd come to visit him in Fremantle Gaol to ask him to finally deny or admit his guilt. Rowles insisted he was innocent, explaining that he'd 'rather die than fight the case anymore'.

On the day before his execution, Rowles handed Curran a letter in which he denied having any knowledge of what had happened to James Ryan and George Lloyd. He told Curran, again, that he had not murdered Carron.

But it was too late. On Tuesday 14 June 1932, reported the Melbourne *Argus*: 'John Thomas Smith, alias 'Snowy' Rowles, was executed at the Fremantle Gaol at 8 o'clock this morning in the presence of gaol officials. He made no statement. Arrangements were made for the body to be privately interred at Karrakatta Cemetery.'

In the years since the Murchison murders the story of Arthur Upfield and 'Snowy' Rowles has captured the Australian imagination. It is part bush yarn, part murder-mystery, part psychological treatise on the mind of John Thomas Smith, a character who thought he was a lot smarter than he was, who couldn't quite tell the difference between fact and fiction. 'Snowy' Rowles is remembered as part larrikin, part idiot, but, like Ned Kelly, is not beyond redemption in our national imagination. We remember him as hard-working, but misguided, prone to flights of fancy, unable to resist the temptation of a £25 cheque, or a motor-truck.

But perhaps the most astonishing aspect of these murders was their source material. Generally the murder inspires the book, or the film, not the other way round. Upfield was never proud of his association with Rowles, but, one guesses, he realised the itinerant stockman had helped launch and sustain his name as a writer. He later wrote his own account of the affair, *The Murchison Murders* (1934). In this booklet he made a comparison between the real and imagined crime (in *The Sands of Windee*), showing how Manning and Bony handled their separate investigations (for instance, Manning found an iron camp oven which he assumed had been used to grind Carron's bones; Bony finds a prospector's dolly-pot which has been used for the same purpose).

Upfield and Rowles have been talked about ever since. In 1993 Western Australian writer Terry Walker published *Murder on the Rabbit Proof Fence*, a detailed re-telling of the story based on years of research. Walker later explained that in 2005 he received a phone call from Louis Carron's grand-daughter in New Zealand. She told him that after their father's murder she and her brother were brought up separately, without seeing each other, in Salvation Army hostels until they were 15. Minnie, Carron's widow, the woman who had returned her gold wedding ring, had recently died aged 94. Walker suggests that Minnie was always a 'strange and difficult woman', which may explain why Brown came to Australia in the first place.

The definitive re-telling of the story came in the form of the ABC's *3 Acts of Murder*, a 95-minute telemovie written by Ian David, starring Robert Menzies as Arthur Upfield, Luke Ford as 'Snowy' Rowles and Nicholas Hope as Detective Sergeant Manning. The movie was promoted with a quote from Arthur Upfield: 'Just because you give someone an idea for murder, does that make you responsible for the crime?'

Upfield never really thought so, but the question must have lingered in his mind, as he remembered his days as a boundary rider on the rabbit-proof fence.

CHAPTER 9

Lasseter's Reef

1930–1931

Lewis 'Possum' Lasseter – Uncertain origins – Man of jumbled moods – The £5 million reef – CAGE, and first plans – The expedition leaves – Forced back to Ilbilla – Women in sun bonnets – Towards Lake Christopher – Lasseter's Cave – 'I would give it all for a loaf of bread' – Possum's other lives

In 1940 world famous Australian singer Peter Dawson published his setting of Edward Harrington's poem *Lasseter's Last Ride*.

> *Now Lasseter sleeps in the great North-west*
> *Where they say the dead sleep sound*
> *But what was the end of Lasseter's quest*
> *And where is the gold he found?*

Today, we know it's still in the ground, if anywhere. Fine specks of gold trapped in Palaeozoic quartz, thrown up in magmatic extrusions resembling sun bonnets and Quakers' hats. Of course, many believe the whole story the work of some long-dead illywhacker, but others, that the suburb-sized reef must exist. When Lewis Lasseter died in 1931 he took his secrets to a desert grave, and no one's even sure of that. Some believe he lived, moved to San Francisco with his dirty mining money, and started a new life (or resumed an old one). Yes, a body was recovered, but whose? In 1957 American journalist Lowell Thomas came to Australia hoping to solve the mystery. He dug up what might have been our great mythological hero, examined the skull, declared the mystery solved. But life is rarely that simple. The beginning and end of this story mixes facts, half-truths, rumours, stories. Adds a twist of drama, waits eighty years and serves up a story nearly as reliable as Ulysses, wandering his own Mediterranean desert, or Tom and Huck, and their Splendid Days and Fearsome Nights. Between all this, the facts are elusive. But as Harrington explained, 'Oh some may jest at his fruitless quest, Or murmur his name in grief, But somewhere out in the great north-west, Lies Lasseter's golden reef.'

Lewis Hubert (Harold Bell) Lasseter ('Das' or 'Possum') was born in 1880 at Bamaganie, Victoria. His mother died early and his father remarried. Adrift as a young man, Lasseter committed a robbery in October 1896 and was sent to a reformatory in Pakenham, Victoria. He escaped in October 1897, around the same time he later claimed to be walking from Alice Springs to the Western Australian goldfields; to have found his gold reef. After making this discovery he stumbled through the desert, lost, before meeting an Afghan camel driver who took him to the camp of a government surveyor named Harding. Harding believed Lasseter's story. In 1900 both men returned to examine the reef and later, unsuccessfully, attempted to raise money for a full-scale expedition.

The timing seems difficult. Lasseter claimed to have spent four years in the Royal Navy before being discharged in 1901. Then he was off to the United States, where he married in December 1903. His early years, especially, are a jumble of beautiful lies. The dates are plastic, and very few sources agree on anything. Was this Lasseter, or history? According to Fred Blakeley, leader of the 1930 reef expedition, Lasseter 'lacked a credible story about anything in all his reminiscences'.

We do know that by 1911 Lasseter was living in Tabulam, New South Wales. He worked a small farm, kept busy with odd jobs and wrote (the great yarn-spinner that he was) occasional pieces for *The Tenterfield Star*. His 'Tabulam Tinklings' were a typically Lasseterian bag of gossip, trivia, social analysis and nation-building suggestions. He was smart, keen, scribbling ideas for everything from disc ploughs to an arch bridge to span Sydney Harbour. At the outbreak of war he sold his farm and moved to Melbourne. Tried to enlist, but was rejected, unfit for service. Never one to be put off, he tried again (claiming to be an engineer) in February 1916 and was accepted, but discharged on 17 October. And again. This time in Adelaide in August 1917. Rejected in November of the same year.

During all this time Lasseter was, apparently, sitting on his 'find'. An enormous reef of gold that might have made his fortune, if he'd 'returned' to the desert to locate his 1897 discovery. This 'man of jumbled moods' waited more than thirty years to act on his revelation, a discovery that surely would have saved him years of struggle, scribbling and roaming the country in search of some sort of purpose.

In 1924 Lasseter married Louise Irene (Rene) Lillywhite in Albert Park, Melbourne. Over the next few years they lived in Sydney and Canberra (where Lasseter worked as a carpenter, including time helping build the new parliament house). 'Possum' (now under the nom de plume of the 'Gleaner') wrote pieces on a variety of topics for *The Canberra Country News*. At the end of 1927 the family returned to Sydney where Lasseter, ironically, worked on the Sydney Harbour Bridge while continuing to invent and register patents, including one for pre-cast concrete.

In 1929 the idea of gold returned. Nothing new. Ever since convict James Daley claimed to have discovered the metal at Port Jackson in 1788 (our first forgery, fragments of gold guinea and belt buckle) Australians have seen gold as the Australian shortcut to wealth, and the good life. Bathurst, Ballarat, Bendigo, Coolgardie and Kalgoorlie. Books such as *An Australian Bush Track* (1896) and *Golden Buckles* (1920) featured outback gold discoveries. Chips Rafferty was still looking in 1949's *Eureka Stockade*. Today, of course, we work the same mine at the RSL, feeding our hopes into pokies, or buying a Jumbo QuickPick at the local paper shop. But back in 1929, with the nation teetering on the edge of a depression, men's minds were starting to wander, and invent.

Lasseter approached the Western Australian government and explained that eighteen years earlier he'd found an enormous gold-bearing reef which assayed out at three ounces to the tonne. All that was needed to secure the gold was £5 million, and an adequate water supply. He offered to survey a route for a pipeline for a fee of £2000 but, not surprisingly, was turned down. Not to be beaten, he approached John Bailey, president of the Sydney branch of the Australian Workers' Union, with a modified story. Now he's seventeen again, wandering the Western Australian–Northern Territory border region, looking for gold. Gets lost. Stumbles through the desert, low on supplies, when he comes across the reef. No water. Horse dead. Saved by a cameleer, who takes him to Harding, who takes him to Carnarvon. Three years later they return to the reef. Decide on a course of action. Both spend years trying to find a backer for an expedition, with no success. Harding dies overseas while trying to raise the money.

Bailey listened attentively. Maybe there was something in it? He sought advice before agreeing to help Lasseter raise the money. Convinced, he formed the Central Australian Gold Exploration (CAGE) Company Limited and appointed himself director. The company's prospectus explained: 'The party will be guided to the reef by Mr LHB Lasseter, the discoverer, who has himself once relocated the area since his original discovery ... The discovery of gold in Australia at this juncture would be of immense value in the stabilising of our national finance.' Perhaps Bailey believed Lasseter could be an economic saviour for the nation and its many unemployed workers. Either way, the idea appealed to hundreds of investors. One pound shares were sold, and £5000 capital raised.

The expedition left Alice Springs on 21 July 1930. Six men, two trucks and a plane. Lasseter was hired for £5 per week as guide. Half a tonne of water, three months' fuel, instruments, maps and radio. The expedition headed west towards Ilbilla. Fred Blakeley, leader, Philip Taylor, mechanic and driver, George Sutherland, Fred Colson, Captain Blakeston-Houston and the pilot, Errol Coote. Almost straight away, Lasseter and Blakeley fell out over directions. Morale dropped. The team wondered why Lasseter spent his time singing hymns and scribbling in his diary. Regardless, Lasseter told them they needed to find land formations resembling the outline of a child and a 'pharaoh's head'.

They headed towards the Warburton Ranges. Haasts Bluff, Putardi Spring, then Ilbilla waterhole, where they set up base camp and started preparing a landing strip, unaware their plane had already crashed. From here, towards Mount Marjorie, near the Western Australian border. Lasseter kept changing directions and Blakeley became furious. They climbed the mountain and Lasseter consulted his map. Now, he claimed, they had to find three hills that resembled women in sun bonnets, walking together. Blakeley reluctantly listened, and they changed direction, south. Later, Taylor said that Lasseter was 'more or less a crank, very aggressive, very self-opinionated and full of large, hopeful visions'. Perhaps Lasseter was acting, full of a feigned confidence to convince his followers. After all, they were expecting gold. What would happen when their faith ran out? Or was Lasseter right? Had he been in the desert as a seventeen year old in 1897?

September. Rough terrain. The expedition was forced back to Ilbilla. Waiting for them was dingo trapper, Paul Johns, and his camels. He offered his services to the expedition but was turned down. Then, Coote arrived in a new aircraft. He took Lasseter up to survey the terrain. An hour in 'Possum' became excited. After landing he told Coote he'd seen the 'three women in sun bonnets'.

The expedition set off again. The country was almost impassable. The mulga shredded the truck's tyres. Blakeley no longer trusted Lasseter. He now believed he'd never set foot in Central Australia. Lewis, Harold, whatever he wanted to call himself, was a con-man. He told Lasseter he intended returning to Hermannsburg Mission.

Lasseter told Johns he'd take up his offer. The pair set off into the desert. Lasseter called to Blakeley, 'If I don't find the gold, I'm never coming back.' Perhaps to save face? Or perhaps because he *was* convinced of his reef?

Lasseter and Johns continued, stopping to rest at a water hole. Lasseter left his companion to scout ahead and when he returned two days later told him he'd found the reef, but refused to reveal the location. Johns wasn't convinced. The pair argued, after which Johns set off alone, convinced, as were the others, Lasseter was delusional.

Lasseter walked towards Lake Christopher with two camels that soon bolted with his food. He'd intended meeting a 'mystery man' named Johansen, or Johanson. This might have been concerning directions to the reef, protection from local Aboriginal people or, perhaps, Johansen might have been Lasseter's source concerning an earlier gold find in the area. A fragment in Lasseter's diary explained, '... engaged to go with the camels that if I did not show up again by the end of November ... they would send a man named Johansen to my relief. As I believe he also stumbled onto this identical reef I had to go right out to Lake Christopher which is 100 miles across the WA border in order to get my bearings ...' Either way, Johansen didn't arrive, having (apparently) been speared to death by local Aboriginal people.

Lasseter was left wandering, starving, thirsty, close to death, when he was found by his own group of Aboriginal people. They took him to *kulpi tjuntinya*, later known as Lasseter's Cave, where he stayed for most of January 1931. As he recovered he wrote in his diary that he'd found the reef (again) and pegged it out. It was close to a scared site, so these indications might not last. After some time he was attacked by the Aboriginal people after their Kurdaitcha man 'pointed the bone' at him. 'Blacks tried to kill me today while I was waiting for a rabbit three spears were thrown but two shots drove them off one spear landed in the tree I had my back against within 3 inches of my neck the other two were on the side ...' As he lingered, alone, forgotten, he wondered if anyone had missed him, and if help was coming.

'Das' tried one more time. In late January he set off, with the help of an Aboriginal family, and with less than two litres of water, to walk the 130 kilometres to Mount Olga, where he hoped to meet the relief party. He wrote, 'I don't suppose I've an earthly chance of surviving I can carry 2 gallons and 3 pints of water but that is hardly likely to take me the 80 miles to Mount Olga and on no food whatever I've brought this all on myself by going alone but I thought the blacks, tho' primitive were fair dealing.'

He soon succumbed. Lying, waiting for death, he still remembered his wife, Rene, and three children, Bobby, Betty and Joy. He recorded, 'Goodbye and God Bless you Rene darling wife of mine and may God Bless the children'. He mentioned he'd like Bob to become a civil engineer. Design bridges, perhaps. Like he had for Sydney (in 1929 he'd unsuccessfully tried to solicit payment for the six months' work he'd put in designing 'the bridge'). He added, 'I am sorry to finish out here and the worry of not knowing how you are faring and knowing how you must be in suspense as to my fate is simply the worst pain of all. Teach the children to believe the best you can of their father and soften the tale of my suffering here. If I could only know what the trouble is all about that no relief was sent or anything done at all ... I want relief and have saved one cartridge but will stick it out as long as possible.' He said he left an 'everlasting curse' on Blakeley for not sending relief. 'How I long to see my children once more to hold their chubby hands to see their laughing faces and hear their baby prattle ... I should never had gone along but I relied on Paul to follow me what good a reef worth millions I would give it all for a loaf of bread ...'

Lasseter walked around 55 kilometres before dying at Shaw Creek in the Petermann Ranges around 28 January.

In early 1931 the Central Australian Gold Exploration Company sent experienced pastoralist Bob Buck to search for the lost prospector. In March, he found Lasseter's body and buried him (he was reinterred in Alice Springs's Pioneer Cemetery in 1958). Years later, Buck seemed reluctant to confirm the body he'd found was Lasseter's. Sixteen year after Lasseter's death, Jack Bailey wrote, 'When Buck reported he had found Lasseter's body or what appeared to be Lasseter's body, the Directors [of CAGE] asked him to sign a declaration to this effect, but Buck refused to do this.

He said he could not swear whether the skeleton was that of a white or black man.'

Perhaps Buck was just unsure? The directors needed a death certificate to prove to the Bank of Australasia that Lasseter was dead, so they might access his papers. Fred Blakely believed there was more to Buck than met the eye. He thought he'd assisted Lasseter out of the country, on his way to America.

In 1931 the *Barrier Miner* (Broken Hill) revealed, 'The discovery has just been made of the use of invisible ink by the late Mr LHB ('Das') Lasseter to protect vital clues in the location of 'Aladdin's Cave', the mysterious gold reef of reputedly fabulous wealth ... The document on which the invisible writing was found was lodged by Lasseter with the Bank of Australasia before he left on his last trip to the interior ...' Lasseter had arranged with his wife, and the company, that in the event of his death or failure to return, the map could be retrieved for 'further clues' to the reef's location. 'When the reef was being mapped from the document [after Lasseter's death] discrepancies were noticed and a close examination showed faint markings. Police experts were able to restore the writing and a second set of directions was brought to light.' These differences were attributed to differences in Lasseter's and Harding's compasses thirty years earlier. The new information was enough to persuade CAGE to commission Bob Buck to lead a second expedition in search of the reef Lasseter had pegged out. Lasseter's secret message read:

The estimated position of this reef is Lat. – S., Long. – E. Group of 3 hills, looking like group of Dickens' women in 'Dombey and Son,' one looks like a maternity case, bearing –, dist. 17 m. Single hill looking like QUAKER, bearing – by –, dist. 20 m. Compass variations at Carnarvon – E. 1897. Only one point on reef from which these two points can be seen. Distant about 3 miles from quartz blow south.

Eventually they too would return empty-handed (except for Lasseter's diary, found buried in his cave).

So who was Lasseter? An eternal optimist? A young man who'd

found, but lost, the world's largest reef of gold? Someone who could convince himself, and others, of a fact, a notion, a lie? Years later, Fred Blakeley said, 'Lasseter is a liar and a fraud.' He had no doubts Lasseter didn't know where the gold was, because the reef didn't exist.

The myth of Lasseter didn't take long to set roots in the desert sands. Novels, songs, and decades of would-be prospectors followed in his footsteps. The first expedition was organised in 1932. Patrick Whelan claimed to have located the reef, and registered thirty-six claims in the Livesey Range with the Western Australian mines department. A company was formed, £3000 worth of shares sold, and an expedition organised. Day one: 22 December 1932. A survey plane set off, but soon crashed, and this was the beginning of a series of misfortunes that beset this, and a dozen other, failed ventures.

And it continues to this day. In 2012 Lasseterians Jeff Harris and best mate Brendan Elliott set off on their fifth expedition. They first learned of Lasseter and his lost gold growing up in Wollongong. As ten year olds they decided one day they'd go looking, and find it. They shook on it, as a hundred others have, and probably will. Harris reckoned this time they were a sure bet. They'd cross-referenced Lasseter's diary with Google Earth and come up with a possible solution. 'I was staying up twenty-four hours a day working on it. Sometimes I'd have a day off work to work on it. I had to keep going until I found the next clue. The missus was quite frustrated, to say the least.'

Does Lasseter get the last laugh? Did he really head overseas after his death, leaving his family, starting a new life? In his 1972 book *Dream Millions* Blakeley suggested this was the case. That Lewis Lasseter was a zelig, changing to suit the times, his circumstances. Did Lasseter, for instance, read Harold Bell Wright's outback novel *The Mine with the Iron Door* (1923) before changing his name? Perhaps, today, little would be known of Lasseter if not for his journey into popular culture. Apart from Dawson's romantic song, Ion Idriess's novel *Lasseter's Last Ride* (1931) turned Lasseter into a sort of early Indiana Jones, romping through the desert in search of treasure. The book ran to seventeen editions. Lasseter became a Phar Lap, Don Bradman, Nellie Melba fixture of the thirties. People choose to remember (and still do) the swashbuckling version of Lasseter, more than the complex man full of unrealised ambitions, struggling to support wives, and children, throughout the lean years of the Depression.

The 10 May 1931 edition of *The Truth* revealed more of the translucent myth, peeling back layers of the mythical man. John Bailey explained he'd received a letter from a Melbourne woman saying she was Lasseter's legal wife. He explained, 'She states that she married him in New York in 1903, and she quotes the number of the marriage certificate.' Lasseter's wife was having none of it. 'I am the legal wife of Lewis Harold Bell Lasseter, having been married to him ... on January 28 1924.' But Lasseter had lived in America (even having become naturalised) from 1901 to 1908. Married Florence Scott on 29 December 1903. Had two children: Ruby and Beulah.

Louise was left to raise Lasseter's three children. Robert never became an engineer but, like his father, spent his life scribbling, inventing, fixing, and searching. Not for the gold, but his father's legacy, laid out in the desert across endless gibbers, lost in the mulga. He was five when his father left home, six when he died. And, like most Australians, has spent years searching for a credible version of the man.

Reading and thinking about Lasseter raises many questions. If, as the evidence suggests, there was never a reef, and Lasseter never discovered it (and wasn't in the desert) in 1897, why did he continue the bluff? Why did he want to lead an expedition to find something he knew didn't exist? Did he intend withdrawing at a crucial moment? Was he planning on acting out his inability to relocate the reef? Did he, when the drama had gone too far, determine to finish his act in the most final way? Lasseter's mind was always working at a thousand miles an hour. Schemes. Inventions. Ideas. Gleanings. Ramblings. Had he decided that his failed ambitions should be, finally, consumed by the desert? Was it to be a hero's death (in his mind, at least)? The tone of his final words suggest this. 'The agony is awful ... I wish to know why everyone has failed me.' Invisible writing. The final promise not to return without the gold. Dickens' women from *Dombey and Son*. A bluff finally called?

People still search, convinced. Believe Lasseter must have been obsessed for a reason. He could've pursued easier schemes, simpler ways of making a few quid. Perhaps the urge to doubt can injure us. The need to believe, sustain. In this sense, Lasseter is still with us (in one of many forms), showing us the way through the desert, towards the seven-, ten- or fourteen-mile reef. Entrepeneur and explorer Dick Smith summed it up this way: 'This is Australia's El Dorado. We need to think there is a mysterious reef that someone has found and no one has rediscovered. It's part of our psyche.'

Bob Buck certainly made up his mind. When interviewed in 1939 he said, 'Lasseter never found a reef of gold in Central Australia. As a matter of fact, Lasseter never visited the sand-hill country until I took his body there for burial. Lasseter imagined the existence of a reef ... after he had read a copy of a novel, printed in 1912. The novel described a group of aborigines [sic] who carried spears with heads of rolled gold.'

As Jeff Harris set off on his latest expedition, he was adamant that *this* time he'd get lucky. And if he didn't? Maybe it wasn't so much the gold as the search. 'What I can prove is Lasseter was a great explorer, and he did find this place. For us, to prove that he was fair dinkum is good enough for me.'

CHAPTER 10

1 2 3:
The Search for Nicholas Bannon

1959

Headlines – Nicholas Bannon and Wilpena Pound – Locals begin the search – Trackers – Footprints – The extended search – '1 2 3' in the sand – The search widens – St Peter's school matron – 30 gallons of stew – A service on the chalet lawns – Hope fades – Two years later – The knotted singlet

On Thursday 29 January 1959 the headline on the front page of Adelaide's daily *Advertiser* trumpeted: 'Wide Search For Lost Boy'. Over the following days the population of Adelaide and Australia read, tuned in, discussed and gossiped over back fences as they followed the frantic search for ten-year-old Nicholas Bannon, who'd wandered away from his family in South Australia's rugged Wilpena Pound. The *Advertiser* knew it was on to a good thing. As the search continued the headlines got bigger: 'Race To Find SA Boy', 'Searchers Pray For Boy, 10', and finally, 'No Hope Held For Boy'.

Nicholas George Bannon, a student at Adelaide's prestigious St Peter's College, was among a group of eight walking through Wilpena Pound late on Tuesday 27 January when he went missing. The group included Nicholas's father, Charles, a master at St Peter's, his mother, Joyce, and his three brothers, John, 15 (later a Labor premier of South Australia), Gregory, 13, and Andrew, five. The group, which had just finished exploring the area, split into two smaller parties on their way back to camp. It was at this stage that Nicholas wandered off. Each party believed the boy was with the other. At the time, Nicholas was carrying no food or water and was wearing only shorts, a light shirt, and sandals that were several sizes too large.

Wilpena Pound is formed by a ring of ancient mountains that create a natural amphitheatre in South Australia's Flinders Ranges. The area is a giant syncline, or fold, in sedimentary rock that is itself full of fossilised coral skeletons from the time when the area was covered in a vast inland sea. The fold runs on a NW–SE axis culminating in the 1170 metre high St Mary Peak on the north-east side of the Pound. The wall of mountains leads down to a crater-like interior that was once thought to be part of an extinct volcano. In the late 19th century agriculture was attempted but abandoned due to low and variable rainfall. Apart from Wilpena Creek, which drains through a break in the mountains called The Gap, there are only a few small waterholes in the Pound.

Within half an hour of his parents noticing him missing a search had begun. Mr G. Hunt, of Wilpena Pound, spent the night on horseback looking for the boy, while the Bannon family and other campers joined on foot. The following morning Constable Max Peters of Hawker organised a more thorough search using campers and local residents. These groups were soon joined by another ten men on horseback. The search continued into the evening of Wednesday 28 January but was stopped by darkness. Flares could not be lit as there was a large amount of dry grass and bush that had been declared a fire risk.

On the morning of 29 January more search parties set out. At 6 am, Ray Warwick, of Holowiliena Station, 70 kilometres from the Pound, started searching the area in his Auster plane. During the day the number of volunteers reached more than a hundred. Walkie-talkies were distributed to as many as possible. A group of Charles Bannon's friends and work colleagues, as well as the St Peter's College scouts, arrived from Adelaide. In a show of intercollegiate support these boys were later relieved by a party of Prince Alfred College scouts. Although the two colleges were fierce sporting rivals, often vying for the mantle of Adelaide's top school, it took an event such as the disappearance of Nicholas Bannon to demonstrate their kinship. During the day the Bannons were also comforted by Patricia Gordon, the wife of St Peter's headmaster, Colin Gordon.

Fears were held for Nicholas's safety from the first night. Although summer temperatures exceeded the old century during the day, at night the area (over 600 metres above sea level) became extremely cold. Nicholas, dressed in light clothing, would have no idea how to survive.

Meanwhile, the boy's footprints were found approximately five kilometres outside Wilpena Pound. It appeared Nicholas had been walking south, dragging a stick. His trail was lost when it passed into an area of grass and timberland outside the Pound. Nonetheless, the tracks encouraged the searchers. Port Augusta trackers Billy Pepper and Johnny Cadell, well known at the time for their roles in the 1957 film *Robbery Under Arms*, joined the search.

By Friday 30 January there were at least 150 men looking for Nicholas Bannon. Mr G. Hunt told the *Advertiser*: 'We split into two parties to cover the outside of the Pound in case he tried to get out, and another party searched inside the Pound.' He explained that a helicopter from Woomera (a rocket testing range 500 kilometres north of Adelaide) had been dispatched to search waterholes in the area. After three days of searching most men were exhausted. 'We are taking a spell tonight so that we will be fresh in the morning. Many of us have had only three hours' sleep in the past 72 hours. It's pitch black outside. We couldn't see the boy if we did go out and we can't light flares ... We might destroy the tracks if we did go in.'

Meanwhile, in the best Australian tradition, Mrs Hunt joined other 'homestead women' to cook meals for the men. The Royal Flying Doctor base at Port Augusta began broadcasting hourly bulletins to the searchers.

During the day a person believed to be Nicholas was sighted from the air. A Department of Civil Aviation pilot by the name of Zwar claimed to have seen a 'still figure' halfway up a 60-metre cliff about ten kilometres south of Wilpena Chalet. Zwar noted the figure was wearing grey clothing similar to that which Nicholas had been wearing on the day of his disappearance. Zwar and three other aircraft continued searching the area but lost track of the figure.

Later, near where the figure had been sighted, searchers found the numbers '1 2 3' written in the sand. Police and Nicholas's parents were unsure if the numbers had any significance. They concluded that the boy, exhausted and delirious, had probably written the numbers while remembering 'something he had read in a book'.

During the afternoon of Friday 30 January, horsemen continued searching the steep slopes of Wilpena Pound but conceded it was impossible to 'investigate every cranny'. Four fresh horses arrived during the afternoon to replace others that had become footsore on the rocky terrain. Ashton Brothers Circus, which was playing in Adelaide's West Parklands during the school holidays, provided a horse transport for the journey.

The police search for Nicholas was being directed from Adelaide by Superintendent Eric Langdon Bonython. On this, the fourth day of the search, he issued a statement: 'He may have become unable to move, either through weakness or injury in a fall. As it is unlikely that he would still be [able] to call for help, searchers would have to be almost on top of him before they could find him in the dense bush.'

Twenty-five police from Adelaide, Port Augusta and Whyalla had joined the search. Back in Adelaide, police, overcome by offers of assistance, were turning away volunteers who did not have their own food and transport. The police commissioner, John Gilbert McKinna, arranged for Engineering and Water Supply Department water-carting trucks to be dispatched to the area.

On Saturday 31 January, as the state continued sweltering through a heatwave, the search continued. One aircraft, an Avro Anson, nearly crashed after it hit an air pocket and plunged earthwards. The pilot, J. Schofield, hit his head on the control panel and his co-pilot,

A.L. Harper, was forced to take the controls as a two-gallon water can tumbled around the cockpit, threatening their safety. The plane narrowly avoided a 300-metre sheer cliff. Eventually air currents and red dust 'willie-willies' made the air search impossible and the planes were told to return to their home base.

The Bannon family was still helping in the search for their son and brother. A staff reporter for the *Advertiser* explained, 'They are showing signs of the extreme strain and suffering they have experienced, but are remaining calm.' By now 70 St Peter's students, masters and old scholars had joined Charles Bannon in the search for his son. The school matron also arrived to help out where she could.

Charles Bannon was a highly respected master at 'Saints'. After moving to Australia from Edinburgh, Scotland, he worked as a painter, ceramic artist, stage designer, printmaker and gallery director. At age 35 he beat a field of 251 entrants to win the prestigious Blake Prize for religious art for his semi-abstract painting 'Judas Iscariot'. At St Peter's College he established a printmaking workshop with Udo Sellbach, and together they later established a printmaking department at the South Australian School of Art.

Bannon loved the outback, and especially the Flinders Ranges where, in 1993, he died. After the disappearance of his son he went on to work with many indigenous Australian artists, and was art advisor to the Northern Territory government from 1963 to 1965.

On Monday 1 January, six days after Nicholas's disappearance, an army unit led by Major F.D. Buckland, an officer experienced in survey work in the Northern Territory, arrived at Wilpena Pound. Thirty-seven men joined another 14 soldiers already on the ground. They started searching large areas of open country and timbered land.

Meanwhile, Murray Valley Coaches, a company owned by Kevin Rasheed, who also owned Wilpena Chalet, donated a bus to transport supplies from Adelaide. The specially converted vehicle was loaded with two tons of food and medical supplies, the result of a police radio appeal on Saturday night. Three hundred loaves of bread were sent from Adelaide, and another 350 from Port Augusta. A small village sprang up at the chalet. Reports described 300 beds being made up from borrowed mattresses and blankets. The Hawker butcher opened his shop and made 30 gallons of hot stew for the searchers. Crystal Cordial sent two trucks' worth of cool drinks.

The *Advertiser* started ramping up its portrayal of the search. 'Help that has been pouring in from all quarters has highlighted the moving human story of the search for the boy.' The newspaper started finding heroes among the gums, like Marree Constable John O'Day, who worked a police radio for 36 hours straight, reluctantly stopping for a six-hour break before starting again.

The next day, Tuesday 2 February, the *Advertiser* reported that '200 weary and footsore men sat in prayer on the lawns of the Wilpena Chalet ... after another gruelling day searching for 10-year-old Nicholas Bannon'. It was apparent that there was little chance of finding him alive. Searchers had been over the same ground again and again. The search shifted to an area south-west of the Pound near Ulowdna Range. In the morning the temperature quickly passed the old century for the fourth day straight as the red sand, densely covered with mallee gums and native pines, as well as a week's worth of foot- and hoof-prints, baked in the sun.

Two Hawker locals, Keith Wallace and Keith Crossman, used four-wheel drive vehicles to re-open a bullock track that hadn't been used for 40 years. This allowed an army truck to bring men and supplies into the Pound. The Civil Aviation Department's Anson, as well as the helicopter from Woomera, were withdrawn from the search because of the dangerous flying conditions. An old Tiger Moth, flown by J.K. Lehman, the president of the Jamestown Aero Club, continued the air search.

That night, nearly a week after Nicholas's disappearance, a short service took place on the lawns of the chalet. Reverend Brook from the Hawker Methodist Church prayed for the lost boy before leading the weary searchers in a rendition of 'Lead, Kindly Light'

The Fierce Country

and 'O God, Our Help in Ages Past'. Hardly anyone knew the words, so most hummed along.

At the chalet there was a real sense of purpose. The local community and towns of Hawker, Port Augusta, and beyond, as well as the whole state were determined to find Nicholas. The men had blistered feet and tired legs, and were being nursed by sisters from the Hawker Hospital. The local 'station women' were cooking meals in their homes and bringing them to the chalet in milk cans and any other type of container they could get their hands on.

Back in Adelaide, Superintendent Eric Bonython said he didn't believe the Anson plane had spotted Nicholas the previous week. Based on what he'd been told by a search party he thought it likely it was just a 'large stone'. The plane's pilot, Mr Zwar, disagreed, and insisted he had seen the boy. He said the figure was kneeling on all fours in an 'apparent state of stupor'. 'The barelegged boy,' he said, 'wearing grey shorts and a dark greenish shirt, was midway up a 500 feet high ridge on the southern side of the Pound, about five or six miles south of Wilpena Chalet.'

By Wednesday 3 February Nicholas Bannon was officially presumed dead. A final search, consisting of 120 men, spent the day on the ground without success. Army personnel searched the area where the boy's tracks had earlier been found. Local Aboriginal men searched Wilpena Creek in case Nicholas had fallen in and drowned. Some clothing was found, including two singlets, but none of it belonged to Nicholas. Charles and Joyce Bannon said they had now accepted that their son would never be found alive. During the day most civilians returned to their towns, or Adelaide, some locals promising the Bannons they'd continue searching the area each weekend until the boy's remains were found.

On Thursday 4 February a small party of searchers had one more go, with no luck. Returning to the chalet that night Johnny Cadell said, 'It is just like that feeling after losing a game. You wouldn't believe we didn't find a thing after all this time.'

Nicholas's distraught parents and family had now accepted the inevitable. Charles Bannon said, 'My wife and I wish to express our deepest appreciation to the people of the outback, and, indeed, all the volunteers, many of whom travelled far and helped not only in the search, but with their sympathy and understanding.'

We can only guess how the other Bannon boys were coping. John, Greg and Andrew had experienced every moment of the tragedy: the afternoon of their brother's disappearance, the frantic search on the first night, the dawning of the magnitude of their predicament as searchers, planes, police and army personnel arrived, the media reports, through to what was perhaps worst of all, the endless hours of waiting and hoping.

Charles Bannon, tired, confused, devastated by the loss of his son, had to hold his family together, as well as praise the efforts of others. 'The officers in charge of the case ... and the other assisting officers, men and black-trackers have been considerate, sympathetic and tireless,' he said.

As the search came to an end, Hawker District Council supervisor John Walladge explained, 'We did the best we could. We know for certain that the undergrowth on the perimeter of the Pound would prevent any child from reaching the hills surrounding it. Because we found no clothing it seems pretty certain he didn't wander far. It wouldn't surprise me if he is within a mile of where he was last seen.' He believed the boy may have climbed a tree and become stuck in foliage, fallen in a waterhole or crawled into a large fox hole.

Police Inspector Horace Sparrow, who had been coordinating the search on the ground, said, 'We don't know any more than when we called off the search on Tuesday.'

Another disaster was narrowly avoided when a police float, returning five horses to Adelaide, overturned north of Hawker. Three passengers were badly bruised and a police instructor was buried under luggage close to kicking horses. The horses were transferred to another float and returned to Adelaide and the float was taken to Hawker for repairs.

On 8 September 1961, two years and nine months after his

disappearance, Nicholas Bannon was found. The *Advertiser* explained, 'A skeleton, believed to be that of a boy, was found on the south side of St Mary Peak in Wilpena Pound yesterday afternoon.'

The skeleton was found by three Victorian tourists who had been bushwalking. They had notified Constables O'Neill and Duthie of the Hawker Police who had then set out for the Pound with coroner F. Teague. They were later joined by Detective Alex Palmer, from Port Augusta. The skeleton, clad in tattered clothing, was then returned to Hawker for examination.

Police found a stick with a fragment of singlet knotted onto it near the skeleton. They believed Nicholas had used this to try and signal aircraft and searchers. Perhaps it was the same stick he had been dragging in the sand on 28 or 29 January. A bushfire had burnt out the area in January 1961 and scraps of clothing near the body were 'charred but recognisable'.

One of the three men who discovered the body described how they had come across the skeleton approximately 800 metres up the side of the peak. These men had just climbed St Mary Peak and were returning to Wilpena Chalet when they made the gruesome discovery.

Nicholas Bannon had perished less than five kilometres from where his searchers had slept on the chalet's lawn, eating stew and humming hymns.

Detective Palmer explained that he believed Nicholas must have been attempting to climb the peak to orientate himself after becoming lost. He said Nicholas showed tremendous courage in climbing as far up the peak as he did.

With the recovery of Nicholas Bannon's body the newspaper reports stopped, and the collective memory of a state, and nation, began to fade. Charles and Joyce Bannon, and Nicholas's brothers, finally had some sort of closure on the events of their tragic 1959 summer camping trip.

CHAPTER 11

'Ran out of Petrel': The Page Family

1963

The road from Shadoxhurst – To Marree – The Birdsville Track – Ernie, Emma and the kids – Avril Howard's reflections – New Year's Day 1964 – 'The Pages – perished in 1963' – Describes the journey north – One of two tracks – 'the idea of north' – In the shade of their Customline – Beside their mother and father – A rushed burial – A pilgrimage

Ernest 'Ernie' Page was sick of life in his small town of Shadoxhurst, Kent. The mechanic wanted a taste of adventure, more opportunities, a new start for his wife, Emma, and their four children. Ernie applied to migrate to Australia as a 'ten-pound Pom'. Then he waited, and waited. One, two, three years, until eventually the letter arrived to tell him he'd been accepted. The Pages started planning their adventure.

In 1959 the family set off on the Orient liner *Orion*. They stopped in France, Portugal, India, Sri Lanka, Singapore and Fremantle before arriving in Adelaide. During the journey in their shiny chromium and bakelite cabin, Ernie and Emma were full of anticipation, as were their three sons, Robert, 15, Douglas, eight, and Gordon, six. Their daughter, Judy, in her late teens, travelled with her fiancé, John Pilcher.

Upon arrival, Judy and John married and found a house in Adelaide. The Pages also lived and worked in town for 12 months before Ernie decided he wanted to 'go bush'. The family started planning their move to Marree, 685 kilometres north of Adelaide.

Today, Marree, an ex-railhead town that still boasts a massive concrete platform as part of its deserted railway station, has the Great Northern Hotel, the Camel Cup and a few houses and shops. Some of the old locos are still scattered around town, some even used as homes. Ernie found a job as a mechanic in a garage owned by Dave Millar, a man he didn't always get along with, about whom we will learn more later.

Marree's population shrank from 600 to 100 after the Adelaide to Alice Springs railway shifted to the west in 1980. With only 150 millimetres of rain each year, plenty of dust and not much to do, Marree was a strange choice for a family from Kent. Still, it must have had some attraction for Ernie, if not Emma and the boys. Perhaps it represented the 'real' outback the Englishman had often imagined. Perhaps it was the perfect place to get away from everything, and everyone, in his quest to start again.

The Pages stayed in Marree for three years, until Ernie decided it was time to move further north, to Queensland, to pursue better job opportunities.

This journey, in December 1963, into the heart of a harsh, unforgiving country – sandhills and gibber plains, rough tracks that could blow away in a matter of days, or hours – would become one of the great, but little known, tragedies of Australian history. The Birdsville Track was no place for a Sunday drive; for the unprepared; for the inexperienced. These were the days before graders removed corrugations. Before decent signage, or emergency communication. It had only been a generation since cars and trucks had ventured north. Prior to this it was just camels and stock. A few generations since drover Percy Burt set up his store at Diamantina Crossing (now Birdsville) to serve as a way out of the Channel Country towards railheads at Marree and Port Augusta.

At the time of his disappearance, Ernie Page was 48 years old, 165 centimetres tall and slightly built. Images of the middle-aged mechanic show a square-faced, flat-nosed man with neatly parted hair and ears burnt by the Australian sun. During his time in Marree, Ernie grew to love the outback and to see himself as a 'bushy'. His wife, Emma, 45, seemed content to continue their adventure north, taking Douglas, now 12, and Gordon, ten. A photo of Emma, standing beside the family's Ford Customline, shows a slight figure with crossed arms, staring at the ground, unwilling to acknowledge the camera, more Coronation Street than main street Marree. The boys, standing beside her, are big-boned and brown-skinned, living the outback adventure their father had invoked.

Robert, now 19, had also inherited his father's sense of adventure and was off jackarooing on Clifton Hills Station, 300 kilometres north of Marree. Judy, in comparison, hated the outback. She had stayed in Adelaide and become a fully-fledged 1960s homemaker. Judy and John would eventually have four children of their own. In 2005, Judy died from cancer, aged 63. At the time it had been 42 years since she had last seen any member of her family. In September 1963, Ernie, Emma and her brothers had visited her in Adelaide before setting off on their ill-fated journey.

In 2010 Judy's daughter, 42-year-old Avril Howard, along with one of her three brothers, Ian, decided to travel to the Birdsville Track to retrace her grandparents' journey, and to replace an old cross that had marked the site of the Pages' outback grave with a memorial stone. She was accompanied by her husband, Keith, and their son, Jordan, 12.

The area has never been advertised. There are no signs or markers along the Birdsville Track, although directions can be obtained from the Birdsville Hotel. The site never attracts more than a dozen tourists a year. The South Australian government has decided against placing a plaque at the site, 88 kilometres south of Birdsville and seven kilometres off the main track.

When I met Avril Howard in Adelaide she told me her mother seldom discussed Ernie, Emma and the boys. But Avril had got the impression that 'Ernest was a man who wouldn't be told', that he moved them halfway around the world in search of new opportunities.

Australians first became aware of the fate of the Page family on

New Year's Day, 1964. Details were sketchy, but it was reported that a family of British migrants had gone missing in the outback. A note had been found in the family's abandoned Ford Customline:

> The Page Family of Marree. Ran out of Petrel. Have only sufficent [sic] water for two days. December 24th.

In the middle of the summer holidays there were few police to search or press to report on the incident. Radio communication was basic and unreliable and there were problems getting searchers to such a remote location, especially in view of heavy, unseasonable flooding along the Diamantina River and Warburton Creek.

After a two-day search the bodies of Ernie, Emma, Gordon and Douglas were found under a coolibah tree near the aptly named Deadman's Sandhill, on a side track off the Birdsville Track. Police deduced the Pages had wandered for two days after they had left their car. They had meandered along a 20-kilometre track towards Clifton Hills before doubling back towards their car. Eventually they had sat down and waited to die. The two boys had removed most of their clothing. Emma, Ernie and Gordon were found sheltered by the tree and Douglas was lying further away, in the open.

The Pages still had food, but no water. Robert's R.M. Williams boots were found nearby but his body was not discovered until the next day, approximately a kilometre from the rest of his family. He had climbed halfway up a sandhill and dug a trench. It appeared he was trying to follow the shade, and seek cool earth.

Police decided it would be too difficult to remove the bodies and the Pages were buried together in a large grave. A small cross was later erected. It said, simply: 'The Pages – perished in 1963'.

The Page family had set off from Marree in their 1957 Ford Customline (known as a 'Big V') on 18 December 1963. Ernie had bought the car under hire purchase from Pointon's Garage in Port Augusta. It had been converted from left- to right-hand drive by a bar that ran under the gearbox, allowing the driver to select gears. Ernie had packed plenty of food and spare jerrycans of water for the trip. He'd gathered his Krico .22 rifle, the family labrador and cat and they'd set off into the night.

As they headed north they passed Lake Harry and crossed the Clayton River. To their east were the gas fields of Moomba and Big Lake, Gidgealpa and Namur, and to their west, the vast, dry expanse of Lake Eyre South and North. It was lightly wooded country, dominated by gibber plains and sandhills that shifted in winds that could change direction and magnitude in hours or minutes. Vast herds of cattle from south-west Queensland and the far north of South Australia regularly moved down the Birdsville Track to the railhead at Marree. In drought years the track itself almost disappeared, sandblasted back to desert. To stray off the track, or to take a wrong turn, was courting disaster. There were only ten cattle stations along the 500-kilometre length of track, so help might be a long time coming.

Meanwhile, the Page's eldest son Robert was heading home for Christmas. He'd arranged time off from Clifton Hills Station and had managed to secure a lift with the famous Birdsville Mail.

Pat Smith had bought the mail run from Tom Kruse, who had transported mail, fuel, medicine and general freight between Birdsville and Marree from 1936 to 1957. Kruse is well known today because of the 1954 documentary *The Back of Beyond* that followed a typical journey along the Birdsville Track, showcasing the characters Kruse met and the difficulties he faced. The two-week trip included stops at remote stations and showed breakdowns, floods and numerous instances of Kruse's Leyland Badger truck becoming bogged in soft sand.

This, though, was not the truck on which Robert Page travelled in 1963. Kruse abandoned his Leyland in 1957 on Pandie Pandie Station, near Birdsville. It wasn't located again until 1986 and was later restored by a group of motoring enthusiasts. Today it can be seen at the National Motor Museum at Birdwood in the Adelaide Hills.

Noel Glass worked for Pat Smith as one of five drivers registered with the Post Master General to deliver mail along the Birdsville Track. Robert Page travelled north to Birdsville with Glass and then asked if he would mind taking him home to Marree for the Christmas break. Glass agreed.

On their way south, Glass and Page ran into another of Pat Smith's drivers, Billy Wilson, who was returning from Cowarie Station, west of the Birdsville Track. They met at the punt that crossed the Cooper Creek. Wilson produced a Kodak Brownie and took a photo of the assembled group. The hazy image shows the almost unrecognisable figures: Billy Wilson, Robert Page, Noel Glass and the punt operator, Ernie Pake.

From there, Glass and Page continued south. As they approached Etadunna, an hour and a half north of Marree, Robert looked at a vehicle approaching them from the opposite direction and said, 'That looks like the old man's car.' Glass slowed and both parties stopped to greet each other.

Robert hadn't known anything about his father's decision to head north. Later, Glass said, 'At the time you had to stop and open a gate, so Ernie pulls up and they both abuse each other for not letting each other know what was happening. So after all the talk, the lad threw his swag on the trailer and away they went.'

While at Etadunna, Noel Glass gave Ernie Page some advice for the journey ahead. He told him to call in at Clifton Hills Station for extra fuel. He explained that 20 metres after the turnoff to the station there were some Shell 44-gallon drums full of fuel. He told him to take what he needed and leave a note at the station explaining what he'd done. He also mentioned there had been recent rains and recommended a side track.

Between Birdsville and Clifton Hills there were two Birdsville Tracks. One, the inside track, followed the Warburton Creek, passing New Alton Downs and Goyder Lagoon. During the wet this track was flood-prone. The outside track took a longer easterly detour between Clifton Hills and Birdsville. Glass told Page to follow the outside track for approximately six kilometres after leaving Clifton Hills, but then to cut across country back to the shorter inside track. This would only add half an hour to the trip and help the Pages avoid the worst of the flooding along the Warburton.

The Pages thanked Noel Glass and continued north. They arrived at the Cooper Creek punt, where Robert met Ernie Pake for the second time that day. Pake helped them across and waved them off, the last man to see them alive.

The Pages drove north, into the night. At some point, close to where the track skirted Goyder Lagoon, Ernie took a wrong turn. The track he chose might have been one left by a French mining survey company, Compagnie Générale de Géophysique (CGG), who had been active in the area over the previous few months. Surveyors from CGG party S6507 had just left the area for their Christmas break. The federal government's Bureau of Mineral Resources had also been surveying the area in late 1963. Furthermore, Noel Glass later explained his fear that a detour he'd made north of Clifton Hills might have been the path Ernie mistakenly followed. Another explanation might have been the presence of tracks left by an oil drilling rig and its crew that had recently shifted from Cordillo Downs, 125 kilometres east of Goyder Lagoon.

Robert might have tried to offer advice or warn his father about the tracks but Ernie, at the beginning at least, was probably convinced he knew where he was going. Ernie did have a reputation for being a 'pig-headed Pom'. Perhaps this spirit, this determination that had led him from Kent to Adelaide to Marree, was the catalyst for his further exploration of the 'idea of north'. Ernie Page was a family man with a whiff of free spirit. Noel Glass would later say that his advice to Ernie, to stop in at Clifton Hill for fuel, 'didn't register'. It was later discovered that Ernie had left or been sacked from his job in Marree because the owner of the garage where he worked, Dave Millar, wasn't happy about him spending all of his time talking to customers. This might explain his decision to leave Marree so hastily in search of new opportunities in Queensland.

Now it was dark, and the Pages had lost their way. They were driving over gibber plains on the edge of the Sturt Stony Desert.

Captain Charles Sturt first encountered this desert in 1844 while trying to reach the centre of Australia. He'd found the 'pavement' of ironstones caused his horses to limp and slowed the expedition. He, like Ernie Page, soon discovered how vast and unforgiving this area was – the treeless, red oxide stone, and sandscape that stretched to the horizon. No plant life except a few grevilleas and saltbush survived in the extreme temperatures.

Ernie found no tracks on the sun-baked earth. But he drove on. All the Pages would have heard was the motor of their 'Big V' and the stones under their tyres. Robert and Ernie must have talked, and argued, and Emma might have tried to reassure the boys. Perhaps Ernie pretended nothing was wrong.

The gibbers, the pebble-sized rocks that carpeted the desert, soon damaged the custom-fitted bar Ernie had welded onto his gearbox. This meant he couldn't change gears. The engine was stuck in second. The next day, Sunday 22 December, Robert tried to help his father repair the bar. They knew that if they had to continue in second they would soon use up all of their fuel.

It's likely that Ernie, perhaps persuaded by Robert, decided their best chance was to try and return to Clifton Hills. They probably spent that Sunday, just a few days before Christmas, waiting beside their car. When they set off, later that day or that night, they had very little fuel, water or food. Ernie kept driving through the night, the car stuck in second, and eventually they ran out of fuel some time on Monday 23 December. By now they were back on the Diamantina floodplain, bogged in sand at Deadman's Sandhill.

Ernie and Robert, spying a windmill a few miles away, set out with a four-gallon drum. They arrived at the windmill at a turkey's nest dam, filled the drum with soak water, then used a long stick to help carry the drum back to the car. Both men had failed to notice two 44-gallon drums full of drinking water left at the windmill for the use of station hands.

'Ran out of Petrel': The Page Family

Back at the car it must have become apparent there would be no festive celebrations in the tropics. No roast, no crackling, no apple sauce. As they exhausted the last of their food and water reality must have dawned. Maybe there were words between Ernie and Emma, and Robert. The boys, perhaps, knew to keep quiet at such times. Ernie must have known what they were facing. He or Robert had already taken the family dog out into the desert, shot it and buried it in a sandhill. As if sensing something, their cat had wandered into the night.

In retrospect it seems that Ernie Page, perhaps full of the bitterness of his sacking, rushed into leaving Marree. But in doing so he left unprepared for a journey through some of Australia's harshest country. Yes, he did have several spare jerrycans full of water, but not enough for four people in case something went wrong. Yes, he did stay with his car for the Sunday and Monday, but then he made the fatal mistake of striking out into the desert.

Perhaps he felt he had no choice. Robert might have told him that no one would come, or even miss them. Ernie had been advised by Noel Glass (who'd noticed the heavy trailer-load full of the Pages' possessions) to stop at Clifton Hills to take on more fuel and water, but he hadn't. He hadn't told anyone about his plans. No one was expecting them at Birdsville. He didn't cross paths with other travellers who might have raised the alarm because no one was on the track during the holidays: no travellers, surveyors, freight runs, no one. He had no map, no satellite communication or mobile phone. Although he understood the outback, he underestimated the vastness of the 'dead centre'.

The Pages rested in the shade of their Customline for two days. Temperatures soared. The heat didn't let up until well after midnight. Trying to rest or sleep in or under the hot car must have been almost unbearable. There was no shelter, no trees, no breeze, no shade. Just hot, baking sun, and the silence of the desert.

Ernie decided they should set out on foot in search of help. Later, Noel Glass would say, 'Ernie worked at Marree and would tell people if they got lost or stranded to stay with their car and yet he broke his own rule. That country is very unforgiving.'

Nonetheless, Ernie believed they could make it back to Clifton Hills. So, on Christmas Eve, he wrote his misspelt note, abandoned their water from the dam, gathered his family and set off.

Perhaps Ernie thought he had no choice. In January 1964 a Sergeant Dowling, one of the police officers involved in the search for the Page family, spoke to the *Sydney Daily Telegraph*, explaining, 'They'd found water and they had camping gear in their trailer which would have enabled them to stay alive if they had stayed near Turkey's Nest. But imagine how they must have felt when no help came after two days. They had a young family with them and they didn't have a bushman's experience ... It's all very well to say, "If the Pages had done this or that", but you have to be there yourself.'

During the day the family managed to walk 30 kilometres in the blazing heat. They meandered, constantly reassessing their path, looking for landmarks that didn't exist. At some point, probably on Boxing Day, or perhaps the day after, the Pages sat down to rest under the small coolibah tree where their bodies were eventually found. By then they were probably too tired and dehydrated to go on. There must have been few words spoken. Their bodies would have started shutting down. They would have eventually slipped into unconsciousness. Their organs would have failed, their hearts stopped beating.

Emma was found under the tree. Aboriginal trackers examined the footprints and found that Ernie and Robert had led her there. Robert had then taken his two younger brothers away from the tree but had returned them to the shade beside their mother and father. He had left his boots and kept walking, realising, perhaps, he was their last chance. But he had only made it another kilometre before dying a lonely death.

The Pages' car wasn't found until Sunday 29 December. Phil McKenzie, heading north from Copley, approximately 120 kilometres south of Marree, was delivering supplies to rabbit trappers when he came across the Customline 60 kilometres south-west of Pandie Pandie Station. McKenzie was also lost, having taken a wrong turn, but his vehicle was in good condition. He was heading to Clifton Hills to 're-orientate' himself. He noticed the note, the empty fuel tank and the drums of abandoned water and knew something was wrong. If Ernie had followed his own advice and stayed with his car this bit of good luck might have saved them. If, perhaps, the Pages had boiled and drunk the water from the dam, or their own radiator. If they'd rigged up the tarpaulin from their trailer as a shelter. If they'd set up camp, and waited.

McKenzie continued to Clifton Hills where he contacted Sergeant Eric Sammon of the Birdsville police. Technical difficulties with the government radio network meant that Sammon could not raise the alarm before New Year's Eve. By then the Pages had already been dead for days.

Sammon improvised. The French survey company's Land Rovers were being stored at the Birdsville Airstrip over Christmas; he borrowed a few and started a search. An RAAF DC3 was dispatched from Edinburgh base just north of Adelaide. Meanwhile, the owner of Kamaran Station, Jack Clancy, used his plane to look for the Pages. A French pilot, Kron Nicholas, flew across from Oodnadatta. South Australian Police and trackers in four-wheel drives also joined the search. On Clancy's final run his spotter, George Morton (from Pandie Pandie Station), saw the bodies of the Page family under a tree.

It was 4 pm on New Year's Eve. Searchers were given directions and made their way to the scene. Don Engleton, the first police officer to arrive, didn't even know Robert existed when he found the four bodies. According to Avril Howard, 'He thought that was the whole family and they were buried the next morning ... but then the trackers saw the prints of another young person heading away [to Deadman's Sandhill]. They could tell by the footprints that Robert and Ernest had brought Emma in [under the tree] and she never came back out. And then the eldest little one [Douglas] walked around in circles until he passed away. It wouldn't have mattered how much water they had with them. It was over 50 degrees, and no amount of water would have saved them.'

It was decided the partly decomposed bodies were too difficult to recover, so Eric Sammon arranged for a front-end loader to be driven from Birdsville to excavate a large grave. This was eventually marked by a circle of rocks. A crew from Pointon's Garage in Port Augusta arrived to repossess the Customline. They refuelled the car but couldn't find the keys. Someone mentioned that they were still in Ernie's pants when he was buried, so they hot-wired the car and drove it back to Port Augusta.

Police originally believed that Ernie had missed a turnoff to Clifton Hills Station because of a sandstorm, but locals later denied there had been any storm. Meteorologists claimed there had been 'dust in suspension' around Birdsville at the time but no one believed this was the real cause of the Pages' death.

The reality was that Ernie had chosen not to stop in at Clifton Hills. He was almost certainly convinced that they had plenty of fuel to get to Birdsville.

The tragedy of the Page family was destined to make headlines across the world, especially England, with its flood of migrants waiting to come to the 'lucky country'. But for Avril Howard, growing up in Adelaide, it wasn't something she heard much about. 'I probably would've asked questions,' she remembers, 'flipped through the scrapbook [of cuttings]'.

But it wasn't until she was pregnant with her first son that she really became interested. She obtained Judy's permission to access coroner's files about the tragedy, then approached State Records for more information. This paper chase led her to the Marree and Port Augusta police stations, both of which had kept files, photos, daily reports and transcripts about the tragedy, but had lost them in the intervening years. Eventually she found Eric Sammon, the ex-Queensland police officer based at Birdsville in 1963. She obtained more information, with the goal of visiting the site of the tragedy.

Years lapsed before Howard, her husband, Keith, youngest

son, Jordan, and brother, Ian, along with his partner Molly and their two daughters, met up on the Birdsville Track in July 2010. Howard said, 'It wasn't until Mum passed away [six years ago] that we started looking into it a bit more ... it made it more of a goal.' She explained that this journey had always been in the back of her mind, but that she hadn't wanted to upset her mum. 'For Mum it was a bit too sensitive to talk about ... being 21 and your whole family dying ... her way was to not talk about it. In herself, there were probably days when she thought about it, but she wasn't consumed by it.'

Later, Noel Glass became disappointed that the Pages' grave was virtually forgotten. He frequently travelled to the area with his son-in-law, Graham Puckridge, and was 'astounded that such a significant and historical site' lay forgotten to all but the most intrepid travellers. He explained that 'many other sites of interest on the track are well signposted with displays providing old photos and historical information ... What happened to the Page family serves as a tragic example of the dangers of outback travel.'

It is easy to read the Pages' story as one of a string of tragedies that have grown out of our misreading, our misunderstanding, of the Australian outback. But it's more than that. The Pages were living, breathing, dreaming people, full of hopes for a future stretching out from their home in Kent to an unrealised life in Queensland. Not much is known of the boys, their hobbies, their favourite songs, the games they played, how they annoyed each other and nagged their parents. Or Ernie, his abilities as a mechanic, a driver, a ten pound Pom who had found, for a while at least, his niche in Marree. Robert, the teenage adventurer, already making a living mustering and branding cattle on an outback station. Or, most mysterious of all, Emma, still standing beside the family car, still staring down at the sand.

When Avril Howard and her family returned to the desert they had trouble finding the site of the tragedy. Eventually 12-year-old Jordan found the spot. The grave had originally been marked by a cross made from the coolibah tree, but this was later replaced with a sturdier, metal cross.

When Howard and her brother found the site it had been, ironically, recently flooded. The old metal cross had come apart so they took it back to the Birdsville Caravan Park and repaired it. Then, using equipment they'd hauled, they laid a small slab and placed a permanent memorial on top. After a few days' work Howard and her brother had done what they'd been planning for so many years: made the pilgrimage to honour their lost family. 'It's South Australia's largest outback tragedy,' she explains. 'If it's not told, then it's all forgotten about. It is my family, but it is also part of our history.'

Most important for Howard are the memories of her own mum, who always remembered Emma as a 'small lady who was always there for the family', who 'didn't want to talk to people about it …'

And why would she? Who could fathom the horror of losing their entire family at age 21? Howard remembers that, 'Mum was ironing … it was on the news. Mum wasn't really listening. Then she was getting phone calls asking if she was okay. Then her friends rang Dad and he came home. She was put on sedatives. They'd only found the four so Mum was thinking, There's hope for Robert … and then Dad recalls the next morning a police officer coming to the house.'

Howard plans to write a book about her family. She also wants to return to the site to lay another memorial where Robert perished. She hopes to use photos of the Customline to track the registration, and see if, miraculously, it might still exist (her father eventually drove to Port Augusta to reclaim it, but later sold it).

Today the Marree garage Ernie worked in is a ruin of crumbling walls. The site of the tragedy is still not marked on the Birdsville Track, and the government wants to keep it that way, to let the family rest in peace. Noel Glass still wants it signposted, as a warning as much as anything.

In truth, it should be, because the memory of the Pages belongs to all Australians.

When Howard was in Birdsville she met Jimmy Crombie, an indigenous man who'd worked at Clifton Hills with her uncle, Robert. After so many years, Jimmy gave her a belt buckle that had once belonged to Robert. He said, 'That belongs to you now.' As it does, in a small way, to us all.

CHAPTER 12

The Faraday School Kidnapping

1972

Flight 232 to the Alice – The views from Faraday – School No. 797 – Mary Gibbs and her students – 'School's over for today, kids' – The ransom note – Boland and Eastwood – A patch of isolated scrub – The drop-off arranged – Escape – Eastwood tries again – The third man – 'the most annoying bastard I'd ever met'

One year in a single image: the teacher, Mary Gibbs, in knee-high boots and a mini-skirt, a white top and cardigan. She is standing beside her students outside the Faraday School; each wearing their own cardy or jumper, ankle freezers and canvas shoes. Haircuts courtesy of Mum's mixing bowl. Two detectives stand at the back, awkward with the attention. But for Lindsay Thompson, Victorian Minister for Education, there is no such dilemma.

It's 1972. In five weeks' time Ansett Airlines flight 232 from Adelaide to Alice Springs will be hijacked, and three weeks after that, Gough Whitlam will wrestle the prime ministership from Billy McMahon. It's been barely a month since 11 Israeli athletes were killed by the Palestinian 'Black September' group at the Munich Summer Olympics. It's a time of dissent. From the first stirrings of the extreme-Left Baader-Meinhof group to the more sedate ravings of *Oz* magazine. The gaps are filled with angst (*Deep Purple* going head-to-head with Donny Osmond), a new cinema (Barry McKenzie exposing himself to the world), living-room dramas (*The Removalists*) and a growing dissatisfaction with established views. Anti-Vietnam War demonstrations have been intensifying for years, and events such as the My Lai massacre have

The Faraday School Kidnapping

galvanised many Americans and Australians against the conflict.

All of this is a long way from Faraday, a small town 38 kilometres south of Bendigo, 116 kilometres north-west of Melbourne. Here, life is simple. The Methodists have been and built a church, but mostly it's weatherboard cottages on acreage, improved pasture, sheep, cattle, gentle hills with granite boulders and plenty of scrub for hiding things (including kidnapped children). There are views to be had: Mounts Alexander and Macedon, and nearby Hanging Rock, another good place for hiding schoolgirls.

The rain has cleared, but 6 October is still a wintry afternoon. It's just after 3 pm, nearly time to go home, and inside the Faraday School (No. 797) teacher Mary Gibbs is busy with a game of musical chairs for her six students: Robyn Howarth, eleven, her sisters, Jillian, eight, and Denise, five, Lynda Conn, nine, her sister, Helen, six, and Christine Ellery, ten.

Luckily, another four children are off with a cold.

The door opens and two men, one wearing a balaclava and holding a rifle, the other a floppy hat and dark glasses, enter the room. One says, 'School's over for today, kids.' Christine thinks it's some sort of joke, someone's dad or brother trying to scare them, but soon realises, from the look on her teacher's face, that this is the real thing.

The two men usher them out of the schoolroom and into the back of a red van. The young ones are scared, but Mary and Christine do their best to comfort them. The kidnappers have left a note:

> RANSOM WILL BE ONE MILLION
>
> 500,000 – $20 NOTES (3 SUITCASES)
>
> 500,000 – $10 NOTES (6 SUITCASES)
>
> ALL CURRENCY MUST HAVE BEEN IN CIRCULATION
>
> AT LEAST 12 MONTHS
>
> PICKUP DETAILS

AT 7.25 PM WE WILL CONTACT LINDSAY THOMPSON
AT RUSSELL ST. POLICE HQ AND MAKE ARRANGEMENTS
WITH HIM.
WE ARE NOT GOING TO WASTE ANYONES TIME
BY MAKING IDLE THREATS SO WE WILL CUT
IT SHORT BY SAYING THAT ANY ATTEMPT
TO TRACE US AND APPREHEND US WILL RESULT
IN THE ANNIHILATION OF EVERY HOSTAGE.

So begins the story of one of Australia's strangest crimes. It was to provide the material for the 1980 novel *Fortress* and a 1986 film of the same name. Abductions have seldom featured in Australian criminal history. The most famous, though, was the 1960 kidnapping of eight-year-old Sydney schoolboy Graeme Thorne. Thorne's father had just won £100,000 in a lottery raising money for the construction of the Sydney Opera House. Stephen Bradley took Thorne as he waited for a lift to school. He demanded £25,000 or 'the boy will be fed to the sharks'. But Bradley panicked, struck the boy on the head and asphyxiated him.

Twelve years later, unemployed plasterers and friends Robert Clyde Boland, 32, and Edwin John Eastwood, 21, have a similar idea: the children will comply, the government will find the money, they'll bolt from their bush hiding hole before anyone has any idea what is happening. Eastwood had been hard up. He'd slipped into petty crime, using a .22 rifle to rob a takeaway and two railway stations. But he needed more money. He shared his plan with Boland, and he agreed. They found a country house, but abandoned the idea. They dug a pit for their hostages, but it collapsed. So they bought an old bread van instead.

The world found out about Faraday via *Sun* journalist Wayne Grant. At 4.40 pm that afternoon he received a phone call. A voice on the other end said, 'I've just kidnapped the teacher and kids from the Faraday school.' Grant later said, 'I couldn't believe what I was hearing. He said the ransom was a million dollars and there

The Faraday School Kidnapping

was a note in the front desk. Then he hung up. I didn't know what to make of it for a little while.'

Grant looked up the location. He rang Bendigo police and told them about the phone call. A policewoman explained they had just received calls from anxious parents reporting their kids missing.

Meanwhile, Boland and Eastwood drove their captives through Elphinstone, Kyneton and Lancefield before finding a patch of isolated scrub. Eastwood left in a car (to call Grant) while Boland let the teacher and children out, telling them to behave. They were given some chips and allowed to move around, all the time watched by Boland. He was holding a flick knife. Years later, Christine Ellery told the *Australian*: 'We pretended like we were on a nature excursion. We picked up leaves, made little boats, just not being emotional. I guess we were all acting because we had to do something and we didn't want to be crying or anxious.'

When Eastwood returned, Mary Gibbs and the children were locked inside the van. The kidnappers told her they were going to collect the ransom. They drove off, leaving the group in the dark.

The Victorian Education Minister, Lindsay Thompson, was already at police headquarters following the progress of the investigation. He told a press conference the government was doing everything possible to secure the return of Gibbs and her students. Their main concern was 'the welfare of those missing'. Victorian premier, Rupert Hamer, told parents (across the state, and nation) the government would pay the ransom.

Thompson returned home to bed but was woken at 3.45 am by Assistant Commissioner Mick Miller. Forty-five minutes earlier he'd received instructions: 'Woodend Post Office at 5 am and no funny business.' The drop-off had been arranged. Thompson agreed. He was picked up and driven north along the Calder Highway towards the small town.

Beside him was a suitcase full of money.

Assistant Commissioner Bill Crowley was posing as his ministerial chauffeur. Crowley had a Derringer pistol hidden, while Mick Miller was under a blanket in the back of the car with a high-powered rifle. Thompson had been told that if there was any trouble he should duck to give Miller a clean shot.

They arrived at the post office. And waited. An old car passed a few times before a man got out and walked towards them. Thompson called out, 'What the hell do you think you're doing walking down the main street of Woodend at 5 am?' Police took the man in for questioning, but he told them he'd been waiting for a friend.

Meanwhile, Mary Gibbs had been busy. She'd kicked out a panel in the back door of the van with her platform-heeled boots. Later she told the *Sun*: 'When they didn't come back before dawn, I thought it is now or never and began kicking at the door.' She explained that Christine and Robin had helped. 'I must admit I hadn't thought of escaping until dawn and the children were desperate to do you-know-what.'

It had been a long day for the teacher: six hours of school, and 15 hours of comforting her students, trying to convince them they'd all be fine, despite her own fears. Ellery explained later: 'Everybody fared quite fine. We all came from very strong families.'

Gibbs described the escape in detail: 'First I got the children to charge the doors, but they were bolted from outside ... Then I got Christine Ellery to hang on to a small chain on the wall of the van. I supported myself on Christine's shoulder, put one hand on the other wall of the van and kicked and kicked and kicked. God knows how many times, but then, bit by bit, things started to give ... It was fantastic. I crawled out and the girls followed.'

She led her six students – tired, frightened, stumbling through the bush – until they found hunters at 8 am.

Their ordeal was over.

Over the next few days police ramped up their manhunt and eventually captured Boland and Eastwood. Gibbs and her students became minor celebrities. Their images appeared in most national newspapers. Robyn Howarth told the *Sun*: 'I was scared they were going to kill us for nothing. They said they had nothing to gain from killing us – and nothing to lose either.'

The Faraday School Kidnapping

The attention didn't hurt Lindsay Thompson's career. He became Victorian premier in June 1981 after winning a Liberal Party ballot to succeed Rupert Hamer. He was a man of the people, son of schoolteachers (although his father died when he was two), raised on a shoestring by his mother before winning a scholarship to Caulfield Grammar. He was Number One ticket holder for Richmond Football Club. He could connect with ordinary people. Jeff Kennett, Victorian premier from 1992 to 1999, said, 'There was no ego attached to Lindsay Thompson. He didn't want a big car, he didn't want a big house, he didn't want the best clothes. He was in one sense the most wonderfully simple person.'

Thompson remembered his role in the Faraday kidnappings as one of the highlights of his political career. 'I've only been a millionaire once in my life,' he said of the Saturday after the kidnappings, 'and all the shops were closed.'

Forty years later journalist Wayne Grant still recalled those days in 1972. He believed Mary Gibbs had done a stand-out job. 'She was quite a small young lady. She had these tanned, knee-high leather boots and she used them to great effect.' He explained that the day and night of 6 October was a sort of loss of innocence. And later: 'There was no such thing as counselling … it was all a matter of family support and friendship support that would have gotten them through.'

Boland and Eastwood went to trial. Eastwood provided evidence against Boland and had three previous robbery charges discounted in return. He was sentenced to 15 years in prison with a non-parole period of ten years. It took three trials to convict Boland: 17 years in prison with a non-parole period of 12 years. During his trial, Eastwood claimed Boland was innocent. His real partner was the man the police had approached in the main street of Woodend early on the morning of 7 October.

Eastwood wasn't finished yet. On 16 December 1976 he escaped from Geelong Prison. Two months later he kidnapped a teacher and nine students from Wooreen Primary School in South Gippsland. He then collided with a truck and took its driver and his partner hostage. A few minutes later he waved down another truck and added its driver and passenger to his collection. Finally, he stole a campervan, and its two female occupants.

Lindsay Thompson knew the drill. He offered himself in exchange for the hostages.

Eastwood was having none of that. He was more confident. This time he asked for $7 million, guns and a supply of heroin and cocaine, as well as the release of 17 prisoners from Pentridge Prison.

That night he fed his hostages and chained them. Next morning, one was missing. He gathered the other 15 and quickly set off. Meanwhile, his escaped hostage had raised the alarm. Eastwood was spotted by police and chased. His Glenrowan moment came at Woodside, where he was shot below the knee and captured.

He pleaded guilty. In November 1977 he was sentenced to another 21 years in prison with a non-parole period of 18 years. This added up to nearly 26 years with 23 years non-parole. He was philosophical: 'I am getting better each time, and I will get it right eventually.'

He was eventually released in 1993.

Today, the name Faraday means one thing to most people. Like Snowtown, it makes the job of getting on with life difficult. But this small town has become part of Australia's folklore. It lost its innocence during a period of widespread social change. It has been written about again and again (Eastwood's *Focus on Faraday and Beyond: Australia's Crime of the Century, The Inside Story*) and turned into fiction and film.

The Faraday School was closed after the kidnapping. The six girls grew up, went their separate ways, and seldom talked about that day and night in 1972. In 2007, Christine Ellery said: 'We just got on with life. It wasn't talked about much.'

Eastwood remains one of the most complex characters in Australian criminal history. At his trial, the Crown Prosecutor, John Howse, asked him to identity the man who had helped him kidnap the children. Despite Boland being present, he said he couldn't. He said Boland wasn't his accomplice. Howse repeatedly asked for a name but Eastwood kept replying, 'I'm sorry, sir, but I refuse to divulge his name.'

Justice Gowans then said: 'What reason have you for refusing to answer?'

'Naturally, this is a serious crime and I have been put in a position where I have to name him and I'd prefer not to.'

'Unless you have some legal justification for refusing to name him, you will have to answer the question.'

Eastwood then said the man was David O'Ryan.

The Crown never presented physical evidence proving Boland's involvement in the kidnapping. Senior Constable Geoffrey Le Conteur, of the Forensic Science Laboratory, told the jury a hair similar to Boland's had been found on one of the kidnapped girls but 'I can't say that it was or that it was not'.

Boland's lawyer, Charles Francis, QC, said: 'Would it be correct to say that at the scene you found precisely nothing which would verify that Boland had been there?'

'Yes, that would be so.'

Meanwhile, police were having trouble finding the mysterious O'Ryan. They traced him to two boarding houses in Darling Street, South Yarra, but neither landlady had heard of him.

Was this man (Eastwood called him 'Meggsie' because of his supposed red hair) a figment of Eastwood's imagination? Was he hoping to get his mate off? Or was Eastwood correct? Had Boland come into the picture some time after the escape of Gibbs and the children, but before their own capture?

When Mary Gibbs came face-to-face with Boland during his trial in March 1973 she identified him as the man who had taken her and the children from the schoolhouse. She had previously identified both men in a line-up. When Boland was asked to put on the hat and sunglasses he was alleged to have been wearing at the time, Gibbs sat back and covered her eyes with her arms. Under cross-examination Boland denied having told work mates the best way to make money was to 'kidnap someone important'. Despite having been positively identified as the buyer of the red bakery van used in the kidnapping, Boland told the jury he'd spent 6 October on a beach with a woman named Susan Buchanan. Despite his father's and lawyer's efforts to find her, they had been unsuccessful. He suggested this was because they had been having an adulterous relationship.

Later, one of the jurors claimed she had received a phone call from an anonymous person offering her $5000 to convict Boland. The caller had threatened her safety if she spoke out.

In his summation, Howse claimed that Eastwood and Boland had abandoned their kidnap attempt because they 'thought it had gone wrong'. He told the jury they'd dumped their rifle in McIvor Creek and a bag full of chains and padlocks in the Campaspe River. Boland's wife claimed these had been used to secure unsafe areas in the childcare centre she ran. Howse claimed the pair planned to keep their chained hostages in a trench they had dug and covered with galvanised iron near Lancefield, but had abandoned this idea.

In his book *Chopper Unchopped*, Mark 'Chopper' Read said: 'Edwin John Eastwood was the most annoying bastard I'd ever met ... some complete mental case had encouraged Ted towards music.' Eastwood had delusions of musical greatness, constantly practising his guitar. 'After some months of this never-ending nonsense I was at the point of cold-blooded murder.' But, he concluded, 'He is a true gentleman and a loyal friend, a strong man and a rare individual within the prison system ...'

Was this man, strumming for hours on end in his cell, 'smiling broadly with his new guitar', still hiding a secret? Did he like to think he was smarter than the police? Was he simple, or, as he told John Howse: 'I smile when I'm nervous. When I'm nervous I smile easily.' Was it really Boland who masterminded the kidnapping?

Like all good crimes, the questions remain. In the end, it's the intersection of outback idyll and city crims that make this a story to remember.

CHAPTER 13

'I Found Peece': Simon Amos and James Annetts

1986

The plaque – Simon, James and their dream – Arrival at Flora Valley – 'some of the blokes were not up to it' – Becoming jackaroos – Simon's Valiant – Nicholson and Sturt Creek outstations – Bore runs – Forbidden visits – The boys disappear – The search – An improbable lead – Bogged to the axle – The body, the bullet, the rifle – Lost on the 'lines' – 'My follt'

The plaque sits close to where two teenage boys died. This is flat, dead country – red sand and spinifex. There's nothing on the endless horizon. Thermometers top out mid-morning and stay there all day. The plaque, fixed to a flat rock, is weather-beaten, corroded and hard to read.

IN MEMORY OF
SIMON AMOS AND JAMES ANNETTS
WHO TRAGICALLY PERISHED ON THE EDGE OF
THE GREAT SANDY DESERT
SOUTH OF HALLS CREEK IN NOV.- DEC. 1986
SAD LOSS NOT FORGOTTEN
BY THE PEOPLE OF THE KIMBERLEYS

This is the classic story of what can go wrong in the Australian outback. Here is the lethal combination of inexperience, lack of preparation, dodgy vehicles and no communication. Simon Amos and James Annetts, 17 and 16 years old respectively, knew nothing about the rugged cattle country in Australia's north-west when they first arrived at Flora Valley Station to work as jackaroos. Over the following few weeks they worked long hours, were paid little and were eventually 'farmed out' to work on remote outstations. This led them to make their most fateful decision: to flee across the desert, in search of their old lives.

Simon Amos and James Annetts had much in common: not particularly academic, in search of new challenges, young, cocky, practical (James had recently become a Queen's Scout) and confident. James, from Binya, near Griffith in New South Wales, still lived at home with his mum and dad, Sandra and Les Annetts. Later, Sandra would describe her son as 'a wonderful boy ... an excellent sportsman ... he was in Boy Scouts. He loved the outdoors'.

Simon Amos, in contrast, was a city boy. He lived in the leafy Adelaide suburb of Tranmere and attended Rostrevor College. His agriculture teacher, Wayne Edwards, reckoned he enjoyed 'getting his hands dirty'. Simon would watch videos of jackaroos at work on outback cattle stations and ask his teacher about the job. He enjoyed working with sheep and cattle at Rostrevor, a passion that led him on a new adventure only a few years later.

Amos and Annetts obtained their jobs through a rural employment agency. They were sent to Flora Valley Station, 100 kilometres east of Halls Creek. At the time, beef prices were low and the industry was depressed.

Flora Valley is a vast property west of the border between Western Australia and the Northern Territory, just off the Duncan Highway. The station covers part of the Open Grass Plain – flat, featureless country covered in native grasses (mainly soft and feathertop spinifex) and isolated steppes of bloodwood, grevillea and acacias. The fauna consists of skinks and geckos, dingoes, dunnarts and spinifex hopping mice, but not much else. To the south is Australia's second largest desert, the Great Sandy Desert.

Flora Valley is surrounded by bores: Coolibah Bore, No. 3 Bore, Nyulasy Bore and 'Sturt Creek', small, isolated spots, hundreds of kilometres from anywhere, that Amos and Annetts would be tasked with maintaining.

Flora Valley's cook, Debbie Davis, later recalled the boys' arrival in August 1986. She remembered Amos wearing seven earrings in one ear and a studded leather wristband and belt. Although he was friendly, quick to crack a joke, willing to fit in, she predicted he'd last one week, and the quiet Annetts, two weeks, perhaps.

A 1988 coronial inquest into the disappearance and death of Amos and Annetts paints a picture of the life the boys led during their first seven weeks on Flora Valley. Debbie Davis's husband, Jonathon Davis, who worked as an overseer at Flora Valley, explained that plumbing and sewerage were often broken and there was nothing for the employees to do after hours. 'There were no TV sets or pool tables,' he said. 'You just did your work, had dinner and went to bed. You were working long hours and doing hard work and some of the blokes were not up to it.'

Let alone a 16-year-old and a 17-year-old, living away from home for the first time.

The boys had to learn quickly, mainly from other station hands. There was no time off for lectures, to learn under safe, controlled conditions. No concessions were made for their age, backgrounds, lack of mechanical skills and aptitude, inexperience handling animals or driving in desert conditions. No one taught them survival skills, what to do if they broke down, became lost or injured. There was no one to make sure they looked after themselves, that they were healthy and happy. They had no one their own age, and no doubt still had some of the silliness and cockiness of adolescent boys.

They worked hard, six days a week, from 7 am until after dark. They were used for unskilled work such as shifting portable cattle yards, and they soon became disenchanted. There were no opportunities to become a 'real' jackaroo. Regardless, Annetts's first letter home in August contained no complaints. He was, he explained, enjoying the life.

The boys found consolation and support in each other's company.

They must have discussed their jobs and general situation. This discontent may have led them to challenge their manager.

Not all the staff were as enthusiastic as the boys. Jonathon Davis told the 1988 inquest: 'Blokes were coming and going all the time. Half of them were good, but the other half weren't worth feeding.'

During his time at Flora Valley, Amos purchased a Chrysler Valiant from another jackaroo. He paid $700 for the red car – he believed red cars were faster – and told Debbie Davis he planned to 'do it up'. He showed her pictures from his *Wheels* magazines and explained how, one day, his car would be on the front cover.

At the end of October, the boys' manager decided to send them to separate outstations, where they would be responsible for the upkeep of bores, fences and troughs, as well as general maintenance. He probably also believed they would work harder if not distracted by each other. Amos would be sent to Nicholson Station, 150 kilometres north-east of Halls Creek, and Annetts to Sturt Creek Station, 100 kilometres south-east of Halls Creek.

Jonathon Davis and his wife left Flora Valley before the boys left.

Over the following few weeks Amos and Annetts, alone, lonely on their out-stations, maintained daily 'bore runs' to make sure windmills were working and stock had access to water. Apart from two daily radio checks, and a weekly trip back to Flora Valley for supplies, they had no contact with the outside world. Their living conditions were poor and they received very low pay. Despite this, Amos was proud of having become a 'manager'. Annetts was not so happy. When he'd left home his mother had told him, 'If you don't like it, let us know, and we'll get you back home again.' He had only ever intended trying the job for four months, before heading home for Christmas, and it's likely his experiences so far helped him make up his mind about a career on the land.

In November 1986 there were only five jackaroos left on Flora Valley. Around this time, Annetts wrote home: 'The new head stockman doesn't show us what to do, he just tells us to do it, and if we make a mistake we end up in all sorts of trouble with the boss.'

'I Found Peece': Simon Amos and James Annetts

The boys took time off to visit each other. During November, Annetts would drive two-and-a-half hours to Nicholson Station to pick up Amos and go swimming in remote gorges.

Nicholson was a big responsibility for a 16-year-old city kid. Amos was running a station that had previously required a team of men. He was working with vehicles, diesel engines and pumps, gears on the windmill. There was a narrow margin of error. Annetts's days too were all work. No wonder, at some point, in late November 1986, they decided they'd had enough.

Some time between the first and third days of December 1986, Amos left Nicholson Station in the company's 1983 Datsun utility. The ute was in poor condition, with failing brakes, broken instruments, a faulty fuel filter and a disabled 4WD function. He headed south to Sturt Creek Station to visit Annetts. He arrived, and they talked, and agreed that enough was enough. It's likely they then decided to return to Adelaide for Christmas. Alternatively, they might have left in order to scout a quick route back to Adelaide, or to visit other stations in search of alternative employment. This might explain why they left behind cash and personal belongings, as well as Amos's vehicle. Among Annetts's effects, police found a hat with his blood splattered on the rim. Sandra Annetts later said, 'We never believed the police theory that the boys had just run away and got lost and died.'

When he couldn't raise the boys on the radio, the manager checked the out-stations. Unable to find any trace of them, or clue to their whereabouts, he contacted police. A small search commenced on Wednesday 3 December but it was not until Friday 5 December that 12 police started scouring the vast area. At the time temperatures were in the mid to high forties. Police would later be criticised for not asking for, and indeed, refusing, offers of outside help.

Les Annetts asked the 1988 inquest into his son's death why several days passed between the boys being reported missing and the search commencing, given they couldn't have lasted more than two days stranded in the desert; why State Emergency Service teams in the Kimberley were not mobilised; and why the offer of a search plane was not taken up.

In April 1987 Les Annetts told Adelaide's *Advertiser*: 'It was a so-called big search, but those boys had no hope. There wasn't enough done.'

After the boys left Sturt Creek Station they most probably drove to Balgo Aboriginal Mission. In the heat of the early summer desert they would have passed to the east of the Wolfe Creek Crater National Park, through 100 kilometres of flat, featureless land, claypans, stunted vegetation, past Selby Hills to the small mission.

Balgo was founded in 1942 and by the time two Sisters of St John of God arrived in 1956 there were 150 Aboriginal people on the mission. The first government teacher arrived in 1961 and soon there was a freshwater bore, a vegetable garden and dormitories. By 1965 there was an administration centre, hospital, bakery, abattoir and a 1000-head cattle operation. By the time Amos and Annetts passed through it was gaining a reputation as a centre for excellence in Indigenous art.

The search for the boys continued through the first two weeks of December 1987. Police covered thousands of square kilometres without finding any trace of their movements. After the official search was called off authorities continued their enquiries in the Northern Territory, Western Australia and South Australia after several reported sightings. Les Annetts believed not enough was being done to find his son during these weeks, and the following months. He travelled to the area to help with the search. When this was called off in mid-December he continued his own private search.

There is a possibility that after leaving their out-stations, Amos and Annetts headed to the Northern Territory before returning to Western Australia. On 6 April 1987 a truck driver approached police claiming that on 10 December 1986 he gave two youths a lift from a remote Northern Territory Aboriginal community to a roadhouse in Katherine. The youths had apparently told him they were station managers on Sturt Creek and Nicholson stations. They explained that their ute had broken down and some Aboriginal people had come along and offered them a lift to their community.

The driver claimed one of the boys said he was going to Sydney and the other wanted to see a friend in Katherine. The police, who still had no idea where the boys might have gone, took the lead very seriously. Chief Inspector Arnold Davies of the Broome Police told media, 'With this information we can check on some serious leads. It is the first solid information we have had yet. However, it is still a big mystery and we are concerned as to why the boys would not have contacted their parents. If we can confirm the story we will request enquiries from the Northern Territory police.'

Davies said he trusted the information from the truck driver because he knew about an engine fault on the boys' ute despite this information not having been made public. Police failed to turn up any information about the boys at the Katherine roadhouse.

The truck driver's claims were never proved. Why would the boys head north when Amos had earlier stated he wanted to be home for Christmas? Who were the boys' friends in Sydney and Katherine? Why did they never come forward? Why did neither boy contact their parents for several weeks (if they'd been picked up on 10 December they couldn't have returned to the desert before 13 or 14 December)? James, especially, knew the importance of keeping in contact. To counter this, perhaps the boys were scared to tell their parents they'd thrown in their jobs.

Immediately to the south and west of Balgo, country that the two boys were now entering, the Great Sandy Desert is scarred by 'lines', or survey tracks, laid down by mining companies. Typically, each grid is eight-by-eight roads, stretching 50 or 60 kilometres, before coming to an abrupt stop. These lines, stretching south towards the Stansmore Range, are put down as a single-use proposition, for the country to be surveyed and tested and, if nothing is found, to be abandoned and forgotten in the sands of time.

It is likely the boys, searching for a shortcut through the desert to Alice Springs, took a wrong turn onto one of these lines. Once on the grid, they were lost. There was no single destination. The grids were a combination of left and right turns that led back on themselves. They were navigating a spider web through the desert, unaware that once lost, there was no way out.

The boys would eventually be found, too late, 100 kilometres south of Balgo, in an area police admitted they had only ever 'partially searched'. The search leader, Superintendent Len Craddock, later explained that this area had been considered 'too remote' when the search had first begun. He said, 'It's a mystery why the boys would have gone out there and we didn't plan on them being so far south when we were looking for them.'

On 26 April 1987 the boys' ute was found 400 kilometres from Flora Valley by a survey team from the Derby mining company, Clan Contracting. It was bogged to the axle. The boys had jacked up the back and put the side-trays under the wheels in an attempt to get out. The engine had eventually failed because of the problems with the fuel filter. They had flattened two batteries trying to free themselves.

The utility, which didn't have a functioning radio, was found close to an abandoned airstrip on a seismic exploration line. The boys had used tools to make an SOS on the roof and a fence post and wood to make a north-pointing arrow on the ground. They had then gathered some provisions, 30 litres of water, and set off in search of help. On 27 April Superintendent Len Craddock confirmed that the utility's number plates matched those of the boys' missing vehicle. Unfortunately, there was no sign of Amos or Annetts.

When told the news, Les Annetts was cautious, explaining, 'Even if the police think they know the number of the car, I have been told there are two possible numbers.' In Adelaide, Simon's family, including his grandmother, Eileen Amos, was even further out of the loop. She told media: 'My husband said we wouldn't know anything about where the boys are until they found that utility.' She said she would ring Halls Creek police to see what was happening.

Police from Halls Creek soon arrived at the scene and started searching for further signs of the boys. They were surprised at how far south the ute was found. They believed the pair had probably strayed off the Tanami Track, searching for a shortcut to Adelaide. Several months before another truck driver had told them he'd met two boys and shared his shortcut from Halls Creek to Adelaide along the Tanami Track. They had unsuccessfully searched the area, unaware of the boys' wrong turn. They concluded that Amos and Annetts must have driven along the survey lines until they had become disoriented, lost, and finally bogged.

On the morning of Tuesday 28 April, the *Advertiser* told its readers: 'Horror Deaths for Outback Pair'. The body of Amos, it reported, had been found with a bullet hole in his head with a .22 rifle nearby. His skeletal remains showed he and Annetts had walked 18 kilometres from their ute before Amos either shot himself or had been shot by Annetts in a mercy killing. Annetts had managed to walk another two kilometres before collapsing. Len Craddock said the boys had 'perished under tragic circumstances'.

Before discovering the bullet hole in Amos's skull, police believed the boys had died of dehydration as they'd attempted to walk back to Balgo Mission. Several empty water bottles were found near Amos's body. Craddock explained they wouldn't have lasted more than two days after leaving their vehicle. 'They had no chance,' he said. 'They were more than 100 kilometres away from the closest civilisation or waterhole and even if they had been able to keep walking they may still have by-passed Balgo by mistake.'

When they heard the news, Amos's parents, Robert Amos and Pat Clark, were devastated. Les Annetts, who was preparing to fly back to Western Australia, said his family was shocked as the previous day's discovery of the ute had given them some hope the boys were still alive. He was still trying to work out how he'd break the news to James's two younger sisters and 14-year-old brother. Sandra Annetts said, 'Now I don't know which is worse – knowing or not knowing. I hate to think what they went through out there.'

Again, Les criticised the search for his son over the previous five months. In March 1987 he had forced the Western Australian police to resume the search by threatening to get the prime minister, Bob Hawke, involved.

The following day, Wednesday 29 April, the nation learned more about the circumstances surrounding the boys' deaths. Western Australian Assistant Commissioner Bob Woodley explained that neither of the boys had left a note and the mystery of their deaths might never be solved. A police spokesman said, 'We are not discounting the theory that he [Amos] shot himself, or was shot in a mercy killing, until we know the result of the detectives' report and the pathologist's report. We will probably never know what happened. They were the only ones out there, and we can only speculate.' He added, 'They have been out there so long we are not sure if he [Annetts] ran out of water, or had plenty, but simply keeled over from the heat.' Another police officer involved in the search said, 'Where we found them was literally a road to nowhere.'

During the day the site was cordoned off and examined for evidence. The skeletal remains of the two bodies, which had been disturbed by dingoes, were then sent to Perth for forensic examination.

On the same day a former employee of Flora Valley Station, Jim Ghilotti, came forward stating that he believed Amos and Annetts had died after getting lost on a 'bore run' – a long, lonely drive on sandy tracks between scattered bores servicing cattle grazing the low spinifex grass.

The manager of nearby Ruby Plains Station, John Boland, said that the boys were too young to be working by themselves, unsupervised, in remote 40-degree conditions. 'A couple of lads like that wouldn't last very long,' he said. 'They were not used to it [the heat]. I've done it myself [worked unsupervised] when I was a kid but I grew up in the area. Usually there'd be an old retired bloke as a caretaker or an experienced hand, but I think they are a bit short over that way.'

A local electrical contractor, Geoff McGlasson, said he believed the boys had got lost on seismic research lines that crisscrossed and abruptly ended. He said, 'It's a very big country, there is no real station out there where they were, nothing out there to tell you where to go. No stations, no signs, no roads, no railway line, nothing ... I have seen that area from the air and I wouldn't want to be lost down there.'

Almost immediately, the federal government announced an inquiry into complaints about low wages, overwork and poor conditions on Kimberley cattle properties.

On 30 April 1987 Sandra Annetts asked for the return of a plastic water bottle searchers had found beside her son's body. Les, by now at the site of the tragedy, had phoned her to tell her about the bottle, on the lid of which James had managed to scratch the words: 'My follt, I always love you Mum and Dad Jason Michelle and Joanne.' As he lay dying, Annetts had also managed a second, fainter message on the side of the bottle: 'Take me back to Flora Valley', written, perhaps, as an ironic comment. Finally, on the handle, he had written 'I found peece'. Beside this he'd scratched a small circle with a dot in the centre which, in scouting terms, meant 'the end of the trail' or 'gone home'.

These messages were especially poignant. Through these few, simple words the public gained some insight into what both boys must have gone through in their last hours. How it must have dawned on them that they were beyond help, how no one except a few Flora Valley staff might realise they were missing and raise the alarm; how there was no water, no shelter, no communications; how they'd been naïve to set out on such a long journey in an unroadworthy vehicle; how they hadn't told anyone where they were going and when they were due. In short, how they'd made every mistake of the inexperienced outback traveller.

Annetts was thinking of his brother and sisters, his mum and dad. He was saying how annoyed he was at his treatment at Flora Valley and how, when he was dead, certain people would have to live with the legacy. Mostly, though, James was saying: It's okay.

Simon and I had a go, but it just didn't work out. His 'peece' was acceptance, the selfless act of trying to console his family after he was gone. Heavy baggage for a schoolboy with a world view forged from Boy Scouts, the streets of Binya, his parents, a few teachers and a love of the outdoors.

A police officer at the scene explained that Les did not want to see the bottle. Sergeant John Hatton said, 'He just broke down. [Les] says that as a scout he's always taken the initiative and I took it that he's saying to Simon it's his fault that they're out there.'

But Sandra Annetts was adamant. 'We have to have that water bottle brought to us,' she said. 'The police are not releasing it yet but we know we just have to have it. We'll possibly keep it somewhere as a reminder. I don't know where. It shows what a fine boy James was. He loved his whole family. He's written each person's name in the family.' She'd been wondering if he'd left a message but wasn't expecting to find one on a water bottle. 'It must have been quite difficult for him to do at the time. That's the type of boy he was. Even at the last minute he was thinking of his family.'

Meanwhile, back in the desert, Superintendent Craddock said he believed the messages became fainter as Annetts became weaker, walking the two kilometres beyond where he'd left his mate's body, all the time dealing with the guilt associated with his belief that he'd caused their stranding (as well as the horror of just having shot Amos, or having seen him shoot himself).

'He must have tried to write some more later on but wasn't able to,' Craddock explained. 'He may not have had the strength. It's tragic. He was probably just trying to get a message to his mum and dad the best way he could. Nobody will ever know the truth. Maybe forensics will come up with something when they examine the rifle.'

There is a certain poetry to the story of Simon and James. Not that they died young, tragically, pursuing their dreams, but more that they had become mates, and were there for each other, right up until, and including, the end.

CHAPTER 14

Clinton Liebelt
1993

The Stuart Highway – Steve and Adele Liebelt – Phoenix has bolted – Clinton's tracks – Description of a sleepless night – The search continues – The bush telegraph – Lewis Vieusseux, 1858 – The Back of Beyond – 'they'd pick him up on the way back' – 1200 people on the ground – A church on a truck – Kirby's Agents Football Club – Crying quietly – The 'Professor'

The Stuart Highway (or 'the track' as it's often called) is a no-nonsense road. It closely follows the path explorer John McDouall Stuart took on his quest to find a north–south route across the continent. It starts on the edge of Darwin's CBD and stretches south for nearly 3000 kilometres. On its way it passes through Katherine, Mataranka, Tennant Creek and Alice Springs in 'the Territory', and Marla, Coober Pedy and the Woomera Restricted Area in South Australia, before arriving in Port Augusta, at the top of the Spencer Gulf.

Along the way there are dozens of roadhouses. Most display their own personality as they compete, in a more or less friendly manner, for the travelling dollar. Aileron Roadhouse, for instance, 130 kilometres north of Alice Springs, is home to the 17-metre sculpture of Anmatjere Man, an anorexic Aboriginal man standing on the hill behind the roadhouse, clutching a spear, in front of a HOLLYWOOD-style sign proclaiming AILERON.

Anmatjere Man was erected in 2005 by Mark Egan. In an interview with ABC Radio he said, 'I got talking to my old mate, Greg Dick, who owns the roadhouse here at Aileron, and he's as mad as I am, so, after we were talking for a while, yeah [we decided] we'll put the big black fella up on the hill.'

This is how it goes in the Territory. Until 2007 the Stuart Highway didn't have a speed limit on its northern stretch. It was only fully sealed in the 1980s. It's a long, featureless asphalt ribbon bisecting the nation, chockers with B-doubles bringing thongs and cucumbers to the north, over-flown by wedge-tailed eagles in search of road kill, trawled by grey nomads pining for the 'quintessential Outback experience'. Sometimes it becomes a landing strip for the Royal Flying Doctor Service, and other times, the setting for murders and tragedies amid the spinifex loneliness.

Most Australians know little about the patches of civilisation along the highway. Daly Waters, 270 kilometres south of Katherine, was the site of Australia's first international airport, refuelling London-bound planes. Later, during World War II, the area hosted Australian and American fighters and bombers that patrolled the north coast. Its small, corrugated-iron pub, decorated with bras, bank notes and banners from all over the planet, is a Territory must-see. Visitors can expect to see ten-pin bowling on the main street, and Australia's least used traffic light.

The roadhouses say much about the character and outlook of those who choose to work in or visit them. Almost nothing can be taken seriously – after all, what's the point? This is the Australia most tourists come to see. Spiders under the dunny seat, loaded dogs. The character of these places is enhanced by an isolation that speaks of mateship by necessity, the importance of sticking together in the face of adversity.

The Dunmarra Wayside Inn, 314 kilometres south of Katherine, is typical of most: petrol, motel accommodation, a bar decorated with the obligatory 'pubobilia' and a small caravan park. Dunmarra started life as a supply station for Overland Telegraph crews, and 27 kilometres south a plaque commemorates, with typical Victorian precision, the day that men working from the north and south came together to complete the line – 3.15 pm on Thursday 22 August 1872:

The Overland Telegraph. This plaque was erected in memory of Sir Charles Todd, Postmaster General of the Province of South Australia. His gallant construction teams, operators, and linesmen ...

The area is named after Irishman Dan O'Mara, a telegraph linesman who wandered into the bush and was lost in the early 1900s. His skeleton wasn't found for years, and when it was (by station owner Noel Healy) local Aboriginal people referred to him as the unfortunate 'Dunmarra'.

In 1988 Steve Liebelt, an ex-Territory policeman, and his wife, Adele, bought Dunmarra. Steve had been tiring of the mental and physical strain of police work and wanted a change. As Robert Wainwright explains in his book *The Lost Boy*, 'The more Steve thought about it the more he liked the idea. Adele was unhappy about his not being home for her and the kids and letting the job take precedence ...'

Dunmarra is located on the eastern edge of the Tanami Desert. This is Australia's third largest desert and, with 400 millimetres annual rainfall, one of our 'wettest', although most of this is lost due to evaporation. The Tanami is covered in spinifex-carpeted sandplains, low-growing acacia, grevillea and hakea, as well as desert bloodwoods and termite mounds. Summer temperatures soar into the high forties and only a few native animal species, such as the little native mouse, can survive. It's not a place for the unwary or unprepared.

The Liebelts soon settled in. They employed Val Brooks, a friend and workmate of Steve's mother, Mary, as governess for their two young sons. In 1988 Greg was five years old, Clinton, three. The brothers were close; a result of the various lonely postings they'd shared. They loved sport, and the outdoors, but Clinton had another side. He was scared of the dark, and would often creep into bed with his parents. He loved his teddy bear, Victor, and a collection of trolls that lived in his room.

After their arrival the Liebelts spent time improving conditions at Dunmarra, planting trees, fixing up the eight motel rooms and ten powered sites. It was a seven-day-a-week job, and although there was a small, itinerant staff, Steve and Adele worked a minimum 12-hour day.

Greg and Clinton soon settled in. 'Miss Val', as she was known, and Adele drove 300 kilometres to enrol the boys at the Katherine School of the Air, and Steve and Adele set up a classroom in an old staffroom at the roadhouse. Miss Val ensured the boys had a regular school day, which included two half-hour radio lessons. Clinton wrote: '7.15: I woke up and got dressed. I had Weet-Bix for breakfast. 8am: Radio lesson, school work. 10 am: Morning tea. 10.30: School ...'). Everyone at the roadhouse took an interest in the boys' education, often stopping their tasks to help out.

Over the next five years the Liebelts learned to love their life at Dunmarra. As Wainwright explains, 'By 1993 they had bought out their business partners and had settled into a life that revolved around the daily rhythm of travel up and down the Stuart Highway.'

Then, on 6 October 1993, everything changed. It was almost lunchtime when Dave and Sandy Langan stopped at Dunmarra to make a phone call and let their two horses, Lady and Phoenix, stretch their legs. As Dave was on the phone just outside the roadhouse he heard his wife call out that Phoenix, spooked by a passing road train, had bolted. Dave ran over to Lady, took her reins but looked up to see Phoenix had already gone, up along the highway and into the bush.

The Langans pitched their tent and stayed the night at Dunmarra, determined to search for the horse the following morning.

The next day Clinton was bored. He pestered his mum, and then Miss Val, but they told him they were busy. Then he wandered outside, fetched his trail bike, told another staff member named Lu Stokes that he was going for a ride, put on his helmet and took off across the concourse. This was nothing unusual. He and his brother often rode on a track around a paddock behind the roadhouse. Steve had warned them to wear a helmet, ride safely, and not cross to the western side of the highway. For a sun-hardened country kid, even one as young as Clinton, trail bikes were one of the joys of outback life.

At 4.30 that afternoon Steve, having helped out in the search for Phoenix, returned to the roadhouse. He was met by Adele who asked him if he'd seen Clinton. He said he'd assumed he was with her. She found Val and Lu but neither had seen Clinton for hours. Steve searched the back paddock but couldn't find his son. He immediately became worried – the boys were under strict instructions to stay within this two-square-kilometre area.

When Steve returned to the house Adele was in tears. Dave Langan had told her he'd seen Clinton on the other side of the highway opening a gate. Dave, unaware that this area was out of bounds to the boy, had helped him chain the gate. Steve guessed that Clinton had been trying to join the group searching for Phoenix. He took Greg's trail bike and immediately started searching the western side of the highway. He soon picked up his son's tracks and followed them. After a while they disappeared into the bush. He stopped; now he was *really* worried. He turned around and headed back to the roadhouse.

Meanwhile, Adele had contacted the family's nearest neighbour, John Dyer, and within half an hour seven men had arrived at Dunmarra. Among this group were three Aboriginal trackers who soon picked up Clinton's tracks around a dam in the western paddock. The men were joined by Steve and they continued following the tracks into the bush in four-wheel drives. Soon after they lost any sense of where Clinton had ridden. Frustrated, they returned to the roadhouse.

Steve and Adele were frightened, worried, aware that this, their worst fear when coming to live in such an isolated location, had been realised. Steve managed to track down constables John White and Sam Robinson at Renner Springs. He told them the news and they returned to their station at Elliott, 104 kilometres from Dunmarra, to plan a search for the next day. By 11 pm a full ground and aerial search had been organised. At midnight both constables headed to Dunmarra to wait. For many, it would be a sleepless night.

Steve had returned to search the east and west side of the highway. He deviated onto dirt roads, and even into bush, setting out lights every hundred metres with a water bottle and one of his son's favourite muesli bars. Next to each light he left a note: *Clinton, stay at this light. There is water in the bottle.* When he arrived back at the roadhouse White and Robinson were waiting for him. They discussed the search, and Adele told them that various friends had already heard the news, including Margie McLean, a nurse from Elliott who was on her way in case Clinton came in during the night.

Steve and Adele spent a sleepless night. Where was Clinton? Huddled beneath a log, beside a dam, crying, afraid of the dark? Whose fault was it? Should they have been watching him more closely? Had he seen Phoenix and started after her? Had he run out of fuel, come off his bike, injured himself? Was he wandering the scrub – back towards them, in the wrong direction? Was he thirsty, hungry, calling out for his mum and dad? He was independent, but he was only eight years old.

No one could wait for morning. At 4 am John Dyer briefed the searchers about the type of country they would face. He told them this huge paddock, called Shenandoah, was covered in thick scrub – lancewood and turpentine – and was nearly impossible to traverse in four-wheel drives. According to Wainwright: 'The bottom line, Dyer told them gravely, was that they probably only had until late in the afternoon to find the boy alive. The ground temperature soared well into the high forties each day, there was no visible surface water and Clinton had taken no supplies.'

At first light Steve, a friend named John White and the three trackers picked up Clinton's tracks and followed them into the bush. Mark Robins, from Tanumbirini Station, arrived at 6.30 am and started an aerial search in his helicopter. Another three fixed-wing aircraft arrived from Newcastle Waters and commenced a grid search. Soon after the helicopter spotted Clinton's trail bike.

Robins landed but there was no sign of the eight year old. By the time Steve and the ground party caught up with the helicopter crew it became apparent that Clinton had forgotten his father's advice that, if he were ever lost, he should stay with his bike. He had wandered off into the bush, in a westward direction, further away from the roadhouse. From his boot prints, they knew Clinton was confused and disoriented.

The searchers continued following Clinton's tracks in a north-west direction. After two kilometres they lost his prints in soft sand and thick scrub. They decided to head back.

Meanwhile, at the intersection of the Stuart and Buchanan highways, nearly 100 people had gathered to help. These included Northern Territory Emergency Service volunteers, army reservists and personnel from the RAAF Tindal air base, as well as dozens of stockmen and locals from roadhouses, Katherine and other small communities such as Mataranka and Larrimah. Nine more Aboriginal trackers had arrived at Dunmarra, and were now following a gas pipeline west of the roadhouse, searching for any sign that Clinton may have crossed beyond this point.

Mark Robins, along with John Dyer, continued searching in his helicopter. Both men would land, spread out and search, then work their way back to the helicopter by listening for its engine. Eventually, through sheer persistence, they found another boot-print four kilometres west of the trail bike.

Back at the roadhouse, dozens more friends, colleagues, and ex-workmates of Steve and Adele, as well as people who had heard about Clinton on the 'bush telegraph', had arrived. Groups of stockmen with their horses were sent out to cover a patch of scrub. Clinton's teacher called to say he was on his way, Clinton's maternal grandparents, Vic and Patricia Stokes, were booked on a flight – everyone dropped whatever they were doing.

Adele, with a group of close friends, was cooking for the growing team of searchers. She was beside herself, replaying every moment of the last few days, still trying to believe it was only a matter of time before Clinton was found. Clint was tough, and smart. As long as he stopped and waited they would find him.

As history shows, the Australian bush and eight-year-old boys don't mix. In her article, 'A City Child Lost in the Bush', Kim Torney describes an incident with many similarities to the search for Clinton Liebelt.

Ferntree Gully, in the Dandenongs, was a popular picnic spot for 19th-century Melburnians. Lewis Vieusseux, the eight-year-old son of Louis and Julie Vieusseux, went missing after a family outing in the bush on 2 January 1858. Lewis, his mother and another man were returning to a hut they'd stayed in the previous night. Lewis was riding ahead of the others on an old stock horse called Taps. Another member of the expedition, Alfred Howitt (who led the expedition to recover the bodies of Burke and Wills), later wrote: 'Lewis and Taps were some little way in front and out of sight and most unfortunately Mrs Vieusseux took the wrong turn – a road leading past the sawmill. Having followed this for a few hundred yards but not seeing Lewis she 'coo-eed' and Lewis answered her from the other track. She then sent the driver …[to] fetch [him] but he misunderstood her and only went as far as [to] see Lewis and then came back to tell her that he had seen Lewis leading the horse. From this moment not the faintest trace of the little boy has ever been found.'

Although Taps was soon found grazing close to the track, Lewis was nowhere to be seen. A search was quickly launched and, as with Clinton Liebelt, friends, relatives and locals pitched in to find the boy before it was too late. But despite everyone's best efforts he could not be found. Howitt described how the search affected the boy's mother: 'She would start up and wring her hands – the tears streaming from her eyes – and exclaim in a tone of such heart rending misery … that my blood seemed to freeze, it was like a horrible dream become as reality.'

Howitt reported that Aboriginal trackers had little success, and he quoted them as saying, 'plenty rain fall him down – no get him track – a little boy too much pull away all about …' He eventually dismissed them by saying, 'They believed that he was dead and that it was useless to look and went off to the Yarra.'

Howitt later wrote that he believed Lewis, having heard his mother, had tried to turn Taps around but the horse, sensing it was close to home, had refused. The boy had dismounted and tried to follow the 'coo-ee' but had been scared into the bush by wild dogs, which 'ran out at him open mouthed as they do to every one ...'

In her article Torney explains the importance of luck in these searches. She describes Howitt's meeting, several days into the search, with a man named Banbury. Howitt later wrote: 'On Saturday night he'd [Banbury] heard a child "a coo-eing and a hollering" in the direction of his hut and had supposed it to be his little boy. On going home he found the child there before him and thought nothing of the circumstance ... On Saturday morning he had seen the prints of a child's foot coming down towards the sawmill from Dobson's.'

Two years later Lewis's skeleton was found by a 'bush cutter'. In the meantime the Vieusseuxs had been sent a fake ransom note and, most probably, suffered the same anguish that Steve and Adele were now experiencing. The story of Lewis Vieusseux was not uncommon. Less than three years after the discovery of his body a six-year-old boy was lost in scrub nearby, and his remains weren't located until years later.

Vieusseux, Liebelt, and hundreds of children have been lost to the Fierce Country in our attempt to 'civilise' it. The anxiety was there in 1966 when Jane, Arnna and Grant Beaumont went missing from their own stretch of suburban sand. A few years earlier, audiences of the 1954 documentary *The Back of Beyond* saw something similar. Here, young outback sisters Sally and Roberta set off into the desert to search for help after their mother falls ill. Sally pulls a billycart full of supplies as Roberta, playing her recorder, follows with their dog. They become lost, before stumbling across their own tracks. Sally realises they're low on water and insists they leave the dog behind. She ties him to a tree as a snake comes over to investigate. Shots of bleached cattle skulls leave us in no doubt. Sally knows they're in trouble but doesn't want to alarm her sister. The narrator explains, 'She told Roberta he needed a rest and they'd pick him up on the way back.'

The documentary was made to show the journeys of the 'Mailman of the Birdsville Track', Tom Kruse, as he delivered the Royal Mail, fuel and other supplies along the 517-kilometre desert stretch. The film, directed by John Heyer and made by the Shell Film Unit, premiered at the Marree Town Hall on 24 July 1954. It showed a side of Australia many of our rapidly urbanising population had never seen and certainly hadn't experienced.

The girls continue, and so does the narration (co-written by Douglas Stewart): 'Two days later their father rode after them, followed their tracks for 27 miles, until they disappeared under wind-blown sand. The children had vanished. What became of them isn't known. Into the ocean of sand they went. All that remains is their story.'

Although the story of the missing girls wasn't relevant to Kruse's journey, Heyer thought it powerful enough to include. Despite a lack of evidence, Heyer claimed it was true, and that he'd learnt it from John Flynn, founder of the Flying Doctor Service. Maybe the truth doesn't matter. The story has all the elements: the mother, left alone while her husband is out working; succumbing to illness; the father arriving, but too late; the search for the kids. The lack of communication. The isolation.

The next morning the concourse in front of Dunmarra was covered in cars, buses and horse floats. Dozens of people woke up in swags, in the front seat of their cars, wherever they could find a spot. The police and army had taken over the roadhouse, setting up command centres to coordinate the 300 searchers and the numerous helicopters and fixed-wing aircraft now involved in the search. Every hour more soldiers and airmen, doctors, NTES volunteers, cooks, friends, and concerned locals were arriving to help out. From the moment Adele asked Steve if Clinton was with him, less than 36 hours before, the search had grown exponentially.

Eventually there would be more than 1200 people on the ground. If volunteers weren't out looking they were helping at Dunmarra, or waiting by a radio or phone, hoping, praying, realising, somehow, that in the outback, whatever happened to one, happened to all.

Clinton's School of the Air mates were worried. Terry Oliver, who lived 700 kilometres away, sent the Liebelts a message of support. 'Clinton is such a true sports kid he'll make it home. You don't have to worry because Clint knows his way around. He'll soon get home to you. I can't think of what to say. He's a great buddy. We play a lot at camp. I have been asking God to bring him safely home to you. Don't give up hope.'

Hundreds were now following grid patterns set out by Superintendent Col Hardman, head of the police special operations unit, which by now had taken control of the search. At 4 pm there was still no sign of Clinton. With only a few hours of light left, Mark Robins landed his helicopter near a gas pipeline that had become the western boundary of the search area. His spotter, Murray Taylor, got out for a look. Then he called out – he'd found footprints. Clinton had taken off his boots and was walking barefoot in the soft sand. Now it dawned on them that the search parties were looking too far east. Soon after a second helicopter found Clinton's jeans not far from his prints. This was a worrying sign. Why had he started to take off his clothes? Trackers and sniffer dogs were brought in, to no avail. Clinton had been out in the scrub, minus food or water, in punishingly hot conditions, for two days. Every minute was crucial.

Dunmarra had transformed into a town. A medical clinic was set up to treat dehydration, sunburn, scratches, eye injuries and sprains. At its most crucial time, the search for Clinton was interrupted when a search helicopter crashed. The camp nurse, Margie McLean, was soon on the scene, treating and stabilising the chopper's two men, who were flown back to Katherine.

On the third full day of searching, with the grid having moved to the west, a police sniffer dog found Clinton's boots half a kilometre away from his jeans. Although this continued to point them in the right direction, it was a bad sign. He was becoming more dehydrated, confused, unsure of where to head or what to do; and worse, the location of his clothing suggested he was starting to wander in ever-widening circles.

Although the search was becoming more desperate, no one was willing to concede. The owner of the Katherine Motel-Hotel started delivering car loads, and then truck loads, of goods to Dunmarra. More volunteers helped run the roadhouse, care for the sick, cook, handle media enquiries, and generally support the Liebelts, as well as Clinton's brother, ten-year-old Greg, who tried to help out around Dunmarra but was suffering his own emotional torment. He and Clinton had always been close; up until a few months before they'd even slept together. Greg had always looked after and protected Clinton, but now there was little he could do.

A portable church arrived on the back of a truck. Pastor Mike Ellemor and his wife began offering help and consolation wherever they could. Soon there were counsellors, psychologists and social workers. It was obvious the physical and mental strain of the search, the not-knowing, would soon take a toll on many. The NTES set up a search chapel and this became a 'quiet spot', a place to go to be with your own thoughts and fears.

The following day, police officer Michael van Heythuysen said, 'In reality, hope virtually has petered out. I think it has dawned on everyone that there's not much chance of him surviving. But everyone wants to finalise the situation by at least finding his body. The response to this has been incredible … I think the whole situation has touched everyone's heart.'

The search continued. A Katherine football team, the Kirby's Agents Football Club, hired a bus, loaded it with food and swags, cancelled their weekend footy match, and the whole team set off for Dunmarra. There was no question of anyone being too busy, tied up at work or home; there was a boy lost, it was as simple as that. Although most of the players must have known it was too late, this didn't stop them coming. It would be a case of what you'd think and feel afterwards – did I do everything I could to help? Might I have made a difference?

A week after Clinton's disappearance the search was still continuing. Col Hardman had so many offers of help he had to turn people away. By now he'd told the media Clinton's chances of survival were 'slim at best'. He explained that 'the searchers are still as keen as ever and they're hoping we can find him alive ... We know he headed west since getting off his bike, but then his boots, jeans, goggles and socks are all over the place. It is impossible to stay on his tracks.'

Nine days after Clinton's disappearance the search was finally called off. Hardman told searchers, 'As much as we would all like to think there is still hope I want you to know that, like all of you, I accept the truth that Clint has not made it ... Don't consider that what has been done here has been a failure. It has been a triumph of people and spirit.'

On the same day a search party found Clinton's helmet. It's likely he'd carried it into the bush as some sort of comfort, and security. Steve boarded the only remaining helicopter and flew to the scene. He knew Clinton wouldn't have dropped his helmet until he couldn't carry on. When he arrived he finally broke down. The sight of the helmet, filled with spear grass from where Clinton had dragged it through the scrub, was just too much.

Meanwhile, the searchers had spread out. The helicopter returned to the air to help. One volunteer, who was only 200 metres from the helmet, noticed an odd shape in the grass. He walked towards it slowly, and then stopped.

It was Clinton.

Steve was alerted and rushed to the scene. As Wainwright explains, '[Steve] could see the stockmen and their horses standing quietly in a half circle in a small clearing beneath five little gums. [They] were crying quietly, holding their hats across their chests in respect. Steve walked to the trees and saw that someone had placed a saddle blanket over the body.' Steve pulled back the blanket and looked at his son, dressed only in his underpants, his skin dark brown, his eyes closed. He held his hand. He tried to hold him but broke down, crying.

Later, Adele would say that the one good thing that came out of the tragedy of her son's death was that it united people, and showed how much even absolute strangers could care for a boy, and family, they'd never met. She said, 'Clinton has renewed our faith in human kindness. Everyone is put on this earth for a reason, and I believe Clinton's task was to bring the people of the Northern Territory together. I don't consider myself a religious person – I can't remember the last time I went to church – but I prayed an awful lot during that week.'

The country kid had walked 23 kilometres before giving up. It had all been a simple mistake – the need to help out in the search for Phoenix, who was, ironically, found during the search. Clinton was probably so fired up he didn't stop to think, to remember all the warnings his father had given him: to stay in his paddock, to use the sun as a guide if he ever got lost, to stay with his bike, conserve his energy, and water. But maybe – after he realised he was lost, after he'd called out for his mum and dad and Greg – he still guessed he'd find his way back, or would be found. What was hardest for Adele, and many others, was the image of Clinton panicking, crying, running through the bush in the wrong direction, desperate to return to them. Later she would say, 'We had to find him. I just couldn't stand having to look out from the shop across into that bush every day knowing he was out there somewhere.'

At his son's funeral, Steve Liebelt spoke of 'the Professor', with his 'cheeky smile, mischievous antics, quick wit and loving nature'. He said, 'Clinton typified the boy from the bush. Though only eight years of age he displayed a maturity at times which belied his age. People who knew him well knew of his passion for adventure, his abundant amounts of energy and his consummate desire to learn more about everything all of the time.'

The church was full to overflowing, and for weeks and months later, the tributes would flow in for a boy who, as his father explained, 'brought peace and happiness to so many people. Few people are able to do this. You have brought so much faith in mankind. Dad's Possum and Mum's Clintypops, rest in peace. You are with us forever'.

CHAPTER 15

Caroline Grossmueller
1998

The road to William Creek – Caroline and Karl – Outback odyssey – Towards Lake Eyre – REMOTE AREAS AHEAD – 'I came upon a number of small fish' – 4WD bogged – Waiting – The return to William Creek – Point of separation – 'trying to get out of this hell' – The death of Caroline Grossmueller

William Creek is a place of extremes. With its ten or so inhabitants and a single pub, it's one of our smallest towns, located on our biggest working cattle station, the 24,000-square-kilometre Anna Creek Station. The 1887 corrugated-iron hotel is an outback icon, complete with the obligatory pin-up board covered with autographed underwear, business cards and messages from across the world.

William Creek is located halfway along the 620-kilometre Oodnadatta Track, an unsealed road that leaves the Stuart Highway at Marla, continues south-east to Oodnadatta, on to William Creek and finally, Marree. The track follows an ancient Aboriginal trading route and the course of the original Central Australian Railway. Along the way travellers find springs bubbling from the Great Artesian Basin, remnants of railway sidings and telegraph repeater stations, gibber plains, saltbush flats and red dunes. The town, which attracts nearly 80,000 tourists a year, is nearly 700 kilometres from Adelaide and 150 kilometres from the closest 'major' centre, Coober Pedy.

It was here, on 6 December 1998, that 28-year-old Austrian tourist Caroline Grossmueller and her boyfriend, 32-year-old

Karl Goeschka, arrived as part of their outback odyssey. They had been travelling Australia for several months, firstly through the Northern Territory, across to Cairns, down the east coast and west into South Australia. Grossmueller – determined to see as much of the 'real Australia' as possible before returning to Europe to continue her studies – and Goeschka had been trawling the country in a Britz Toyota four-wheel drive. Although the vehicle was perfect for outback conditions, the pair knew very little about driving in remote and difficult areas.

Grossmueller and Goeschka headed to the William Creek Hotel for a drink. As the hotel's owners, Malcolm and Helen Anderson, were away, the pair talked to their son and told him they wanted to travel to Halligan Bay, 60 kilometres east of William Creek, to see Lake Eyre. He invited them to register their names in a 'search and rescue' book. Since he couldn't find the current book he started a new one. This system of 'signing in' and 'signing out' gives locals some idea about who's in the area. Unfortunately it seems Grossmueller and Goeschka may have believed this system was some sort of official check, and that it would, if necessary, alert police or searchers to their presence.

Later, Malcolm Anderson told the press his son had tried to talk the pair out of taking the trip to Lake Eyre during this, the hottest part of summer. He explained that his son believed the couple hadn't gone to Lake Eyre. 'We had no reason to believe they were out there, even though there was a note. If they don't turn up we ring the police and they get the shits with us when we find they are safe and sound and halfway to Melbourne. It makes it very hard to do the right thing sometimes.'

The Andersons, originally from Melbourne, had first stopped at the William Creek Hotel in 1989 on their way to Broome. In a 2000 *Australian Story* for the ABC they explained how the local publican happened to tell them he was thinking of selling up. They had jumped at the opportunity. They had grown to love the pub, the town, the few locals and the stream of tourists. Helen explained, 'It's a totally different way of living. You can walk along one of the shopping centres in Melbourne and you'll look at a person and they'll just have this dead look on their face ... But here, everyone's in happy mode because they're all on holidays having a good time.'

That night, Grossmueller and Goeschka camped out near the hotel. The next morning, 7 December, they set off for Lake Eyre. Their 4WD contained enough food and water to last for weeks. It was early summer, with daytime temperatures often exceeding 50 degrees. As the pair travelled along a remote side road that ran off the Oodnadatta Track they would have seen saltbush, a few stunted shrubs, red sand, dry creeks, but not much else. They must have known they weren't likely to see anyone this far from civilisation, and that they were a long way from help, medical aid or companionship. Still, they were determined to see the Dead Heart.

As they drove they passed a sign that warned about this 60-kilometre stretch of track. It told travellers they *had to* sign in at the William Creek Hotel. Under bold letters that said 'WARNING, REMOTE AREAS AHEAD' the sign reminded anyone roaming this stretch of outback they needed a tool kit, tow rope, and plenty of water. It warned of wandering livestock, flash floods and bad roads. Most importantly, it stressed, 'NEVER LEAVE YOUR VEHICLE'.

Later, Malcolm Anderson said the track to Halligan Bay should have been closed. 'You just don't go down that track in a one vehicle situation. I don't go down that track unless I have to ...' A former tour operator, Adam Plate, said on this 'dead-end road, there might not have been anyone there for a month, the road just goes straight into a salt pan'.

Now the couple was entering real 4WD country. The only problem was, they'd had no training or experience in operating their vehicle under such conditions. They arrived on the west bank of Lake Eyre North later that morning. The north and south lakes, or saltpans as they are most of the time, cover an area of 9500 square kilometres. At 15 metres below sea level, Lake Eyre is the lowest point in Australia and occasionally fills with flood waters from the Channel Country in western Queensland. The lake fully fills about four times each century, with a four-metre flood every decade and smaller floods every few years. During these times the area is teeming with birdlife and many species of fish. But most of the time, as was the case when Caroline Grossmueller and Karl Goeschka arrived at Halligan Bay, it's just salt, leftover from an ancient inland sea, stretching out to the horizon.

The explorer Edward John Eyre first attempted to reach the centre of Australia in 1839. He got as far as Lake Torrens, to the south of Lake Eyre South, before having to change course and follow the Flinders Ranges to the aptly named Mount Hopeless, where he abandoned his mission and returned to Adelaide. Australia's greatest inland explorer, John McDouall Stuart, wasn't so easily put off. His third expedition managed to reach Lake Eyre in November 1859. Upon his arrival he wrote in his journal:

> After breakfast went to examine the shore ... found it to be caked with salt, with ironstone and lime gravel. When flooded, at about fifty yards from the hard beach, the water will be about three feet deep. I tried to ride to the water, but found it too soft, so I dismounted and tried it on foot. At about a quarter of a mile I came upon a number of small fish, all dried and caked in salt ... I should think this a sufficient proof of the depth of water.

Grossmueller and Goeschka decided to camp near a 400-litre emergency water tank beside the lake. To help create a windbreak, Goeschka manoeuvered their 4WD into position beside the tank. In doing so he drove into soft sand and became bogged. Alarmed, but not panicked, they attempted to free themselves by deflating their tyres. Goeschka, unsure of what he was doing, did not deflate the tyres sufficiently to have any effect. He then attempted to dig the vehicle free. Since he didn't have a long-handled spade he improvised with a plate, with no luck.

Eventually the couple pitched their tent and settled in for the night, sleeping as best they could. There was no need to worry, yet.

Apart from the water tank, their 4WD contained another 50-litre tank. They had plenty of food and the folks at the William Creek Hotel, they believed, would report them missing when they didn't return.

Little did they know that no one had, or would, notice them missing. After Malcolm and Helen Anderson's return from a holiday, they found the old travellers' register and checked to see if anyone had signed in. There were no names. Grossmueller and Goeschka's names were in the new book that the Anderson's son had started.

The travellers waited another two days, taking shelter beside their vehicle from the extreme temperatures. After a third day of waiting they became convinced they'd been forgotten. They remembered being told it could be six weeks before anyone came along. So, after a day of 50-degree-plus temperatures, they decided to set out in search of help, ignoring the most important rule of outback survival: always stay with your vehicle.

Perhaps Grossmueller had reasoned that it was only 60 kilometres. For an experienced mountain walker this was no ordeal. Perhaps they believed it was their only option. Ironically, they had enough food and water to keep them alive for weeks. This was no Page family, or Amos and Annetts, stranded without water. This was just a case of bad judgement. Later, Goeschka said, 'We should have stayed with the car.'

At 4 pm on 9 December the pair started walking back to William Creek. They had been keeping a log that, after its translation, showed they hadn't taken this decision lightly. Grossmueller had estimated they could walk four or five kilometres an hour during the night, meaning they would be back at the William Creek Hotel before the heat of the following day. What she hadn't counted on was their state of exhaustion, the weight of the water they would have to carry and the type of sandy terrain they would have to cover.

The couple had estimated they'd need one litre of water for every ten kilometres covered. Again, enough for normal bushwalking, but not for the desert. After five hours they stopped to rest and realised a third of their water was already gone. They rested for five hours before carrying on for another hour, at which time they were forced to stop again.

It was 3 am and Goeschka, unable to walk with the pain from an ankle injury he'd incurred trying to remove their 4WD from the sand, decided he couldn't go on. He later explained that his companion was determined to make it to William Creek. 'She desperately wanted to go on,' he said.

Helen Anderson later told the *Australian*, 'He tried to get her to go back but she wouldn't go back.'

They decided to separate, thereby breaking the second golden rule of outback survival. At 4 am Caroline took nine litres of water in two containers and set off into the desert, wearing Goeschka's hiking boots. Goeschka remained in their tent for the rest of that day. He only had one litre of water left. Deciding he'd probably die if he stayed, he then started back to the 4WD.

Caroline Grossmueller's final hours would have been marked by exhaustion, a splitting headache, delirium and the inability to walk or use her muscles. All brought on by intense dehydration. Accompanied by the impending realisation of what was happening to her. Along the way she managed to stop and scribble several notes, which she attached to signs.

> Help! Had to leave boyfriend alone due to health problems with less water.
> (5–10 km past sign WC-50 – direction Lake Eyre. Myself still trying to get out of this hell heading towards William Creek, which 2 inhabitants simply forgot us.
> Please try to find us!

Thirty kilometres along the William Creek–Halligan Bay track, Caroline Grossmueller succumbed to the intense heat. She simply stopped walking, collapsed and never got back up. Her body, unable to supply her organs and cells with the water they needed, shut down. The Krebs cycle, a stage of tissue respiration that converts foodstuffs into energy, carbon dioxide and water, stopped working.

Grossmueller died on 11 or 12 December, about the same time Goeschka was arriving back at the 4WD. She'd managed to walk only half the distance to William Creek, slowed down, perhaps, by the weight of the water still in the containers she carried. Nonetheless, the water hadn't helped. It was just too hot. On the ABC's *Australian Story*, Malcolm Anderson explained, 'The overseas tourists, the foreign tourists, they travel in outback Australia and find it very difficult with the harsh environment here especially in summer. You can come unstuck very easily.'

His wife, Helen, was touched by Grossmueller's death. 'She walked past bores, she walked past water troughs for the cattle,' she told the ABC. 'They had a 400-litre water tank where their car was and I think it was if not full probably half full.' She explained that most tourists have no idea what they're in for. 'So you just do the best you can and sometimes it's not good enough. It was shocking, yeah. That is the worst feeling that I've really had when we found what had happened.'

Goeschka waited beside the 4WD for several more days, managing to keep cool and hydrated. On 15 December, five days after the couple had set off from Halligan Bay in search of help, two German tourists discovered Caroline Grossmueller's body. They quickly returned to the William Creek Hotel, alerted the Andersons and waited for police to arrive from Coober Pedy. This group then started for Halligan Bay.

Several hours later they arrived at Lake Eyre and found Goeschka sheltering in the shade of his vehicle. Later, in an Austrian television interview, he said that when they had become bogged, 'We thought, it's okay, someone will come.' He described the track to Halligan Bay as 'good to drive on' but said, 'I made a mistake – the tyres were embedded.'

But they weren't. Upon arriving it took experienced outback police only ten minutes to deflate the couple's tyres and drive the 4WD out of the soft sand. It could have been so simple, if only

Grossmueller and Goeschka had sought or been given instruction on the use of their vehicle. Later, coroner Wayne Chivell explained: 'Mr Goeschka was aware of the benefit to be gained by deflating tyres. He said he allowed 30 seconds for each tyre. That was obviously insufficient ...'

Goeschka was taken back to the William Creek Hotel where Helen Anderson, speaking to a staff reporter for the *Australian*, described him as 'physically fine, but very distressed over Ms Grossmueller's death'. He told hotel staff that he and Caroline had been together for 11 years and that they'd arrived in Australia in October.

After Grossmueller's death an inquiry was mooted. Some of the possible areas of concern were the use of the 'search and rescue' book, its reliability, ways to make it more foolproof; the fact that many tourists don't have a friend or relative to 'nominate', to tell when they should be back from a certain area, before an alarm is raised; the lack of equipment (including communication and GPS systems) and training given to tourists who hire 4WDs and campervans.

A post-mortem was carried out on Grossmueller's body in Adelaide on Friday 18 December 1998. A provisional finding stated that the final year medical student had died from heat exhaustion. Coroner Chivell suggested this finding would lead to an inquest as the death raised public safety issues.

Several years after Caroline's death Karl Goeschka returned to William Creek to place a memorial to his partner.

> Caroline was tragically taken in this area while travelling the outback. A precious life ended all too soon. Your spirit will live on forever.

There is also a small white cross and a stone memorial along the Halligan Bay track near where Grossmueller died, a reminder, and warning, to all outback tourists, that this is not forgiving country.

CHAPTER 16

Robert Bogucki
1999

43 nights in the desert – Riding around Australia – Sandfire Roadhouse – Wandering the desert – Ray and Betty become worried – Gunslinger arrives – Murray Gavey succumbs to the heat – Bogucki is found! – 'scratched the itch' – Evan Muncie and the man dressed in white

When he was a troubled 15-year-old, Alaskan Robert Bogucki decided one day he would, like Jesus, head into the wild – to test his faith, to explore his relationship with God. It would be another 18 years before Bogucki got the chance to experience his 40 days and 40 nights in the desert (in his case, 43); to have his questions answered. And when it was all over, the searches concluded, the newspaper articles written, he said, 'It's still going through my mind the things I've seen and experienced. I feel satisfied that I stretched that edge, whatever it was that sent me out there in the first place. The only feeling I have right now is a feeling of confidence that God will take care of me.'

In 1999, 33-year-old Bogucki took time off from his job as a fireman in Fairbanks, Alaska, to ride a bike around Australia. Somewhere along the way, as he travelled from Perth up the west coast along the Great Northern Highway, he saw a map showing Australia's second biggest desert, the Great Sandy Desert, an area of nearly 300,000 square kilometres, surrounded by the Pilbara and southern Kimberley regions, and the Gibson and Tanami deserts. With its nine-month summer, feral camels and endless spinifex grass, this seemed just the place to lose yourself, for better or worse. At last, he knew the time had arrived. Throwing aside all common sense, he decided where his bicycle journey would take him next.

After a long, hot ride, Bogucki arrived at the Sandfire Roadhouse, 1910 kilometres north of Perth. He avoided telling anyone about his plans. Later he explained he'd decided to ride across the Great Sandy Desert to Fitzroy Crossing, a small town approximately 500 kilometres from the roadhouse. After his rescue he said, 'I wanted to spend a while on my own with nobody else around, to make peace with God.'

Bogucki set off on his odyssey on 11 July 1999. He didn't have enough food or water for the long journey through one of Australia's harshest landscapes. Common sense must have told him he had almost no chance of completing his trek. Daytime temperatures in the desert are some of the hottest in Australia and there are few permanent water sources. Apart from goannas, kangaroos, bilbies and marsupial moles (not that Bogucki had the skills to catch them) there was nothing to eat. Later, police would be at a loss to understand his actions. Superintendent Steve Roast, from the Broome police, summed up most people's views of the American. 'We have to face the facts. Mr Bogucki went out there alone. It was an extremely irresponsible thing for him to do.'

Bogucki's parents, Ray and Betty, received a postcard at their Miami home from their son on 20 July and assumed all was well. But it wasn't. By then Bogucki had been wandering the desert for nine days. He later admitted he had run out of food a few days into his trek and had survived by eating small native plants. Then, on 26 July, tourists found his camping gear and bike abandoned several kilometres along the east–west aligned Pegasus Track, a 'line', or mining survey track, put down by Pegasus Metals, leading into the Great Sandy Desert.

The next day, 27 July, a land and air search for the missing trekker got underway. Police planes, four-wheel drives and Aboriginal trackers tried to ascertain his position. A combination of soft sand and dense scrub made it difficult for searchers to follow his tracks. The operation continued for 12 days, at which time police, believing he'd either hitched a ride out of the area or perished, called off the search.

Ray and Betty Bogucki refused to accept their son was lost. They believed Robert had the skills and will to stay alive. They also thought he might be attempting to avoid discovery as part of his 'quest'. They contacted the 1st Special Response Group (1SRG), a privately run emergency search and rescue organisation based at Moffett Field, California, and asked for help. 1SRG – its motto 'Anytime, Anywhere' – usually responded only to requests from 'government agencies or recognised humanitarian, disaster relief, or search and rescue organisations'. But, after talking to Ray and Betty Bogucki, 1SRG realised it could help.

Within days of the request 1SRG was on its way to Australia. Over the coming few weeks this distinctly American organisation would irritate police, locals and searchers with its gung-ho methods and attitudes.

The group, led by cigar-smoking, larger-than-life figure Garrison St Clair ('Gunslinger'), consisted of eight searchers and three dogs. Upon their arrival local police weren't interested in helping. They were suspicious of these 'cowboys' who were unfamiliar with the desert. The last problem they needed was another eight missing persons, and another desert search. Likewise, car-hire firms in Broome wouldn't rent the Americans a vehicle – several four-wheel drives had been damaged in the earlier search. Eventually the ever-determined St Clair managed to hire a tourist coach from a Broome hotel. Police concerns regarding 'Gunslinger' seemed vindicated when 1SRG bogged their vehicle just outside Broome and the local State Emergency Service was called to free them.

Also, by now, police were suspicious that Bogucki was deliberately evading them, either to test his survival skills, or because he had a US publishing deal in mind.

Bogucki had been in the desert for well over three weeks. Most locals believed there was no chance he could still be alive. But he was, walking 15 to 30 kilometres per day, eating fruits and flowers from native bushes, drinking muddy water from creeks. This wasn't the hottest time of year, but it was still punishing.

History suggested this was the case. Charles Wells and George Jones of the Calvert Expedition had perished close by just over a hundred years earlier, and lost jackaroos Simon Amos and James Annetts had suffered a similar fate only 12 years before. This country demanded respect and caution. Bogucki, the apparently level-headed fireman, had showed neither. Deep down, most believed this 'new age Yank' had it coming.

The warnings had been there. Murray Gavey had been working at Kununurra in the East Kimberley region of Western Australia. In 2004 Gavey attempted to cross the Great Sandy and Gibson deserts on a motorbike, setting out from Kununurra and heading south to the Aboriginal community of Yagga Yagga (400 kilometres south of Halls Creek) where he stopped for fuel. Once there, locals tried to dissuade him from continuing his journey, seeing how he was low on petrol – Yagga Yagga only stocked diesel – and the track he was travelling was rough and overgrown, avoided even by locals.

Like Bogucki, Gavey was determined. He left Yagga Yagga on 29 September with limited fuel and water supplies, heading for the small community of Kirwirkulla, 300 kilometres south. When, several days later, he failed to arrive, his wife reported him missing. A large land and air search commenced. Gavey's body was eventually found inside his tent at a makeshift campsite. He had no fuel or water, and he'd been riding on a flat tyre for some time. A police spokesman said, 'It's pretty inhospitable out there – a lot of sand dunes, some of them 150 foot high, and very easy to get lost because of the number of little side tracks.'

'Gunslinger' St Clair eventually persuaded Western Australian police to help 1SRG in their search. The group set up a base camp on the edge of the Edgar Range, a series of hills and gorges approximately 200 kilometres south-east of Broome. St Clair believed this area, west of Geegully Creek, a tributary of the Fitzroy River, was the country Bogucki would have had to cross on his way to Fitzroy Crossing.

1SRG picked up from where the Aboriginal trackers had left off. They used a combination of searchers, dogs, and trackers in helicopters to accelerate their search, but three days later they had found nothing. Then, with the Americans on the verge of giving up and heading home, a media helicopter sighted some of Bogucki's belongings abandoned on a blue tarpaulin. Along with a T-shirt, boxer shorts, empty water bottle, sunscreen, tent and Bible, searchers found a notebook containing confused, rambling thoughts. Broome police said, 'They're the thoughts of a bloke obviously in isolation. It goes all over the place.'

The following day, Monday 23 August 1999, after 43 days in the desert, and following 28 days of searching, Bogucki was found alive wandering gorges in the Edgar Range. A Perth Channel Nine news crew in a chartered helicopter made the discovery. In all, Bogucki had travelled 400 kilometres from the Sandfire Roadhouse. Although he was confused and disoriented, he was in good health. In an interview close to the creek in which he was found, Bogucki appeared surprised, but coherent. Watching the footage today it appears the Alaskan wasn't truly aware how close he'd come to death.

On hearing the news of Bogucki's discovery, St Clair said, 'I think he wanted to be found. He said he thought he was in trouble several days ago, so he lightened his load.'

Bogucki was flown to Broome, and admitted to the Broome Hospital, where medical staff said they couldn't believe how good he looked. He'd lost 20 kg and had severe sunburn and blistering, but his only real injuries were scratches on his feet and back.

Bogucki told hospital staff he had 'scratched the itch' that had led him into the desert. He said, 'I just wanted to spend a while on my own, just nobody else around, just make peace with God I guess.' He promised never to repeat his odyssey, but police weren't happy, having invested large amounts of time and money in the search. Eventually, though, they declined to press charges.

When asked if he'd found 'enlightenment' Bogucki replied, 'Before I started out I really didn't know what I was looking for. I really felt alone, not desperate but just without hope at some point.' From his hospital bed, he explained that, 'I feel bad that a lot of people came looking for me, that there was so much spent in time and effort, and I really appreciate it ...'

Western Australian Premier Richard Court wasn't so understanding, insisting Bogucki pay for part of the search. 'What he did was quite reckless. To set out on something, knowing that there would be a significant risk, not properly informing authorities as to what and how you were going to do ...'

Which is the key to understanding Bogucki's actions. Did he really have no idea what he was in for as he rode away from the Sandfire Roadhouse? Did he think God would lead him through the desert? Did he have a death wish or, as some asked afterwards, did he have a few roos loose in the top paddock?

Premier Court had made up his own mind. 'I certainly hope that he and his family are prepared to pay for a significant part of the search, and I certainly wouldn't like to see someone profiting from that sort of experience without making sure the bills were paid here.'

In the years since Bogucki's odyssey the rumoured book has never appeared. Perhaps we need to take Bogucki at his word, and try to understand that this was just an 'itch' that needed scratching. Nonetheless, the scale of the American's irresponsibility was breathtaking: the time wasted, the police resources tied up, the cost and efforts of State Emergency Service volunteers, not to mention Ray and Betty Bogucki, worried sick about their son.

But perhaps Bogucki's disappearance was a re-affirmation, a reminder to all of us that life is precious. As the fireman later said, 'There's just been an amazing outpouring of concern, and I'm sorry that people had to go to so much trouble.'

Bogucki's is one of the great survival stories. He stayed alive for six weeks on nothing more than tea brewed from gum leaves, native berries and murky water. Still, there are even more amazing survival stories.

On Tuesday 12 January 2010 a 7.0 magnitude earthquake hit the small Caribbean country of Haiti, with its epicentre approximately 25 kilometres west of the capital, Port-au-Prince. Hundreds of thousands of homes and businesses were destroyed and somewhere between 92,000 and 300,000 people killed, making this the sixth deadliest earthquake ever recorded.

On 7 February, 28 days after the quake, a 28-year-old man, Evan Muncie, was pulled from the rubble of an apartment building two weeks after authorities had called off the search for survivors, and 11 days after the last survivor had been rescued. Although he had lost 14 kilograms no one could believe he had survived so long without water. Muncie, later dubbed the 'miracle of Haiti', now holds the record for longest survival without an obvious water source.

When asked how he'd managed to survive, Muncie explained that he'd been given water by 'a man dressed in white'.

Perhaps Bogucki, as he set off from the roadhouse, knew something we don't.

CHAPTER 17

The Disappearance of Peter Falconio

2001

Falconio arrives – Sets off with Joanne – The orange Kombi – Bradley John Murdoch – 'a vehicle backfiring' – Lees fights off Murdoch – Light from the torch – Vince Millar, and his B-triple – Refuge at Barrow Creek – The police search – Lees: 'I didn't know there was a rule book' – Murdoch captured – Describes the trial – Cruel, and unstable

Twenty-eight-year-old Peter Falconio was born and bred in West Yorkshire, but his name has become Australian myth, alongside other victims of the Fierce Country: Robert O'Hara Burke, Ludwig Leichhardt, even nine-week-old Azaria Chamberlain, tragically taken by a dingo at Uluru in August 1980. Falconio was no stranded jackaroo, or foreign mystic seeking God in the desert – he was an engineer, out to see the world with his 27-year-old girlfriend, Joanne Lees. Both grew up in Huddersfield, West Yorkshire, where they first met in a nightclub in 1996. The following year Joanne moved in with Peter at Brighton, in the south of England, and it was here they started discussing and planning their first overseas trip.

Peter Falconio was a graduate of the University of Brighton. He worked in construction and was always fascinated by buildings, technology and construction sites. In 2008, on the ABC's *Enough Rope*, Joanne Lees told interviewer Andrew Denton, 'Yeah, when I got my photos developed from travelling around the world, it would be like, you know, the Opera House, the Harbour Bridge, and then I'd just find a construction site, construction site. So that did make me laugh, but that was his passion.'

In 2000, Falconio's parents, Joan and Luciano, and his three brothers – Nicholas, Paul and Mark – farewelled their son and brother when he and Lees left England on a trip to Thailand, Singapore and Australia. Luciano and Paul could never have guessed that by July 2001 they would be flying to Australia's Red Centre to take part in the search for Peter. But by then one of the strangest crimes in Australian history would have played out on a lonely stretch of the Northern Territory's Stuart Highway, thousands of kilometres from the green hills of Huddersfield.

After Falconio's disappearance, Lees said of her partner, 'Pete was my best friend. He was a wonderful person. He was popular, he got on with everybody. He was very close to his mum and to his family. They were an Italian family ... Pete's dad comes from a village in Italy ... Pete was very chilled and relaxed and quite casual, which I loved about him, that quality.'

After travelling through Asia and spending five months living and working in Sydney, Falconio and Lees decided to hit the road, to see the 'real' Australia. Lees, who had made many new friends and enjoyed living at Bondi Beach, was at first reluctant to move on. Later, she would admit to having had a 'fling' with another backpacker, Nick Reilly, while living in Sydney. Although this indiscretion had nothing to do with the disappearance of Peter Falconio, the media would later use it as an indication of her character. As she later explained, 'It was used as an attempt to discredit me throughout the committal but it was irrelevant [to] what happened to Pete and I on the Stuart Highway.'

On the evening of Saturday 14 July 2001, Lees and Falconio were heading north along the Stuart Highway, travelling from Alice Springs to Darwin in their now famous orange Volkswagen Kombi, purchased in Sydney in May 2001. Joanne Lees was moved by the countryside, its vastness, and emptiness. She later commented, 'I thought it was beautiful. That is the beauty of the outback. That's what appealed to Pete and I to travel there ...'

They had just passed through a small town called Ti Tree, 193 kilometres north of Alice Springs. Ti Tree has a population of almost 1000 mostly Anmatyerre people. It is a service centre for scattered cattle stations, the Barrow Creek community to the north and several Aboriginal out-stations, the biggest of which is the poetically named Utopia. Although this is dry country, Ti Tree is best known for its horticultural produce, grown on Ti Tree Farm. Apart from fruit and vegetables, Ti Tree has a roadhouse, school and police station, but not much else.

It was approaching 8 pm, and it was dark. Peter noticed another vehicle coming up behind them, fast. A white utility eventually caught up and pulled onto the right-hand side of the road as if to overtake. The driver sped up until he was beside them. Then, he slowed to keep pace. Lees and Falconio looked at him, and noticed he was motioning to them, pointing to the back of their Kombi and trying to say something. Lees later said, 'The man was looking across into our vehicle ... He was wearing a blue baseball cap and a dark T-shirt with a check shirt over the top with long sleeves.'

Unsure of what to do, frightened, aware of their isolation, Falconio made the decision to slow down and pull over. The other vehicle followed suit, parking close behind the Kombi. Falconio got out, leaving the door ajar and the engine running, and went back to see what the other driver wanted. Lees, meanwhile, moved over to the driver's seat, and watched Falconio talking to the man. She heard him tell her partner there were sparks coming from the back of their vehicle.

Falconio returned to Lees, grabbed his cigarettes, and told her to rev the engine. He returned to the rear of the Kombi and she depressed the accelerator. Then, Lees later explained, she heard a noise 'like the sound of a vehicle backfiring'. Seconds later the other driver was standing beside the Kombi window. He was holding a revolver, and pointing it at Joanne Lees's head.

Lees would later recall this moment with horror. The man, 43-year-old Broome mechanic Bradley John Murdoch, was an intimidating figure. He had a hard, sun-bleached face, a high chin, and cold eyes; his thin lips, and the fine wrinkles across his forehead, might have belonged to a local farmer, but there was darkness in his features.

Murdoch was an outcast, a criminal who ran drugs between Broome, in north-west Western Australia, and South Australia. He had form: a 1980 conviction for death by dangerous driving; a 1995 conviction for shooting into a football crowd; and a 2002 arrest in South Australia for allegedly raping a 12-year-old girl and assaulting her mother.

Murdoch told Lees to switch off the engine. She fumbled with the keys, but was shaking so much she couldn't turn them in the ignition. Murdoch opened the door, forced her across to the passenger seat, got in and turned it off. He pushed her head down, pulled her hands behind her back and secured them with cable ties. He then forced her from the Kombi and attempted to tie her feet and gag her with electrical tape, some of which became tangled in her hair. She later explained, 'I fought for my life. And when I was on the ground I just didn't want him to bind my feet together, so I just kicked frantically to keep them apart.'

Lees remembered kicking and screaming as Murdoch attempted to bind her feet. She tried to grab his testicles, but then he punched her in the face, and she stopped, stunned. While she was groggy, he lifted her from the ground and walked her back to his utility. He used his hand to stop her looking at the spot where her partner lay.

Murdoch's ute had a canvas-covered canopy. He lifted this, produced a sack which he slipped over Lees's head, then opened the door to his own vehicle and pushed her into the passenger seat. Luckily, in doing this, the hood came off. Lees became aware of a dog sitting beside her; she remembered that it neither licked nor sniffed her. It just stared ahead, as if it, too, knew its place. She asked Murdoch if he'd shot Peter, and he replied, no. She asked if he intended raping her.

Again, no.

Some time after this (Lees's recollection was confused), she

The Disappearance of Peter Falconio

ended up lying in the back tray of Murdoch's vehicle on what felt like a mattress. As she waited she heard cars passing on the highway. Whether she was taken from the passenger seat and placed there, or whether she climbed through an opening from the front of the ute, is unclear. By now she must have assumed the worst: that the sound she heard when she revved the engine was a gunshot; that her partner was dead (or else he would have said, or done, something); that this man only wanted to keep her alive until he had time to rape her.

But then, Lees later explained, she was overcome with resolve. 'When I was laid in the back of his vehicle, his ute, I had an image, I realised that I wasn't just going to die – that man was going to rape me ... it was as if I'd just woken up and I just found some strength, some energy, and I just knew what I had to do, and I could hear him the other side of the canopy of his ute ... and I think he was doing something to Pete, and that's when I took the moment and made my escape.'

Lees managed to slide her body towards the back of the vehicle. With her hands still tied she wriggled until her feet dropped from the tray and she was able to sit up. She jumped from the utility, making noise in the gravel, and started running for the scrub. Tripping and staggering through the undergrowth, she went 30 metres before hiding behind a bush. Then she curled up into a ball, waiting, listening to her own heart pounding. She could hear her tormentor's footsteps coming her way, and see the light from his torch searching the bush.

Then he retreated, walking back to the road, returning to the Kombi and driving off into the night. Lees didn't know what to think. If he'd left his ute, he'd be back. Maybe there were two of them, and they were playing a trick? She could still hear cars passing, but nobody stopped. She stayed completely still, waiting. Afterwards, she couldn't remember how long she'd been there. A few minutes? A few hours? Time had no meaning.

Some time later she heard Murdoch return. Again, she heard something heavy being dragged along the gravel. She wondered if it was her partner, being loaded into the back of the ute, to be taken to some isolated place where he could be buried. Eventually Murdoch got into his own vehicle, started the engine, and drove off. Perhaps it was another trick. Perhaps he'd gone for help. Or maybe, with the threat of passing traffic, of being discovered, he'd decided to leave.

Lees later told police she believed she waited beside the road for approximately five hours. During this time she managed to bring her hands up under her legs so they were in front of her body. Taking lip balm from her pocket, she lubricated her wrists and managed to completely remove the cable ties.

After several hours, she decided to act. She knew she would be vulnerable if her attacker returned at first light. Her worst fear was pulling over a vehicle, only to discover it was the same man, so she decided to flag down a road train. 'I think I was driven by the fact that I needed to get help for Pete. I felt that he was close by somewhere and would be injured, and I just wanted to raise the alarm ...' She was cold, bruised, covered in cuts, and terrified, wearing nothing more than a T-shirt, board shorts and sandals, suffering from shock, unsure if she had any chance of surviving her ordeal. Only hours before she'd been sitting in her Kombi, cruising the Stuart Highway, her eyes open for new sights and sounds. Now her whole world had changed.

Listening for the sound of a truck, she eventually emerged from the scrub and approached the highway. At approximately 10.30 pm she flagged down a B-triple road train on its way from Darwin to Adelaide. At first the driver, Vince Millar, thought he'd hit the stranger standing beside the road, waving her arms. After bringing his truck to a stop he got out and walked back, worried about what he'd find. Instead, Joanne Lees came running towards him along the highway. He tried to calm her, but she was distraught, screaming about being kidnapped, and her boyfriend taken.

The truck's other driver, Rodney Adams, who'd been resting in the sleeper, heard the commotion and got out to investigate. Both men tried to console Lees, to make sense of what she was saying. They talked about taking her to the police in Alice Springs, but she told them there was a closer station at Ti Tree.

Millar moved the truck to the side of the road, disconnected the trailers, and drove up and down the highway looking for clues. He eventually found fresh tyre tracks near a white gate. Then, Lees told them, 'I became very fearful and I mentioned to them that we needed to be very careful because the man had a gun, and that's when they decided, Right, we just need to go and get the police.'

They reconnected the trailers and drove to the Barrow Creek Hotel. Strangely, when they arrived at 2 am, a mid-year New Year's Eve party (a Barrow Creek tradition) was just finishing. Millar and Adams introduced Lees to the hotel's owner, Les Pilton. Lees recalled: 'I just wanted to go to the police station. I didn't want to be there and I was in a state of shock ... I just wanted the police to ... get involved and arrive and take over the situation and launch an investigation and search for Pete, but I ended up waiting there for about six hours for the police to arrive.'

Les Pilton attempted to phone the Ti Tree police but got an answering machine. Then he rang the Alice Springs police and handed over to Millar to explain the situation. Eventually Lees confirmed the story to the duty officer. Alice Springs police immediately set about gathering a group of officers to travel to Barrow Creek.

Lees was comforted by Barrow Creek's apprentice chef, Catherine Curley. She and Pilton helped the shocked girl clean her scratches with alcohol wipes. They lit a fire to keep her warm. At last she agreed to lie down in one of the hotel's guest bedrooms. But she couldn't sleep and returned to the front bar.

At approximately 4.30 am a group of police arrived from Alice Springs. They spoke to Millar, Adams and Lees separately, gathering each version of events. Lees described the man who had attacked her and Falconio, as well as his utility. Police immediately circulated these descriptions. Realising this man could have already travelled a long way they ordered roadblocks north and south on the Stuart Highway, east on the Barkly Highway and west on the Buchanan Highway.

Police sealed off an area within a 20-kilometre radius of the crime scene, determined to preserve any forensic evidence. Lees's clothes were gathered for examination. When she took a shower and found a long hair, possibly belonging to Murdoch, she gave it to them.

Later that day, Sunday 15 July, as an aerial search of this stretch of the Stuart Highway was beginning, Lees was taken to Alice Springs by police. Les Pilton's partner, Helen Jones, who had also been comforting and helping Lees since her arrival at the roadhouse, offered her a room in Pilton's mother's house in Alice Springs. Here she would be out of reach of the media who had already picked up on the story. Upon her arrival in 'the Alice' Lees was taken to hospital for treatment of her wounds.

On the Sunday evening, Lees still hadn't contacted her or Peter's parents to tell them what had happened. Perhaps she was hoping for some news before calling; perhaps she just couldn't bring herself to tell them. Either way, back in Huddersfield, Lees's parents, watching the Sunday morning news, saw a story about a couple who had been kidnapped in Australia, near Alice Springs. They contacted Joan and Luciano Falconio to share their concerns, before approaching local police in Huddersfield. The police confirmed their worst fears. The kidnapped tourists were Joanne Lees and Peter Falconio.

Peter's father and one of his brothers, Paul, decided to fly to Australia straight away. When they arrived in Alice Springs on the Wednesday morning they still didn't know if Peter was dead or alive, what was being done to find him, who the attacker was, if the police had any leads, how Joanne was faring, and why, out of the thousands of tourists who used the Stuart Highway every year, their son and brother had become the victim of what Roger Maynard, a *Times* journalist who was covering the case, called 'another example of the dark side of Australia'.

Talking on the ABC's *Lateline* program on the Wednesday evening Maynard said, 'The fact is ... a lot of very unpleasant things have happened to young tourists in Australia over the past ten years.' He invoked the Ivan Milat 'Backpacker' murders and the recent Childers hostel fire that had killed 15 young people (including six from Britain), as well as other assaults and murders on backpackers. He concluded, 'Now, of course, we have this latest drama, which is probably one of the most horrific stories that I've ever had to cover in Australia.'

Upon their arrival, Luciano and Paul Falconio were briefed by police in Alice Springs. Then, still jetlagged and worried sick about Peter, they faced a press conference full of local and British media. Luciano described his son as a 'wonderful boy, not because he's my son, but he is a wonderful boy. He's very clever, and he is a very loving person, to everybody'.

Luciano refused to believe that his son was dead. He had been taken, kept somewhere, perhaps, but he would fight, resist, and escape. 'That's my feeling,' he told reporters. 'He is still alive. Otherwise I won't [*sic*] be here if he wasn't.' These were his public thoughts, but one can only guess what he and Paul were thinking. Paul asked the public to come forward with any information.

Lateline also spoke to Rodney Adams, whose memory of that Saturday evening was still fresh. He said: 'The chap was apparently coming and going in and out of the scrub, three or four times, shining a torch around looking, and then he moved the car into the scrub ... and, at that point, she was watching from the far side of the road in fear of her own life.'

Meanwhile, as Luciano and Paul were talking to the media, Lees returned to the crime scene with police to re-enact the events of 14 July. The immediate area was cordoned off and Lees, still traumatised, 'walked through' the horror that was still fresh in her mind. Northern Territory Police Commander Max Pope explained that 'there may just be little bits and pieces which [are] in the back of her mind and re-enacting what transpired that night may assist us further'. He admitted, 'It's a long shot, but we'd be criticised if we didn't take this step. And it's a very traumatic thing for Joanne to [have to] do ...'

Back at the press conference, Paul Falconio told reporters that Joanne was 'very distraught and upset'. Although he and his father had only talked to her by phone since their arrival, Paul said 'she was very tearful and found it very difficult to speak'. When asked why he thought his brother had been so 'incautious' on that Saturday night, Paul replied, 'He's a trusting guy ... he's been to Thailand, Cambodia, and various other places. So it's not like he's, you know, he hasn't been anywhere before.'

Lees had already provided police with a description of her attacker. This image was used to help search closed-circuit footage from pubs, service stations and supermarkets in an arc hundreds of kilometres from the crime scene. Eventually police found what they were looking for – a man matching Lees's description re-fuelling his white, canopy-covered utility at a service station north of Alice Springs early on Sunday 15 July.

Lees was protected by police and the Falconios. Her absence from the public spotlight in the first week after Falconio's disappearance gave media, domestic and international, licence to invent. She later told Andrew Denton: 'I chose to sort of grieve in private, or – and I guess all I can say is I was a victim of violent and serious crime and had no support or guidance. I didn't know there was a rule book or manual on how to behave.' When she did appear at her first press conference, she was criticised for wearing a T-shirt with the words 'Cheeky Monkey'. It was the only top the police hadn't taken for forensic investigation.

To some, Lees seemed cold, distant, and many couldn't understand this. Why wasn't she in tears, hysterical, pleading for help? The ghost of Lindy Chamberlain was invoked. To others it seemed the media, and sections of the public, hadn't learnt much since 1980. Lees, trapped in a nightmare, had no idea people wanted to think the worst: Peter was a drug runner and had been killed; she herself had killed her partner; he had run off; she was some sort of mental deficient, spinning a story. But the answer was simple. She later explained that although her tough countenance was 'the Yorkshire girl in me', she was worried because 'my mum was ill ... and I didn't want her to see me crying on the news'.

Lees was numb. For many months, she said, she couldn't grasp that the situation was real. 'I just felt that I would wake up and I was in a nightmare situation.'

Police investigators soon found unknown blood on the back of Lees's T-shirt; also, blood on the highway near where Falconio was taken. But not everyone was happy with their progress. The Falconios, and Lees, waited three months before police released the image of Bradley John Murdoch and his vehicle, and three months before they found Lees's lip balm and some of her bindings near the crime scene. Lees later said, 'Mistakes were definitely made but it was a unique situation for them. It's probably the biggest investigation that they will ever have, so I'm not critical of that.'

Lees waited in Alice Springs for nearly a month for a breakthrough, an arrest, anything of substance. The day before she was due to return to England, police asked to interview her. At the interview, she said, she started to feel like a suspect. 'They asked me to clarify inconsistencies in my statement, but there were no inconsistencies. It seemed as if they were trying to get a confession from me.' She later discovered police had bugged her hotel room. When she confronted them they claimed it was only in case her attacker tried to make contact.

Almost 18 months after her ordeal on the Stuart Highway, Joanne Lees received a phone call from Australian police informing her that they had arrested a suspect for the murder of her partner. When they forwarded a photo of Murdoch, Lees immediately recognised him as the man who had tied her up on that cold July night in 2001. Murdoch had been arrested outside the Adelaide Magistrates' Court on a Northern Territory police warrant on charges of murdering Falconio and attempting to abduct Lees. He had just been acquitted on sex charges against a 12-year-old girl and the assault of the girl's mother. Murdoch was placed in custody. His lawyer, Grant Algie, then opposed extradition to the Northern Territory.

Algie argued that Murdoch's arrest was unlawful, and that he would be mistreated by Territory police. Chief Magistrate Kelvyn Prescott overruled the objections and returned Murdoch to the Northern Territory. Algie argued that another member of Murdoch's defence team, Mark Twiggs, should be allowed to accompany the Broome mechanic to Alice Springs because, 'It would be too easy for allegations subsequently to be made by detectives in relation to offhand, unguarded statements made by Mr Murdoch.' This request was also denied.

Bradley Murdoch was born in Northampton, Western Australia, 450 kilometres north of Perth. He worked as a mechanic and truck driver, but at the time of the Falconio murder was ferrying drugs from Adelaide to Broome. In 2005, Lindsay Murdoch, a *Sydney Morning Herald* journalist, described him as 'tough, foul-mouthed, with his front teeth missing and his arms covered in tattoos. He admitted using amphetamines while driving trucks. He admitted not paying his taxes.'

One of Murdoch's former friends in South Australia described him as 'a dangerous animal' who is 'capable of anything'. He said that after the Falconio disappearance, Murdoch was agitated about the search, spending most of his time sipping amphetamine-laced tea and smoking marijuana. One of Murdoch's ex-girlfriends, Beverley Allen, said that after 'Big Brad' returned from his July 2001 trip to Adelaide, 'He wasn't very happy. He was very strung out, very stressed. He'd had to come back a different route.' She explained that he 'suspected somebody had been following him on that occasion and he had to deal with it'.

The trial of Bradley John Murdoch began in Darwin's Supreme Court in late 2005. Northern Territory Chief Justice Brian Martin heard prosecutor Rex Wild explain that Murdoch was 'cunning, alert and meticulous'. His DNA had been found on Joanne Lees's T-shirt and the crime was entirely pre-meditated – he had taken the time, for instance, to make 'handcuffs' from cable ties. After the murder and abduction, Murdoch had driven 1800 kilometres (mostly on the little used Tanami Track) in 18 hours, avoiding police roadblocks. As Lindsay Murdoch reported, 'Wild suggested that Murdoch – high on amphetamines that he sipped from cups of hot tea and sugar – became paranoid about a couple in an orange Kombi van that he had seen two or three times during his marathon drive.'

Murdoch testified that at one of these meetings, at a Red Rooster shop in Alice Springs, some of his blood must have got on to Lees's T-shirt. He claimed he was innocent. Yes, he admitted, he had been trafficking drugs, but had never met Falconio or Lees. He also admitted being in Alice Springs on 14 July, and owning a .357 Colt and a palm-sized Beretta pistol. He denied the utility caught on closed-circuit footage at the Alice Springs petrol station on the evening of 14 July was his vehicle. He claimed to have been towing a camper trailer.

Over the course of the nine-week trial, 85 witnesses and 300 exhibits were produced in an attempt to explain the events of 14 July. Joan and Luciano Falconio sat in court every day, listening, searching for answers, studying the man they were convinced had killed their son.

Murdoch's lawyers claimed their client had no reason to kill a pair of innocent British backpackers. Where was Falconio's body? How had Murdoch avoided the numerous police roadblocks? Where was the murder weapon, the spent cartridge, and why was there so little blood at the crime scene?

Despite all this, Lees's positive identification of Murdoch as her abductor, and Falconio's killer, was going to be difficult to refute. 'I'd recognise him anywhere,' she told the court.

Eventually, in December 2005, after eight hours of deliberation, a jury found Murdoch guilty of the murder of Peter Falconio, and the assault and deprivation of liberty of Joanne Lees. The ABC's Anne Barker said there was a 'collective gasp from the courtroom' when the guilty verdict was announced. 'In the front row,

Peter Falconio's mother, Joan, threw her head back and sobbed uncontrollably. Joanne Lees in the seat behind her clutched Peter Falconio's older brother Paul and hid her face in his arms.'

Later, outside the court, Lees said, 'The past four years have been very traumatic for myself and for the Falconio family and to see justice done today eases a great burden for us all.'

Murdoch showed no emotion as the verdict was read. He simply turned to his girlfriend, Jan Pitman, and shrugged. His lawyer, Grant Algie, said, 'Obviously we're disappointed in the result … we have instructions from our client to lodge an appeal.'

Chief Justice Martin sentenced Murdoch to life imprisonment. As he discharged the jury he told them he agreed with their verdict. By now there seemed little doubt in anyone's mind that Bradley Murdoch was guilty.

Soon after, the Falconio family and Lees publicly pleaded with Murdoch to reveal where he had buried Falconio. Lees said, 'I would like Bradley John Murdoch to seriously consider telling me, Joan and Luciano and Pete's brothers, what he has done with Pete.'

But Murdoch never has, and likely never will, come clean about the murder of Peter Falconio. In the years since his conviction much has been learnt about the character, and history, of this outback criminal. He was even re-invented as a demonic, grinning murderer in the film *Wolf Creek*.

Murdoch was cruel, and unstable. At the time of his arrest, in front of Adelaide's Sir Samuel Way court building, he had just been acquitted of the rape of a 12-year-old girl. He'd been arrested in a supermarket carrying a pistol in a shoulder holster, and only failed to draw it because he was carrying groceries. Police later found 'a shotgun, a rifle with telescopic sights, a crossbow, ammunition … knives, a cattle prod, handcuffs made from cable ties … rolls of tape, gloves, tins of cannabis', as well as cash, in his vehicle.

Murdoch destroyed the lives of a pair of happy-go-lucky 'Poms' who were, like thousands before and since, just out to explore the vast, empty landscape that fills the Fierce Country.

CHAPTER 18

'We believe he is sinless': The Murder of Imran Zilic

2008

> Prayers from the Koran – 'Shetan means the devil' – Aliya and Imran in Coober Pedy – A history of Aliya and Mirsada – Zilic in a dugout – 'Mummy, I want to come home' – Kidnapping his son – Flight from the Coober – Zilic arrested at last – The search for Imran – Premeditated, or insane? – 'the best part of my life'

On 30 May 2008 a small wooden coffin was lowered into a grave at Perth's Karrakatta Cemetery. It was aligned so that three-year-old Imran Zilic could face Mecca. Then Imam Burhan Selim recited prayers from the Koran as the mourners, gathered in a circle around the grave, bowed their heads and cried. 'We believe he is sinless,' Imam Selim said, describing the boy who only a few weeks earlier had been murdered by his own father.

Imran's mother, Mirsada Halilovic, was comforted by a large group from Perth's Bosnian community. At the completion of the ceremony a small wooden board bearing Imran's name was placed at the head of the grave. Imam Selim reminded the mourners of Imran's youth and innocence, and how they had all been deeply shocked by his death. A spokesman for the Western Australian Bosnian Islamic Society told mourners, 'A young life is gone for nothing ... Maybe he is the lucky one who goes straight to Paradise.'

The story of Imran Zilic is a warning. If the death of this wide-eyed, oval-faced little boy is to serve any purpose, or provide any consolation, it will be in our increased understanding of mental health issues. Before he went to trial for the murder of his son,

Imran's father, Aliya, pleaded not guilty on the grounds of mental impairment. Psychiatrists confirmed Aliya suffered from paranoid schizophrenia. He had come to believe that his son was possessed by the devil. He later explained, 'Shetan means the devil ... You've got shetan and you've got shetin, the devil's helpers ... he [Imran] was doing this most weird stuff on the bed [that] a three-year-old child doesn't do ... he was making some marks with his hands and ... flipping his legs up and down on the bed.'

This, he explained, is why he had decided to kill his son.

'I drove about 40 kilometres out of town. I placed him to the spot where I was going to kill him. I didn't want to think about it much at all. I just wanted to relieve his suffering.'

Zilic explained how he had then struck his son, knocking him unconscious, so he wouldn't 'feel the knife'. Then he placed him on the ground, cut his throat and 'put him down the shaft' – a seven-metre-deep opal mine 47 kilometres south of Coober Pedy, on the Stuart Highway.

Zilic returned to his dugout in Coober Pedy, cleaned the knife he'd used to cut his son's throat, packed his few belongings and set off for the Northern Territory. He was next seen that night (Wednesday 23 April) at the Mount Nancy Motel on the outskirts of Alice Springs. He paid $69 for a room with a double and single bed. The next morning he left.

By now Imran had been reported missing by his mother in Perth, from whom Zilic had taken the boy for a two-day access visit on Sunday 20 April. When police searching for the father and son questioned a motel employee she said she had not seen the boy with Zilic. 'He was just like any normal customer,' she said. 'Nothing special.' Police were alarmed but hoped Zilic had left Imran with someone in Coober Pedy.

Aliya Zilic was born in Melbourne to a Bosnian father and Croatian mother. In the early 1990s his family moved to Perth where he worked for a time as an electrical engineer. In his early twenties he was arrested trying to board a plane, carrying a Koran, after running across the tarmac. He was treated for this episode at Graylands Hospital in Perth and later released to his parents' care. They became increasingly concerned when his behaviour continued to deteriorate, wandering the house shouting and banging doors. He was returned to Graylands and placed on anti-psychotic medication.

Zilic met Mirsada Halilovic in 2000 and they married two years later. By the time Imran was born in 2004 Zilic was using marijuana and harder drugs to help him cope with his illness. Apart from believing someone was putting messages in his head he told people he was Jesus. In 2007, Mirsada took Imran and moved in with her parents. Although Zilic pleaded with her to come back she would not expose Imran to her husband's drug taking and erratic behaviour.

Alone and unsupported, Zilic's illness worsened. In 2008 he decided to leave Perth. The journey east would only compound his problems: the isolation and lack of friends and family and support for his illness put him on a trajectory that would end in tragedy.

Upon arriving in Coober Pedy in March 2008, Zilic rented a one-bedroom dugout in Van Brugge Street. Coober Pedy is a small opal-mining town 850 kilometres north of Adelaide. It is incredibly isolated and, in summer, incredibly hot. The town is best known for its subterranean homes, art galleries, shops, hotels, churches and mines. It looks and feels unique, attracting tourists and filmmakers from all over the world. With its 45 different nationalities and a reputation for tolerance and personal freedom, Coober Pedy made the perfect refuge for Aliya Zilic.

But neighbours observed his erratic behaviour over the next few weeks. He told them he was 'troubled by his thoughts'. Eventually, upset by a dream that 'someone was abusing Imran', he decided to return to Perth to see his son. On 19 April 2008 he set off across the Nullarbor.

Caroline Overington, a journalist for the *Australian*, retraced Zilic's steps in 2010. She discovered that along the way he was pulled over by police for speeding. He told them he was in a hurry 'to pick up his son as he was not happy with the way the boy's mother was treating him'. They searched his car, finding a kitchen knife in the glove box. Although he told them it was for opening cans, they confiscated it. Overington explained that 'they called Perth police, who told the boy's mother that her husband was three or four hours east of the city, intent on seeing Imran'.

Zilic arrived at Mirsada's parents' house early on the morning of Sunday 20 April. He told her he wanted to take Imran to visit his brother, who lived close by. She agreed to let him go for two days. As they left, Imran was upset and crying. She phoned them the next day and he was still upset, saying, 'Mummy, I want to come home.' Mirsada didn't think Aliya would harm him. 'No, he loved him very much,' she later explained. 'He always thought it was the best thing that happened to him.' Of the phone conversation on 21 April she explained, '[Aliya] put Imran on the phone and Imran was crying and wanted me. I started crying. Aliya said he would call me back later, but he never did.'

By now Zilic and Imran were on their way back to Coober Pedy. They were seen at Norseman, 730 kilometres east of Perth, and Ceduna, 800 kilometres west of Adelaide. On the evening of Monday 21 April they stopped for the night at the Poochera Hotel on South Australia's Eyre Peninsula.

After Zilic's arrest on 1 May in Kununurra, Western Australia, for the abduction of his son (eight days before his body was found), Major Crime Squad investigators from Adelaide flew to Poochera to help local police search for any trace of the missing boy. They had no idea he had already been dead for a week, sitting in the bottom of a Coober Pedy mineshaft. Caroline Overington spoke to Poochera Hotel barmaid Heidi Lynch who had helped Zilic on 21 April. 'He behaved strange, like he was on something,' she said. 'He came in, and said he wanted a room, and I got him a key. He had a drink. The little boy was with him. I tried to make small talk and he brushed me off.'

Lynch described how Zilic took Imran to their room, but then re-emerged to get something from his car. 'The boy started screaming, went hysterical. So the dad went back in there, and

'We believe he is sinless': The Murder of Imran Zilic

suddenly it all went quiet, and I mean really quiet.' An hour later Lynch and a gardener discovered the room was empty, and the Zilics had gone.

This raises the possibility that Zilic murdered his son in their room at the Poochera Hotel. Forensic investigators later examined the door handle and found Imran's fingerprints all over it. Perhaps Zilic had returned to the room, lost his temper with his frightened son, killed him, panicked and fled Poochera. Perhaps, on the way to Coober Pedy, he had invented the story of Imran's satanic possession, stopped at the mineshaft on the way into town, cut his throat and dumped him, fine-tuning his story about inner voices and his own mental incapacity.

Zilic was back in Coober Pedy late on 21 April or early 22 April. He was next seen at Coober Pedy Hospital, where he visited a doctor on 22 April. Imran was not with him. He told the doctor he hadn't slept for three days and was prescribed anti-psychotic medication. He then went to a pharmacy to fill the script. It is reasonable to assume that he never took his medication, or that if he did, it had no affect. It is most likely, therefore, that Imran's murder must have taken place on 22 or 23 April.

Later, police would find the washed steak knife that Zilic used to kill his son and a large amount of the boy's DNA in the dugout.

Over the next week Zilic drove north, fleeing Coober Pedy. On the evening of 23 April he stayed at the Mount Nancy Motel in Alice Springs. On the 25th he booked a room but didn't stay at the Gunamu Tourist Park at Timber Creek, and by 26 April he had arrived at the Hidden Valley Tourist Park at Kununurra, on the Western Australian and Northern Territory border. His mental state had continued to deteriorate. Richard Hewitt, the proprietor of the park, remembered him screaming and crashing about in his room. When he confronted him, 'He was yelling that close to my face, right up close. I had to ask him to leave.'

Zilic moved to a different caravan park where he was visited by police on 28 April. After confirming his identity, and explaining that his son had been reported missing by Halilovic, they asked where the boy was. He told them he'd left him with his mother in Perth. They explained they'd checked and that wasn't the case. A detective returned to see him the following day and demanded to know what he'd done with Imran. He told them he didn't know where his son was, and said, 'Have you investigated the fact that the mother is working with Lucifer?'

On the morning of Thursday 1 May Zilic tried to leave Kununurra and was arrested by police. Again, he told detectives he'd never left Perth with Imran. As Caroline Overington later explained, 'He was shown images of himself, carrying Imran, from the security cameras from the Norseman BP ... At first he denied it was him, saying it was a "photograph that can be manipulated in 100 million ways".'

On the morning of 2 May Adelaide's *Advertiser* told its readers: 'Father held, but no sign of missing Perth boy Imran Zilic'. The nation read about the ongoing search for Imran with bated breath. It didn't look good: paranoid schizophrenic father stealing his son, driving thousands of kilometres with him, then suddenly fleeing north without the boy. By now Zilic had also told police he'd dropped his son at his parents' home in Perth, but Imran's grandfather, worried sick about the boy, denied this. He told the media, 'No, I didn't see him but I have no comment.'

Detective Inspector Doug Barr, heading the investigation, said there had been no sightings of Imran or Aliya in Coober Pedy but they had evidence to suggest they'd been there. He told journalists that Zilic was not being cooperative. Asked if he thought Imran was dead, he replied that this was a 'worst case scenario'. He pleaded for 'anyone in that area who has seen the boy to contact police'. He also explained that Imran's mother was distraught. 'It is concerning. You can imagine a mother without a child and who doesn't know where he is for just five minutes, never mind for eleven days.'

An Aboriginal tracker helped police search mines, shafts and caves around Coober Pedy. This was no mean feat. The Coober Pedy Precious Stones Field, which supplies the vast majority of the world's opal, covers an area of nearly 5000 square kilometres. There are hundreds of thousands of exploratory shafts dotting the red sand landscape, each with their own slagheap. Barr admitted that it would be impossible to check them all.

South Australian Police declared the case a major crime. State Emergency Service volunteers helped search the town and opal fields. A helicopter was brought in to cover more ground. A description of Zilic and his car, a four-wheel drive Nissan Dualis, was circulated. Detectives retraced Zilic's journey across the Northern Territory, driving the 680 kilometres from Coober Pedy to Alice Springs, and the 1500 kilometres from the 'Alice' to Kununurra. They stopped at pubs, motels and shops along the way, following up any sightings.

On Friday 9 May everyone's worst fear was realised. Imran Zilic's family were told the boy's body had been found down a mine shaft just outside Coober Pedy. Doug Barr explained, 'We were given a number of pieces of information, we've searched a number of locations and it culminates today in the finding of this small child.' At first, nothing was revealed about the manner of Imran's death. Barr said, 'It's not appropriate I comment on the investigation specifically, police will be up at Coober Pedy this afternoon and we will expect to try and remove the body later tonight or tomorrow.' A pathologist and forensic team were on site, he said, and they were preparing to charge an interstate suspect (Zilic). He refused to clarify if police believed Imran was dead before he was dropped down the shaft.

On Tuesday 13 May Zilic, who had since been returned to Graylands Hospital in Perth under a mental health order, appeared before the Perth Magistrates Court charged with murder. South Australian Police applied for his extradition. Meanwhile, Mirsada Halilovic told the media she and her family were devastated. 'He was the sunshine in my life,' she said, 'the thing that made me happy when I got up in the morning. You could not ask for a more loving boy. He was perfect, how can he be gone?' She hadn't yet thought about a funeral, but said, 'Imran, I want you to know that

I love you so much, even more now. I will love you forever, until the day I die. You [will] never be forgotten.'

On Thursday 29 May, Imran's body was released by the coroner and flown to Perth. The following day a service was held for him at Mirrabooka Mosque in Perth's northern suburbs. Sajit Smajic, president of the Western Australian Bosnian Islamic Society, told the press that Imran's death had united local Bosnian, Croat and Serb communities for the first time since the Balkan wars of the early 1990s.

Police and prosecutors now faced a question. Was Aliya Zilic guilty of the premeditated murder of his son, or was he insane? When Zilic looked at his son, did he really see a child possessed by 'Shetan'? As he drove south out of Coober Pedy, walked Imran to the mine shaft, knocked him unconscious and cut his throat, did he really think this was the only way to end the boy's suffering?

Or was Zilic cleverer than that? There were suggestions he knew exactly what he was doing. At the Poochera Hotel, Heidi Lynch heard the boy crying in his room, before the noise suddenly stopped. Zilic was seen carrying the boy, limp (asleep, unconscious, dead?) from his room. Why did Zilic flee Coober Pedy? Why did he spend a week lying to people about what had happened to his son (claiming the boy was in Perth at his grandparents' or mother's house)? Why had he gone to the trouble of hiding his son's body in a mine shaft? Why had he shaved off his beard when he was arrested in Kununurra? How did Zilic think so clearly in the depths of his mental anguish, especially considering he later told prosecutors he had lost his memory during some of this time?

Either way, it was Zilic who told police where they'd find his son's body. It was Zilic who sketched a map for them. It was Zilic who told them he believed the boy was dead when he put him down the shaft.

A forensic report could not categorically give the boy's time of death. When he was found he had already been down the shaft for over a week. The coroner could only say that Imran had died some time between 20 and 24 April, well within the time frame of his trip from Perth and arrival in Coober Pedy.

Bill Watson, the man who saw Zilic carrying his son to his car at Poochera, later explained, 'I gave the statement and that's when they [the police] told me: "You're in the box seat, Bill. You're the last person to see him alive." And I had to say, "I can't be sure he was alive. He was limp, like he was unconscious."'

In May 2009 Aliya Zilic pleaded not guilty to his son's murder in the Supreme Court of South Australia. His claims of mental impairment were tested by several psychiatrists who all agreed that he was suffering from paranoid schizophrenia. Under South Australian law to be found not guilty he needed to prove that at the time of the murder he was not in control of his actions or didn't know what he was doing was wrong.

Zilic was tried by judge alone. His lawyer, Bronwen Waldron, told Justice Margaret Nyland that Zilic's psychosis 'obliterated any sense of what he had done and what he was doing'. Prosecutor Jim Pearce explained that Zilic was a drug addict and schizophrenic who believed his wife was 'working for the devil'.

On 26 March 2010, after listening to submission for three days, Justice Nyland found Zilic not guilty of his son's murder by reason of mental impairment. She said the matter was 'not easy to resolve' but found Zilic was unaware his 'conduct was wrong'. She made a supervision order that he be detained for life in a psychiatric hospital. Under this order Zilic could ask to be released from custody in the future.

When Caroline Overington spoke to Zilic's uncle in July 2010 and asked how Zilic was faring, he said his nephew was doing 'amazingly well, when you consider what happened. He is much better now'.

Imran's mother, Mirsada Halilovic, was not doing well. On 30 June 2009, unable to cope with the loss of her son, she committed suicide in her Alexander Heights home in Perth. Earlier, on 11 January 2009, she had written on her Facebook page:

'Rest in peace, my beautiful son. I love you and I miss you every second of every day. Thank you for being the best part of my life, nothing will ever be the same without you. You were my sunshine, my life, my everything. May our dear Allah look after you now. Love you. Mum.'

CHAPTER 19

Wake in Fright: The Fierce Country Made Real

Walkabout – *Wake in Fright* – Grey Nomads – Kinglake – This brittle, brilliant continent – Shoots of green thought

In James Vance Marshall's 1959 novel *The Children* (later republished as *Walkabout*), a teenage girl and her younger brother wander the desert in search of help, and civilisation, after surviving a plane crash. As the book opens the children huddle together at night, 'their backs to an outcrop of rock. Far below them, in the bed of the gully, a little stream flowed inland – soon to peter out in the vastness of the Australian desert'. Water is a metaphor for life, slowly evaporating as it follows the low ground of the dead heart of this ancient continent. It is, of course, an Aboriginal person who saves them. Later he dies due to a tragic misunderstanding that could itself be a metaphor for what white Australians still haven't learnt about the Fierce Country.

Two years later, Kenneth Cook had a similar vision in his novel *Wake in Fright*. The Christmas holidays have arrived and schoolteacher John Grant farewells his class in the small outback town of Tiboonda ('a variation of hell'). Ahead of him lie six weeks in Sydney ('between the Pacific Ocean and the Great Dividing Range, where Nature deposited the graces she so firmly withheld from the west'). But first comes the train, an overnight stop in Bundanyabba, a two-up game that is really a 'dream of the devil', a lost pay cheque and the slow realisation that we can never escape our own country. In Cook's novel, Australians are reduced to their 'animal customs, their sexual rapacity', and that despite their 'overpowering hospitality' they have become ugly.

When John Grant looks out his schoolroom window he is filled with pleasure. Not that he likes what he sees. Rather, he perceives what he'll be glad to escape. This 'schoolteacher was a coastal Australian' and had no affection for 'the shimmering haze ... marked by a broken fence ... the silent centre of Australia, the Dead Heart'. Cook graphically showed a world most Australians in 1961 would only wish to navigate in words and pictures. Things have changed, and now hundreds of thousands of Australians and international visitors seek out this 'hell', where the only joy Cook's fictional pupils could find was to 'play in the dust, or perhaps tease the wild camels'.

Australians have taken a long time to warm to the idea of Australia. Now, tribes of Grey Nomads, backpackers in beat-up cars they've bought in yards on the edges of our big cities, families in four-wheel drives, all head towards the Dead Heart, hoping to find more than landscape: a reckoning, an understanding, an awakening to the possibilities of this country. It's almost as though the visions of Henry Lawson and Banjo Paterson, Marshall and Cook, have outlived their usefulness; as though we are not happy, anymore, being at odds with ourselves.

But the legacy of the last 200 years will be hard to shake. We are still tempted to see our country as some sort of marauding monster, a Martin Bryant strolling the grounds of Port Arthur, waiting, patiently, for someone to come his way. Then there is a fire, or flood, and in the headlines, the realisation we are the aliens, the ones who choose to build our homes in the bush, along flood-prone rivers.

The Fierce Country holds no malice, but neither pity. It just sits, and bakes, and waits. We do the rest. We provoke it when we mine above its aquifers. Weaken it, and ourselves, when we leave mountains of asbestos to blow away in the wind. Misunderstand it when we see it as nothing more than a resource. Resent it when it takes our children.

On Saturday 7 February 2009 extreme temperatures (a record 46.4 degrees in Melbourne), strong northerly winds (in excess of 100 kilometres per hour) and a dry fuel load combined to cause one of the worst natural disasters in Australian history. 'Black Saturday' as it became known was a collection of almost 400 individual fires that broke out at various locations across Victoria, including Bendigo, Horsham, the Dandenong Ranges, Central Gippsland and Wilsons Promontory. By the time the fires were out, 2030 homes had been destroyed, 173 people killed and 414 injured.

The largest front swept through an area north-east of Melbourne, including the towns of Kinglake, Narbethong and east to Marysville. Most of the damage and loss of life occurred between midday and 7 pm, but fires continued burning and spreading into the evening, fanned by a south-westerly wind change. Several of these fires would not be fully contained until early March.

One Kinglake resident, Tina Wilson, was trapped in her home with her children Krystal, 15, Nathan, 13, and Tegan, 6, as the front approached. She rang the fire brigade for help and they told her to stay in her house. She called her partner, Sam Gents, to tell him she was trapped by the fire. He later explained, 'She rang me up and said, Look, I'm going to go next door – the house has got sprinklers on the roof and we'll be fine, and I'll call you soon.'

But they never made it next door. Tina Wilson and her family died in their home, consumed by a fire described by Jen Wilson, Tina's mother, as 'by no means normal. Houses don't normally explode. They don't normally vaporise'. Wilson told New Zealand television this fire had no precedent even for longtime locals, many of whom were completely unprepared for the speed and ferocity of the flames, some of whom perished through suffocation as the fire consumed all available oxygen. 'In the past,' she said, 'if you told someone to stay in the home they could walk out even if it catches fire, that is correct advice 99.9 per cent of the time.'

Jen Wilson was not alone in losing family members that day. Kinglake recorded 38 fatalities. But, she explained, 'The community has just poured out all their love and support to us, because Tina is a special person and her children are special.'

The Fierce Country, perhaps, is in our minds as much as anything. If it's not a threat, a malevolence preying on our children, and mates, it's a challenge, a barrier. In Patrick White's 1955 novel *The Tree of Man*, the life of a young couple, Amy and Stan Parker, is juxtaposed with an ancient landscape they set out to conquer. 'Then the man took an axe and struck at the side of a hairy tree, more to hear the sound than for any other reason.' The sound of civilisation; of progress. 'He looked at the scar in the side of the tree. The silence was immense. It was the first time anything like this had happened in that part of the bush.' It's as though Stan realises he is just a visitor, a maker of temporary worlds.

If the wilderness (the place where children are lost), the rivers (swept away), the forests (consumed by fire), and the drought-affected farms (inviting suicides at rates far beyond the national average) can all be made to yield, then we will all prosper, apparently. The ravenous dingoes, the amphetamine-addicted mechanics, the rogue elements – living beyond the reach of the law – will, as the frontiers recede, go the way of the rogue Irishman Kelly, disappearing in a whiff of iron-clad folklore.

What started with Frederick McCubbins's *Lost* in 1886 (a painting inspired by the disappearance of 12-year-old Clara Crosbie in the bush near Lilydale in 1885), persisted with the disappearance of three teenage girls near Victoria's Mount Macedon on St Valentine's Day 1901. Real or imagined, has it ever really mattered? Prime Minister Harold Holt, lost off Portsea Beach in 1967, was a sort of tailor-made myth. Ludwig Leichhardt or Voss? Ned Kelly or Sid Nolan's visored boxes?

The Fierce Country is a quick look through the dunny door of outback history. There are hundreds more, lost in the bush, never missed; drowned, washed into one of our three great oceans; murdered, buried in shallow graves thousands of kilometres from anywhere. Time settles over this brittle, brilliant continent, reclaiming us. Floodwaters drop and dust storms disperse; cotton farms are reclaimed by scrub, and Herefords left to wander beside the rabbits, foxes and other mistakes. All this before we, like *The Tree of Man*'s Stan and Amy Parker, understand that 'in the end there were the trees. The boy walking through them with his head drooping as he increased in stature. Putting out shoots of green thought. So that, in the end, there was no end'.

Sources

Newspapers

Advertiser
    'Oscar Station shooting case. A fight with natives. An Aboriginal killed', 22 March 1897
    'Wide Search for Lost Boy', 29 January 1959
    'New Lead in Search for Boy', 30 January 1959
    'Number Clue in Big Search', 31 January 1959
    'Race to find SA Boy', 2 February 1959
    'Searchers Pray for Boy, 10', 2 February 1959
    'No Hope Held for Boy', 3 February 1959
    'Search for Boy Ends', 4 February 1959
    'Skeleton Find at Wilpena', 8 September 1961
    'Boy's Skeleton, Police Believe', 9 September 1961
    'Horror deaths for Outback pair', April 1987
    'Clues from truckie on lost youths', 6 April 1987
    'Missing boys – utility found bogged near desert airstrip', 27 April 1987
    'Bullet may have killed desert victim Simon', 29 April 1987
    'Mother pleads for her son's farewell message', 30 April 1987
    'Ninety years ago a similar tragedy in the Outback', 4 May 1987
    'One Wrong turn and their fate was sealed', 10 March 2011

Age
    'Boland's not the man: kidnapper', 20 March 1973
    'No evidence of Boland at scene: expert', 28 March 1973
    'Boland puts on all alleged Faraday kidnap outfit', 30 March 1973
    'Boland to be sentenced Friday', 19 December 1973
    'Parents to sue over son's desert death', 6 September 2002

Argus (Melbourne)
    'Murchison Inquest', 11 February 1932
    'Murchison Murder Case', 15 March 1932
    'Murchison Trial', 19 March 1932
    'Murchison Tragedy', 30 March 1932
    'Murderer's Appeal', 27 May 1932
    'Afraid to Tell Truth: Condemned Man's Story', 6 June 1932
    'Murderer to Hang', 13 June 1932
    'Rowles Executed', 14 June 1932
    'Murder in the Outback', 18 June 1932

Australian
    'Cry for help in vain in the hot, red Outback dust', 17 December 1998
    'In the footsteps of Burke and Wills', 26 January 2002
    'Time Capsule: Entire School Kidnapped', 6 October 2007
    'Insane … or evil?', 24 July 2010
    'Eight dead, 70 missing as flash floods strike Queensland', 11 January 2011

Barrier Miner (Broken Hill)
    'Lasseter's Gold Reef. Location protected by use of invisible ink', 30 July 1931

Brisbane Courier
    'Mysterious Disappearance of a Boy', 7 January 1899
    'Murder at Oxley', 9 January 1899

Cairns Post
    'The Gatton Tragedy: Old Crime Recalled', 10 December 1928

Canberra Times
    'Teeth from fire: Identified by dentist', 10 February 1932

Daily Telegraph
    'Lasseter's Reef Declared to be a Myth', 7 October 1939
    'Imran Zilic's father faces court after boy's death', 13 May 2008

Herald Sun
    'The day kidnappers Edwin John Eastwood and Robert Clyde Boland took the Faraday School Hostage', 5 October 2012

Independent (UK)
    'Mystery of man's walk on wild side', 24 August 1999

Kalgoorlie Wester Argos
    'A later account. Natives surrounded', 25 March 1897
Maitland Daily
    'The Breelong Blacks', 29 October 1900
Mercury
    'Queensland: The Triple Murder: Further Details', 30 December 1898
Mildura Weekly
    'Another lonely death in the SA outback', 15 January 2010
    'Out of Fuel, out of hope', 23 July 2010
NT News
    'Alice motel link to missing boy', 5 May 2008
Queenslander
    'Police and Trackers at Work', 31 December 1898
South Australian Register
    'A settler murdered by Aboriginals', 20 March 1897
Sydney Morning Herald
    'Death of a Murderer', 9 April 1897
    'The Gatton Tragedy: No Clue to the Murderers', 30 December 1898
    'No Legal Aid for Parents of Dead Jackaroo', 9 January 1988
    'Raging Row Before Youths Left for Death', 5 February 1988
    'Station Conditions Hard, Inquest Told', 31 May 1988
    'Paranoid, armed and deadly', 15 December 2005
    'Haunted by the mystery of Lee Ellen's last hours', 8 November 2009
    'Google puts gold on map for mates seeking Lasseter's Reef', 10 November 2012
Telegraph (UK)
    'Australia: if you're crook, do the locomotion', 16 January 1999
Truth
    'Dead gold-seeker claimed as husband by two women', 10 May 1931
West Australian
    'Murder by natives. Police constable Richardson killed. Two station hands shot', 12 November 1894
    'Queensland Tragedies', 11 January 1899

Books, Journals and Magazines

Elder, Bruce, *Blood on the Wattle*, New Holland Publishers, 1998

Cousins, Emily, 'Mountains Made Alive: Native American Relationships with Sacred Lands', 'Cross Currents', Winter 96/97, Vol. 46, Issue 4

Dormer, Ray and Whalen, Julie, 'An Almost Incredible Academy – the Boys Prison on Point Puer', (workshop paper, 2003)

Hersey, S.J. *Endangered by Desire*. 'TGH Strehlow and the inexplicable vagaries of private passion' (thesis, 2006)

Hill, Barry, 'Journey to Horseshoe Bend' by TGH Strehlow, *The Monthly*, book review, 2016

Horne, Benjamin, 'Benjamin Horne's report on Point Puer Boys' Prison, to His Excellency Sir John Franklin K.C.H. and K.R. Lieut. Governor of Van Diemen's Land, Point Puer, March 7, 1843'

Lasseter, Lewis Hubert, diary

Maynard, Roger, *Where's Peter? Unravelling the Falconio Mystery*, Harper Collins, 2005

Murgatroyd, Sarah, *The Dig Tree*, Text Publishing, 2002

National Railway Museum, *On Shed at Port Dock*, 1997

Peters, Allan, *Recollections: Nathaniel Hailes' Adventurous Life in Colonial South Australia*, Wakefield Press, Adelaide, 1998

Pierce, Peter, *The Country of Lost Children: An Australian Anxiety*, Cambridge University Press, 1999

'The Problem of Consolation in the Country of Lost Children', Society for Studies in Religion, Literature and the Arts, 2001

Ramsland, John, 'The myth and reality of Point Puer', History of Education and Children's Literature, III, 1 (2008)

Stewart, Douglas, *Collected Poems*, Angus and Robertson Publishers, 1973

Torney, Kim, 'A City Child Lost in the Bush', La Trobe Journal, No. 74, Spring 2004

Walsh, G.P., Governor, Jimmy, *Australian Dictionary of Biography*, Melbourne University Press, Vol. 9, 1983

Wilson, Paul and Simmonds, James Wulf, *Murder in Tandem: When two people kill*, Harper Collins, 2000

Wainwright, Robert, *The Lost Boy*, Allen and Unwin, 2004

Walker, Terry, *Murder on the Rabbit Proof Fence*, Hesperian Press, 1993

Walsh, G.P., 'Lewis Hubert Lasseter (1880–1931)', *Australian Dictionary of Biography*, (Vol. 9), Melbourne University Press, 1983

Weidenback, Kristin, *Mailman of the Birdsville Track*, Hachette Australia, 2003

Websites

www.abc.net.au
   'Toddler's body found in mineshaft', 9 May 2008
   'Channel under fire over Bogucki actions', 24 August 1999

www.adbonline.anu.edu.au
   Australian Dictionary of Biography: Online Edition. 'Strehlow, Carl Friedrich Theodor'

www.news.bbc.co.uk
   'American found after outback odyssey', 23 August 1999

www.diamantina-tour.com.au
   'Bejah Dervish and the Calvert Expedition'

www.gattonmurders.com

www.kangaruni.com

www.legacyview.com
   'Bejah Dervish', Legacyview Dictionary of Biography

www.pathologists.com.au
   'Inquest Likely After Outback Death', 19 December 1998

www.perthnow.com.au
   'Mother of mineshaft boy Imran Zilic found dead in Perth', 30 June 2009

www.portarthur.org.au

www.samemory.sa.gov.au
   'Taking it to the edge: Calvert Expedition', State Library of SA

www.stuff.co.nz

www.trutv.com
   'Never to be released: Crimes of Kevin Crump and Allan Baker'

www.sapolicehistory.org
   'Little Boy Lost', July 2008

www.simpsondesert.fl.net.au
   'Birdsville or Dust'

www.watoday.com.au
'Father cleared of mineshaft death', 26 March 2010

Television, Radio, Film and Song

AM, ABC Radio, 'Murdoch found guilty in Falconio murder trial', 14 December 2005

Crime Investigation Australia, 'No Mercy: The Killing of Virginia Morse' (Season 2, Episode 2)

Enough Rope, ABC Television (Episode 124: Joanne Lees), 9 October 2006

First Australians, SBS Corporation, (Episode 5: Unhealthy Government Experiment)

Jandamarra's War, ABC Television, 2011

'Lasseter's Last Ride', Peter Dawson and Edward Harrington, 1940

Lateline, ABC Television, 'Search continues for missing British tourist', 18 July 2001

Tea and Sugar Train, Commonwealth Film Unit, 1954

The Back of Beyond, Directed by John Heyer, Shell Film Unit, 1954 (accessed through the National Film and Sound Archive)

The 7.30 Report, ABC Television, 'Family holds hope for missing tourist', 18 July 2001

The World Today, ABC Radio, 'James Annetts's parents appeal to the High Court', 3 December 2001

Acknowledgements

Spud's Roadhouse once had a RESTAURANT sign. At some point it lost its final T. I was looking forward to seeing the RESTAURAN. It was 2012, and I was on a National Year of Reading tour. We arrived at the Pimba landmark, 480 kilometres north of Adelaide, but the sign had been replaced. It was a minor Dig Tree moment, but we continued across the concourse, big enough to land a Dreamliner. Went inside, to the kept-dark refuge from the desert. Found plenty of licence plates from Vancouver and West Virginia. Cold, cold beer. Autographed bras.

We continued. Next stop Roxby Downs: quarry sunsets, bandicoots and kites, skyfire and Sturt's Desert Pea (still gets a laugh). My surely-you-can-keep-the-dining-room-open-till-ten publicist and miracle-worker Bethany Clark drove east across the cattle grates. It was all foreign. Country I somehow knew, but had never seen. And the thought occurred to me. This is where it's all happened.

Another book. About the rough, rubbing surface between man and country. Michael Bollen would edit, Julia Beaven would oversee the book, and Michael Deves would look after the text.

And here it is. The Adelaide *Advertiser* published an earlier version of the Page family chapter. *Inside History* magazine featured the Tea and Sugar, Snowy Rowles, Harold Lasseter and the Point Puer boys' prison chapters. *Tracer* magazine published the Carl and Theodor Strehlow chapter. The *Adelaide Review* published the Daisy Bates section of Chapter 1. Douglas Stewart and his *Birdsville Track* poems were a constant reference and inspiration. Sexton Blake, Roy Eccleston, Wayne Edwards, David Knight, Cassie Mercer, Eden Cox and Luke Stegemann were all in for a penny and a pound.

Incredible Floridas
Stephen Orr

As Hitler's war looms, famous Australian artist Roland Griffin returns home from London with his family to live a simple life of shared plums and low-cut lawns in the suburbs.

In the yard: a daughter, and a son, Hal, growing up with a preoccupied father who is always out in his shed stretching canvases and painting outback pubs. An isolated man obsessed with other people and places. Everything is a picture, a symbol. Even Hal, the boy in the boat, drifting through a strange world of Incredible Floridas.

As the years pass, Roland learns that Hal is unable to control his own thoughts, impulses, behaviour. The boy becomes the destroyer of family. The neighbourhood is enlisted to help Hal find a way forward. Child actor, a clocker at Cheltenham Racecourse, an apprentice race caller. *Incredible Floridas* describes Hal's attempts at adulthood, love, religion, and the hardest thing of all: gaining his father's approval.

'While the distinctive life of time and place comes across vividly through the interactions of a believable cast of characters, the deeper attractions of the novel come from the way Orr has woven tragic young Hal into the magical tapestry of Rimbaud's famous poem, *Le bateau ivre* (*The Drunken Boat*)'
– Katharine England, *Advertiser*

'A haunting novel of quiet power, with strikingly etched dialogue, *Incredible Floridas* is the work of a literary craftsman at the top of his game.'   – Cameron Woodhead, *Age/Sydney Morning Herald*

'The author has captured beautifully the slow-moving nature of an Australian town in the 1950s with all its colloquialisms and latent sexism …'   – Rod McLary, Queensland Reviewers Collective

For more information please visit wakefieldpress.com.au

DATSUNLAND
Stephen Orr

A long-deserted drive-in, waiting for a rerun of the one story that might give it life; a child who discovers his identity in a photograph hidden in his parents' room ...

Stephen Orr's stories are happy to let you in, but not out. In *Datsunland*, his characters are outsiders peering into worlds they don't recognise, or understand: an Indian doctor arriving in the outback, discovering an uncomfortable truth about the Australian dream; a family trying to have their son's name removed from a Great War cowards' list; a confused teenager with a gun making an ad for an evangelical ministry.

Each story is set in a place where, as Borges described, 'heaven and hell seem out of proportion'. There is no easy escape from the world's most desperate car yard, or the school with a secret that permeates all but one of the fourteen stories in *Datsunland*. Here is a glimpse of inner lives, love, the astonishment of being ourselves.

'When Orr nails it, his writing is piercing, brutal, powerful, both in respect to his unflinching gaze and his wielding of plain English like a weapon. You as a reader will survive, but not without blunt force trauma to show for it.'   – Sam Cooney, *Australian*

'[Orr's] stories in this first collection tend to stop very effectively just short of the punchline, leaving the reader testing their own breathtaking interpretation of his implications.'
– Katharine England, *SA Weekend*

'At its best, the writing is insightful and strangely beautiful ... Orr holds the collection together with an impression of force and linguistic brutality.'   – Catherine Noske, *Australian Book Review*

For more information please visit wakefieldpress.com.au

Time's Long Ruin

Stephen Orr

Nine-year-old Henry Page is a club-footed, deep-thinking loner, spending his summer holidays reading, roaming the melting streets of his suburb, playing with his best friend Janice and her younger brother and sister. Then one day Janice asks Henry to spend the day at the beach with them. He declines, a decision that will stay with him forever.

Time's Long Ruin is based loosely on the disappearance of the Beaumont children from Glenelg beach on Australia Day, 1966. It is a novel about friendship, love and loss; a story about those left behind, and how they carry on: the searching, the disappointments, the plans and dreams that are only ever put on hold.

Winner, Unpublished manuscript award, Adelaide Festival

South Australian winner, 2012 National Year of Reading awards

'In *Time's Long Ruin* [Orr] has conjured up the suburban claustrophobia of the Fifties and added to it streaks of ... darker pigments. His Thomas Street, Croydon – particularly on hot days, when no one has enough to do and everyone gets on each other's nerves – is Adelaide's very distinctive version of Winton's *Cloudstreet*, Malouf's *Edmondstone Street* and White's *Sarsaparilla*; but the quality and vividness of Orr's evocation of those stultifying times ensures he can hold his head high in such illustrious company. *Time's Long Ruin* is a compelling page-turner.'   – Richard Walsh

For more information please visit wakefieldpress.com.au

The Hands

Stephen Orr

He didn't look like he could jump a bull, but she knew he could. It was all in the hands, he'd often explain. The will. The bloody mindedness.

On a cattle station that stretches beyond the horizon, seven people are trapped by their history and the need to make a living. Trevor Wilkie, the good father, holds it all together, promising his sons a future he no longer believes in himself. The boys, free to roam the world's biggest backyard, have nowhere to go.

Trevor's father, Murray, is the keeper of stories and the holder of the deed. Murray has no intention of giving up what his forefathers created. But the drought is winning …

Longlisted for the 2016 Miles Franklin Literary Award

'Orr's ability to capture characters and the way they interact with each other is truly impressive … It's pretty darn perfect.'
– Sue Terry, *Whispering Gums*

'*The Hands* has the scope of a Greek tragedy – not only in its focus on the violence underlying familial relationships. Ineluctable fate seems to press on a family forced into painful reflection. The encroaching desert is, like the Greek Moirai, remorseless …'
– Josephine Taylor, *Australian Book Review*

'The triumphant culmination of a five-book fascination with the dynamics of (family) groups as they function in extreme and often liminal situations … Orr slides seamlessly in and out of his different characters' heads … always moving the story efficiently along …'   – Katharine England, *Advertiser*

For more information please visit wakefieldpress.com.au

Wakefield Press is an independent publishing and
distribution company based in Adelaide, South Australia.
We love good stories and publish beautiful books.
To see our full range of books, please visit our website at
www.wakefieldpress.com.au
where all titles are available for purchase.
To keep up with our latest releases, news and events,
subscribe to our monthly newsletter.

Find us!

Facebook: www.facebook.com/wakefield.press
Twitter: www.twitter.com/wakefieldpress
Instagram: instagram.com/wakefieldpress

www.ingramcontent.com/pod-product-compliance
Lightning Source LLC
Chambersburg PA
CBHW022017220426
43663CB00007B/1109